Apple
PRESS

MW00836964

The Dylan Reference Manual

**The Definitive Guide to the New
Object-Oriented Dynamic Language**

Andrew Shalit

With contributions by David Moon and Orca Starbuck

Addison-Wesley Developers Press
Reading, Massachusetts • Menlo Park, California • New York
Don Mills, Ontario • Harlow, England • Amsterdam
Bonn • Sydney • Singapore • Tokyo • Madrid • San Juan
Paris • Seoul • Milan • Mexico City • Taipei

ISBN 0-201-44211-6
1 2 3 4 5 6 7 8 9-MA-0099989796
First Printing, September 1996

Library of Congress Cataloging-in-Publication Data

Shalit, Andrew.
    The Dylan reference manual : the definitive guide to the new object-oriented dynamic language/ Andrew Shalit.
        p.   cm.
    Includes index.
    ISBN 0-201-44211-6
    1. Dylan (Computer program language).   I. Title.
I. Apple Computer, Inc.
QA76.73.D95S47   1996
005.13'3—DC20   96-31568
                                                            CIP

Contents

Preface   **About This Book**   ix

Chapter 1   **Introduction**   1

Background and Goals   3
Language Overview   4
Manual Notation   6

Chapter 2   **Syntax**   7

Overview   9
Libraries and Modules   9
Bindings   10
Macros   10
Bodies   11
Definitions   11
Local Declarations   12
Expressions   13
Statements   15
Parameter Lists   16
Lexical Syntax   16
Special Treatment of Names   20
Top-Level Definitions   21
Dylan Interchange Format   21
Naming Conventions   23

Chapter 3   **Program Structure**   25

Modules   27
Libraries   28

Chapter 4   Program Control   31

Overview   33
Function Calls   33
Operators   35
Assignment   38
Conditional Execution   39
Iteration   40
Nonlocal Exits and Cleanup Clauses   41
Multiple Values   42
Order of Execution   43

Chapter 5   Types and Classes   47

Overview   49
The Type Protocol   49
Classes   52
Slots   57
Instance Creation and Initialization   64
Singletons   71
Union Types   72
Limited Types   73

Chapter 6   Functions   77

Overview   79
Parameter Lists   84
Method Dispatch   95
Operations on Functions   100

Chapter 7   Conditions   101

Background   103
Overview   105
Signalers, Conditions, and Handlers   105

Exception Handling   107
Condition Messages   112
Introspective Operations   114

Chapter 8   ## Collections   115

Overview   117
Collection Keys   118
Iteration Stability and Natural Order   118
Mutability   119
Collection Alteration and Allocation   119
Collection Alignment   120
Defining a New Collection Class   121
Tables   122
Element Types   124
Limited Collection Types   126

Chapter 9   ## Sealing   131

Overview   133
Explicitly Known Objects   133
Declaring Characteristics of Classes   134
Declaring Characteristics of Generic Functions   135
Define Sealed Domain   135

Chapter 10   ## Macros   141

Overview   143
Extensible Grammar   147
Macro Names   148
Rewrite Rules   150
Patterns   151
Pattern Variable Constraints   157
Templates   159
Auxiliary Rule Sets   161

Hygiene   161
Rewrite Rule Examples   165

Chapter 11   **The Built-In Classes**   185
_____

Overview   187
Objects   187
Types   189
Simple Objects   195
Numbers   197
Collections   206
Functions   238
Conditions   244

Chapter 12   **The Built-In Functions**   255
_____

Overview   257
Constructing and Initializing Instances   258
Equality and Comparison   267
Arithmetic Operations   274
Coercing and Copying Objects   287
Collection Operations   294
Reflective Operations on Types   343
Functional Operations   346
Function Application   350
Reflective Operations on Functions   351
Operations on Conditions   357

Chapter 13   **Other Built-In Objects**   367
_____

Other Built-In Objects   369

Chapter 14   The Built-In Macros and Special Definitions   371

Overview   373
Definitions   373
Local Declarations   389
Statements   393
Function Macros   409

Appendix A   BNF   413

Lexical Grammar   414
Phrase Grammar   420

Appendix B   Exported Names   431

Exported Classes   431
Exported Functions   432
Exported Constants   434
Exported Defining Macros   435
Exported Statement Macros   435
Exported Function Macros   435

Glossary   437

Index   452

About This Book

This book is the complete specification and reference of the Dylan programming language.

The book is divided into three parts: chapters 1 through 10 describe the overall structure and semantics of the language; chapters 11 through 14 provide a reference describing every class, function, and syntactic construct in the language; appendices contain the BNF for Dylan's syntax, a listing of names used by the Dylan language, and a glossary of terms.

The book will be of interest to users of Dylan, as well as to those who have a general interest in object-oriented programming and modern programming languages. It is not, however, a tutorial. Beginning programmers who want to learn Dylan may wish to begin with another book before moving on to this volume.

Introduction

Contents

Background and Goals   3
Language Overview   4
Manual Notation   6

Background and Goals

Dylan is a general-purpose, high-level programming language, designed for use in application and systems programming. Dylan includes garbage collection, type-safety, error recovery, a module system, and programmer control over runtime extensibility of programs.

The name "Dylan" is a portmanteau of the words "dynamic" and "language." Dylan is designed to allow efficient, static compilation of features normally associated with dynamic languages.

Dylan was created out of the belief that programs have become too complex for traditional static programming languages. A new generation of software—software that can be built quickly and enhanced over time—requires higher-level programming tools. The core of these tools is a simple and expressive language, one that protects the programmer from low-level implementation details, but still produces efficient executables.

Dylan was designed from the ground up with a thoroughly integrated object model, syntax, and control structures. It is not source code compatible with any existing languages, and can therefore be more internally self-consistent. At the same time, Dylan's syntax and object-model allow a high-level of integration with libraries written in other languages such as C and C++.

Dylan avoids providing multiple ways of doing the same thing. Quite the opposite, the language often uses a single construct to achieve several ends. For example, Dylan's type declarations improve the efficiency and readability of programs, they ensure type safety, and they provide the basis of polymorphic dispatch, the basic mechanism of object-oriented flow of control.

And while simplicity of language is very important, it should not and need not come at the price of expressiveness. Multi-method dispatch is an example of a Dylan feature that makes the language more powerful and simultaneously makes Dylan programs easier to understand.

Dylan demonstrates that a programming language can be highly expressive, can encourage the use of appropriate abstraction, can make programming more productive, and can make the programming process enjoyable, all without sacrificing the ability to compile into code that is very close to the machine, and therefore very efficient.

Language Overview

Dylan is written in a very regular syntax. In addition to making the language easier to read and write, the layered composition of the syntax supports a macro system that is language-aware. The macro system does not simply perform text substitution, but rather performs syntax fragment substitution. This allows the extension of the language within bounds that are safe, semantically well-defined, and in accord with the "syntactic flavor" of the language.

Bindings (Dylan's analog to variables) are lexically scoped and fully resolved at compile time. Binding names are not retained in running programs. The module system allows bindings to be private or shared. Names can be changed upon import to a module, so the possibility of irreconcilable name conflicts among separately developed modules is eliminated. Modules can provide multiple interfaces to the same code base, decreasing the chance of exposing a client to inappropriate interfaces.

Flow of control is supported through polymorphic function calls, a variety of conditional and iteration constructs, and a nonlocal transfer mechanism with protected regions.

All objects are first class, including numbers, classes and functions. This means that all objects can be used as arguments to functions, returned as values, and stored in data structures, and all are subject to introspection. All objects are typed, and type-safety is guaranteed, either through compile-time or runtime type checking. There are no facilities for deallocating objects. Objects are deallocated automatically when they can no longer be reached by a program.

Types are used to categorize and specify the behavior of objects. An object may be an instance of any number of types. Classes are a particular kind of type used to define the structure and inheritance of instances. Every Dylan object is a direct instance of exactly one class, and a general instance of that class and each of its superclasses. The root of the class hierarchy (and of the type hierarchy) is a class called <object>.

Values associated with an instance are stored in slots of the instance.

Classes do not define scopes for names. Names are scoped by modules and local binding declarations.

Functions are the active portions of Dylan programs. Functions accept zero or more arguments and return zero or more values. Functions are specialized to accept arguments of particular types, and will signal an error if they are called with arguments that are not instances of those types. The return values of functions are similarly type-checked.

A method is a basic unit of callable code. When a method is called, it creates local bindings for its arguments and executes a body in the resulting environment. A method can be called directly by a program or indirectly through a generic function that contains it.

A generic function contains a number of methods. When a generic function is called, it finds the methods that are applicable to the arguments, and passes control to the most specific of those methods.

Slots are accessed through functions. This ensures that instances present an abstract interface to their clients, which assists both in polymorphism and in program redesign.

Sealing declarations allow the programmer to declare portions of the class hierarchy and set of functions to be invariant. This supports the enforcement of protocols, compile-time resolution of polymorphic behavior, and efficient inline slot access. Portions of a program that are not sealed can be extended at run time or by additional libraries.

Dylan includes a number of predefined libraries, including an exception system, collections, arithmetic, higher-order functions, and introspection.

The exception system is object-based. It uses calling semantics (thereby allowing recovery) but also provides exiting handlers.

The collection system includes a number of predefined collection classes and operations built on a simple iteration protocol. Additional classes defined in terms of this protocol have access to the full suite of collection operations.

Arithmetic is fully object-based and extensible.

A library of higher-order operations on functions supports function composition.

A library of introspective functions supports the run time examination of objects, including classes and functions.

Manual Notation

This manual uses a small number of typographic conventions:

- `Monospaced font` (Courier 12) is used to indicate text that should appear verbatim in programs.

- *Italic font* is used to name parameters, placeholders for actual program text.

- References to entries in the BNF are given the same name as in the BNF, and are followed by a subscripted italic *bnf*.

- **Bold** is used for the first use of terms.

- **Bold** is also used for meta-syntactic punctuation, as follows:
    - **[ ]** Contents are optional
    - **{ }** Contents appear once
    - **{ }*** Contents appear zero or more times
    - **{ }+** Contents appear one or more times
    - **|** A choice between the item on the left of the vertical bar and the item on the right of the vertical bar, but not both.

If a comma appears between a right curly brace and the following asterisk or plus sign, it indicates that multiple occurrences of the contents are separated by a comma. There is no comma after the last occurrence.

If a semicolon appears between a right curly brace and the following asterisk or plus sign, it indicates that multiple occurrences of the contents are separated by a semicolon. A semicolon following the last occurrence is optional.

Sample Dylan code is shown in `small monospaced font`. When the return value of an expression is shown, it is preceded by an ⇒.

Chapter 10, "Macros," and Appendix A, "BNF," each use a distinctive notation, described at the start of the chapter and appendix.

Syntax

Contents

Overview   9
Libraries and Modules   9
Bindings   10
Macros   10
Bodies   11
Definitions   11
Local Declarations   12
Expressions   13
Statements   15
Parameter Lists   16
Lexical Syntax   16
Special Treatment of Names   20
    Escaping Names   20
    Function Call Shorthand   20
Top-Level Definitions   21
Dylan Interchange Format   21
Naming Conventions   23

Overview

This chapter describes the syntax and structure of a Dylan program, from the outside in. This is one of the two defining characteristics of Dylan. The other is the set of objects on which a Dylan program operates; objects and their types are discussed in the following chapters. This section is only an overview; language constructs briefly mentioned here are explained in detail in later sections. A formal specification of Dylan syntax appears in Appendix A, "BNF."

Libraries and Modules

A complete Dylan **program** consists of one or more **libraries**. Some of these libraries are written by the programmer, others are supplied by other programmers or by the Dylan implementation. A library is Dylan's unit of separate compilation and optimization. The libraries that compose a program can be linked together as early as during compilation or as late as while the program is running. Program structure inside of a library is static and does not change after compilation. However, many Dylan implementations provide an incremental compilation feature that allows a library under development to be modified, while the program is running, by modifying and recompiling portions of the library.

A library contains one or more **modules**. A module is Dylan's unit of global name scoping, and thus of modularity and information hiding. A module can be exported from its library; otherwise it is internal to that library. A library can import modules from other libraries. Only an exported module can be imported.

A module contains zero or more source records and a set of bindings.

A **source record** is an implementation-defined unit of source program text. For example, in a file-based development environment each source file might be one source record. As another example, in an interactive Dylan interpreter each executable unit of programmer input would be a source record. The source program text in a source record is a body, a grammatical element used in several places in Dylan.

Bindings

A **binding** is an association of a name with a value. The bindings in a module persist for the life of the program execution. The scope of such a binding is its module. That is, the binding is visible to all source-records in the module. A module can export bindings and can import bindings from other modules. Only an exported binding can be imported. A binding is visible to all source-records in a module that imports it.

A binding may be **specialized**. This restricts the types of values that may be held in the binding. An error will be signaled on any attempt to initialize or assign the binding to a value that is not of the correct type.

A binding is either **constant** or **variable**. A constant (or read-only) binding always has the same value. In contrast, a variable (or writable) binding can have its value changed, using the assignment operator : =. Most bindings in a typical Dylan module are constant.

Macros

A **macro** is an extension to the core language that can be defined by the programmer, by the implementation, or as part of the Dylan language specification. Much of the grammatical structure of Dylan is built with macros. A macro defines the meaning of one construct in terms of another construct. The original construct is the call to the macro. The replacement construct is the expansion of the macro. The compiler processes the expansion in place of the call.

Portions of the call to a macro are substituted into part of the macro definition to create the expansion. This substitution preserves the meanings of names. In other words, each name inserted into the expansion from the macro call refers to the same binding that it referred to in the call, and each name inserted into the expansion from the macro definition refers to the same binding that it referred to in the definition.

A macro is named by a binding and thus is available for use wherever that binding is visible. There are three kinds of macros: defining macros, which extend the available set of definitions; statement macros, which extend the available set of statements; and function macros, which look syntactically like function calls but have more flexible semantics.

Bodies

A **body** is a sequence of zero or more constituents. When multiple constituents are present, they are separated by semicolons. When at least one constituent is present, the last constituent can optionally be followed by a semicolon; this allows programmers to regard the semicolon as either a terminator or a separator, according to their preferred programming style.

A **constituent** is either a definition, a local declaration, or an expression. Definitions and local declarations form the structure of a program and do not return values. In contrast, expressions are executed for the values they return and/or the side-effects that they perform.

Definitions

A **definition** is either a call to a user-defined defining macro, a call to a built-in defining macro, or a special definition. Typically, a definition defines a binding in the module containing the definition. Some definitions define more than one binding, and some do not define any bindings.

A **user-defined defining macro** is a macro that defines a definition in terms of other constructs. A call to a user-defined defining macro always begins with the word `define` and includes the name of the defining macro. This name when suffixed by "`-definer`" is the name of a visible binding whose value is the defining macro. The rest of the syntax of a call to a user-defined defining macro is determined by the particular macro. Some definitions include a body. Advanced programmers often define new defining macros as part of structuring a program in a readable and modular way.

A **built-in defining macro** is like a user-defined defining macro but is specified as part of the Dylan language. There are eight built-in defining macros: `define class`, `define constant`, `define generic`, `define domain`, `define library, define method, define module,` and `define variable.`

A **special definition** is a definition construct that is built into the grammar of Dylan. There is only one special definition: `define macro`.

An implementation can add new kinds of definitions as language extensions. Such definitions may be implemented as special definitions. However, they will more commonly take the form of user-defined definition macros that are the values of bindings exported by implementation-defined modules.

Local Declarations

A **local declaration** is a construct that establishes local bindings or condition handlers whose scope is the remainder of the body following the local declaration.

Unlike module bindings, local bindings are established during program execution, each time the local declaration is executed. They persist for as long as code in their scope is active. Local bindings persist after the body containing them returns if they are referenced by a method created inside the body and a reference to the method escapes from the body, so that it could be called after the body returns. Unlike module bindings, local bindings are always variable. However, since a local binding has a limited scope, if there is no assignment within that scope, the local binding is effectively constant.

A local binding shadows any module binding with the same name and any surrounding local binding with the same name. The innermost binding is the one referenced.

Macros cannot be shadowed. Hence, the name of a local binding cannot be the name of a macro.

There are three kinds of local declaration: local value bindings (`let`), local method bindings (`local`), and condition handler establishment (`let handler`).

The **local value bindings** construct, `let`, executes an expression and locally binds names to the values returned by that expression.

The **local method bindings** construct, `local`, locally binds names to bare methods. These bindings are visible in the remainder of the body and also inside the methods, permitting recursion.

The **condition handler establishing** construct, `let handler`, establishes a function to be called if a condition of a given type is signaled during the execution of the remainder of the body or anything the body calls. The handler is disestablished as soon as the body returns. Unlike the other two kinds of local declaration, `let handler` does not establish any bindings.

Expressions

An **expression** is a construct that is executed for the values it returns and/or the side-effects that it performs. The "active" portions of a Dylan program are expressions. An expression is either a literal constant, a named value reference, a function call, a unary operator call, a binary operator call, an element reference, a slot reference, a parenthesized expression, or a statement.

An **operand** is a restricted expression: it cannot be a unary or binary operator call nor a symbol literal. The other seven forms of expression are allowed. Operands appear in situations in the grammar where an expression is desirable but the full generality of expressions would make the grammar ambiguous.

A **literal constant** directly represents an object. Literal constants are available for numbers, characters, strings, symbols, boolean values, pairs, lists, and vectors. For example:

number	`123, 1.5, -4.0, #x1f4e`
character	`'a', '\n'`
string	`"foo", "line 1\nline 2"`
symbol	`test:, #"red"`
boolean value	`#t, #f`
pair	`#(1 . "one")`
list	`#(1, 2, 3)`
vector	`#[1, 2, 3]`

Literal constants are immutable. Attempting to modify an immutable object has undefined consequences. Immutable objects may share structure. Literal constants that are equal may or may not be identical.

A symbol can be indicated in two ways: as a keyword (for example, `test:`) or as a unique string (for example, `#"red"`). The difference is purely syntactic; the choice is provided to promote program readability.

A string literal can be broken across lines by writing two string literals in a row, separated only by whitespace; they are automatically concatenated (without a newline character).

A **named value reference** returns the value of a visible binding given its name; for example, `foo`. The referenced binding can be a module binding (either constant or variable) or a local binding established by a local declaration or by a parameter list. The value of the binding must not be a macro.

A **reserved word** is a syntactic token that has the form of a name but is reserved by the Dylan language and so cannot be given a binding and cannot be used as a named value reference. There are seven reserved words in Dylan: `define`, `end`, `handler`, `let`, `local`, `macro`, and `otherwise`.

A **function call** applies a function to arguments, and returns whatever values the function returns. The function is indicated by an operand and can be a generic function, a method, or a function macro. The arguments are separated by commas and enclosed in parentheses. For example, `f(x, y)`. For readability, the comma can be omitted between the two arguments in a keyword/value pair, for example `element(c, k, default: d)` is a function call with four arguments.

A **unary operator call** consists of an operand preceded by one of the two unary operators: − (arithmetic negation) or ~ (logical negation); for example, `− x`. A unary operator call is actually an abbreviated notation for a function call.

A **binary operator call** consists of two expressions separated by one of the binary operators: + (addition), − (subtraction), * (multiplication), / (division), ^ (exponentiation), = (equality), == (identity), < (less than), > (greater than), <= (less than or equal), >= (greater than or equal), ~= (not equal), ~== (not identical), & (logical and), | (logical or), or := (assignment). When binary operator calls are chained together, they are grouped by rules of precedence and associativity and by parentheses—for example, `(a − b) * x + c * x ^ 2`. A binary operator call is actually an abbreviated notation for a function call or function-macro call. The rules of precedence are given in Table 4-1, "Operators," on page 37.

An **element reference** consists of an operand that indicates a collection and an expression in square brackets that indicates a key. Instead of a key, there can be multiple expressions separated by commas that indicate array indices; for example, `c[k]` or `a[i, j]`. This is actually an abbreviated notation for a function call.

A **slot reference** is another abbreviated notation for a function call. It consists of an operand that indicates an object, a period, and a named value reference that indicates a one-argument function to apply to the object. Typically the function is a slot getter but this is not required, as in `airplane.wingspan`.

A **parenthesized expression** is any expression inside parentheses. The parentheses have no significance except to group the arguments of an operator or to turn a general expression into an operand; for example, `(a + b) * c`.

Statements

A **statement** is a call to a statement macro. It begins with the name of a visible binding whose value is a statement macro. The statement ends with the word `end` optionally followed by the same name that began the statement. In between is a program fragment whose syntax is determined by the macro definition. Typically this fragment includes an optional body; for example, `if (ship.ready?) embark(passenger, ship) end if`.

A **statement macro** can be built-in or user-defined.

A **user-defined statement macro** is a macro that defines how to implement a statement in terms of other constructs. Advanced programmers often define new statement macros as part of structuring a program in a readable and modular way.

A **built-in statement macro** is like a user-defined statement macro but is specified as part of the Dylan language. There are nine built-in statement macros: `begin`, `block`, `case`, `for`, `if`, `select`, `unless`, `until`, and `while`.

An implementation can add new kinds of statements as language extensions. Such a statement takes the form of a user-defined statement macro that is the value of a binding exported by an implementation-defined module.

Parameter Lists

Several Dylan constructs contain a **parameter list**, which describes the arguments expected by a function and the values returned by that function. The description includes names, types, keyword arguments, fixed or variable number of arguments, and fixed or variable number of values. The argument names specified are locally bound to the values of the arguments when the function is called. The value names specified are only for documentation.

The syntactic details of parameter lists are described in "Methods" on page 426.

Lexical Syntax

Dylan source code is a sequence of tokens. Whitespace is required between tokens if the tokens would otherwise blend together. Whitespace is optional between self-delimiting tokens. Alphabetic case is not significant except within character and string literals.

Whitespace can be a space character, a tab character, a newline character, or a comment. Implementations can define additional whitespace characters.

A **comment** can be single-line or delimited. Although comments count as whitespace, the beginning of a comment can blend with a preceding token, so in general comments should be surrounded by genuine whitespace.

A **single-line comment** consists of two slash characters in a row, followed by any number of characters up to and including the first newline character or the end of the source record. For example, `// This line is a kludge!`

A **delimited comment** consists of a slash character immediately followed by a star character, any number of characters (including complete single-line and complete delimited comments), and finally a star character immediately followed by a slash character. For example, `/* set x to 3 */`.

A single-line comment may appear within a delimited comment; occurrences of slash-star or star-slash within the single line comment are ignored.

A **token** is a name, a #-word, an operator, a number, a character literal, a string literal, a symbol literal, or punctuation.

A **name** is one of the following four possibilities:

- An alphabetic character followed by zero or more name characters.

- A numeric character followed by two or more name characters including at least two alphabetic characters in a row.

- A graphic character followed by one or more name characters including at least one alphabetic character.

- A "\" (backslash) followed by a function operator or another name.

An **alphabetic character** is any of the 26 letters of the Roman alphabet in upper and lower case.

A **numeric character** is any of the 10 digits.

A **graphic character** is one of the following:

$$! \& * < = > \mid \wedge \$ \% @ \_$$

A **name character** is an alphabetic character, a numeric character, a graphic character, or one of the following:

$$- + \sim ? /$$

The rich set of name characters means that name and operator tokens can blend. Thus Dylan programs usually set off operators with whitespace.

Implementations can add additional characters but programs using them will not be portable.

A **#-word** is one of #t, #f, #next, #rest, #key, or #all-keys. The first two are literal constants, the others are used in parameter lists. Implementations can add additional implementation-defined #-words, but programmers cannot add their own #-words.

An **operator** is one of the following:

+	addition
–	subtraction and negation
*	multiplication
/	division
^	exponentiation
=	equality
==	identity
<	less than
>	greater than
<=	less than or equal
>=	greater than or equal
~=	not equal
~==	not identical
&	logical and
|	logical or
:=	assignment
~	logical negation

Programmers cannot add their own operators.

A **number** is a decimal integer with an optional leading sign, a binary integer, an octal integer, a hexadecimal integer, a ratio of two decimal integers with an optional leading sign, or a floating-point number. The complete syntax of numbers is given in "Numbers" on page 418. Note that the ratios are not included in the Dylan language. The ratio syntax is reserved for future expansion and for implementation-specific extensions.

A **character literal** is a printing character (including space, but not ' or \) or a backslash escape sequence enclosed in a pair of single-quote characters '.

A **string literal** is a sequence of printing characters (including space, but not " or \) and backslash escape sequences enclosed in a pair of double-quote characters ".

A **backslash escape sequence** is a backslash followed by a character or character code. A backslash escape sequence in character and string literals allows quoting of the special characters ', ", and \, provides names for control characters, and allows Unicode characters to be specified by their hexadecimal codes.

The control characters are:

a	alarm
b	backspace
e	escape
f	form feed
n	newline
r	carriage return
t	tab
0	null

Unicode characters are represented by a series of hexadecimal digits enclosed in angle brackets. If Unicode does not explicitly define the character represented by the hexadecimal digits, the meaning in Dylan is undefined. If an implementation is not able to represent the entire Unicode character set, and the number specifies a character that is not representable in the implementation, an error must be signaled.

For example: `"\<44>\<79>\<6c>\<61>\<6e>" = "Dylan"`

A **symbol literal** is a keyword or a unique string. A **keyword** is a name followed immediately by a colon character ":". A **unique string** is a sharp sign "#" followed immediately by a string literal.

Punctuation is one of the following:

( )	parentheses
[ ]	square brackets
{ }	curly brackets
,	comma
.	period
;	semicolon
=	defaulting/initialization
::	type specialization
==	singleton specialization
=>	arrow
#(	list/pair literal
#[	vector literal
?, ??	macro pattern variables
...	macro ellipsis

Note that some tokens are both punctuation and operators. This ambiguity is resolved by grammatical context.

Note also that some punctuation tokens (for example, period and equal sign) are capable of blending into some other tokens. Where this can occur, whitespace must be inserted to delimit the token boundary.

Special Treatment of Names

Escaping Names

The escape character (\ ) followed by any name or operator-name has the same meaning as that name or operator-name, except that it is stripped of special syntactic properties. If it would otherwise be a reserved word or operator, it is not recognized as such.

For example, \if and if are names for the same binding, but \if is treated syntactically as a named value reference, while if is the beginning of a statement. Similarly, \+ and + refer to the same binding, but the former is treated syntactically as a named value reference, and the latter as an operator.

For reserved words, this allows the names of statement macros to be exported and imported from modules. It does not allow them to be used as the names of local bindings, nor does it allow them to be executed. (That is, they cannot be used as bindings to runtime values.)

For operators, it allows the operator to be used where a named value reference is required, for example as the name in a method definition, as an argument to a function, or in a `define module` export clause.

Function Call Shorthand

Dylan provides convenient syntax for calling a number of functions. These include the operators, the array reference syntax, and the singleton syntax.

In all cases, the syntax is equivalent to a function call (which can be a function macro call) whose function is a named value reference to the name of the function in the current environment. The syntax does not automatically refer to a binding in the Dylan module.

Top-Level Definitions

Dylan's built-in defining macros and special definitons can only be used at top level. When the expansion of a user-defined macro includes a call to a built-in defining macro or special definition, the user-defined macro also can only be used at top level.

A constituent is at **top level** if and only if it is a direct constituent of a body, no preceding constituent of that body is a local declaration, and the body is either the body of a source record or the body of a `begin` statement that is itself a constituent at top level. When a constituent appears inside a call to a macro, whether that constituent is at top level must be determined after macro expansion.

The effect of the above rule is that a constituent at top level is not in the scope of any local declarations, is not subject to any condition handlers other than default handlers, and is not affected by any flow of control constructs such as conditionals and iterations. This restriction enhances the static nature of definitions.

Dylan Interchange Format

The **Dylan interchange format** is a standard file format for publishing Dylan source code. Such a file has two parts, the **file header** and the **code body**. The file header comes before the code body.

The code body consists of a source record.

The file header consists of one or more keyword-value pairs, as follows:

- A keyword is a letter, followed by zero or more letters, digits, and hyphens, followed by a colon. It contains only characters from the ISO 646 7-bit character set, and is case-independent.

- A keyword begins on a new line, and cannot be preceded by whitespace.

- All text (excluding whitespace) between the keyword and the next newline is considered to be the value. Additional lines can be added by having the additional lines start with whitespace. Leading whitespace is ignored on all lines.

- The meaning of the value is determined by the keyword.

- Implementations must recognize and handle standardized keywords properly, unless the specification for a keyword explicitly states that it can be ignored.

- When importing a file, implementations are free to ignore any nonstandard keyword-value pairs that they do not recognize.

- When exporting a file, implementations must use standard keywords properly. Implementations are free to use nonstandard keywords.

- The definition of a keyword may specify that the keyword may occur more than once in a single file header. If it does not, then it is an error for the keyword to occur more than once. If it does, it should specify the meaning of multiple occurrences.

The file header cannot contain comments, or other Dylan source code.

Blank lines may not appear in the file header. A blank line defines the end of the file header and the beginning of the code body. The blank line is not part of the code body. (A "blank line" is a line consisting of zero or more space or tab characters, ending in a newline character.)

The following standard keywords are defined:

`language:` *language-name*   [Header keyword]

The source record in the file is written in the named language. The only portable value for this keyword is `infix-dylan`.

`module:` *module-name*   [Header keyword]

The source record in the file is associated with the named module. This keyword is required.

author: *text*	**[Header keyword]**
copyright: *text*	**[Header keyword]**
version: *text*	**[Header keyword]**

These are provided for standardization. They are optional, and can be ignored by the implementation.

A typical Dylan source file might look like this:

```
module: quickdraw
author: J. Random Rect
        Linear Wheels, Inc., "Where quality is a slogan!"
        rect@linear.com
copyright: (c) 1995 Linear Wheels, Inc., All rights reserved
version: 1.3 alpha (not fully tested)

define constant $black-color = ...
```

Naming Conventions

Several conventions for naming module bindings help programmers identify the purposes of bindings. In general, the names of bindings do not affect the semantics of a program, but are simply used to improve readability. (The exceptions to this rule are the "-definer" suffix used by definition macros, and the "-setter" suffix, described later in this section.)

■ Module bindings used to hold types begin and end with angle brackets.

```
<window>
<object>
<character>
<number>
<stream>
<list>
```

■ Variable module bindings begin and end with asterisks.

```
*parse-level*
*incremental-search-string*
*machine-state*
*window-count*
```

■ Program constants begin with a dollar sign.

```
$pi
$end-of-file
```

■ The names of most predicate functions end with a question mark. Predicates are functions that return a true or false value.

```
subclass?
even?
instance?
```

■ Operations that return a value similar to one of their arguments and that also destructively modify the argument end in a !. (It will often also be the case that destructive and non-destructive variations of the function exist.) ! isn't a universal warning that an operation is destructive. Destructive functions that return other values (like -setter functions and pop) don't need to use the ! convention.

```
reverse!
sort!
```

■ Operations that retrieve a value from a location are called **getters**. Operations that store into a location are called **setters**. In general, getters and setters come in pairs. Setter binding names are derived by appending "-setter" to the corresponding getter binding name. This convention is used to generate setter names automatically, and it is used by :=, the assignment operator, to find the setter that corresponds to a given getter.

```
element      element-setter
size         size-setter
color        color-setter
```

Program Structure

Contents

Modules   27
   Defining Module Bindings   27
Libraries   28

Modules

Modules are used for creating large-scale namespaces of bindings. The bindings accessible in a module are visible to all the code within the module (except where shadowed by a local binding). Only the bindings explicitly exported are visible from outside the module.

Some languages have module systems with distinct support for exporting variables, functions, types, and classes. Dylan modules operate only on bindings. Because functions and classes are commonly named by bindings, access to them is controlled by controlling access to the bindings that name them. By exporting the binding naming a class or function, a program has effectively exported the class or function. If the binding is not exported, then the class or function is effectively private.[*]

A module definition defines the imports and exports of a module, and may specify bindings owned by the module. A complete description of module definitions is given on page 380.

Defining Module Bindings

A module consists of a set of bindings. A binding may be **owned** by a module, or a module may **import** the binding from another module by **using** the other module. Modules **export** bindings to make them accessible to other modules. Only exported bindings can be imported by other modules.

Module-use relationships may not be circular. To create a common set of bindings for a group of modules, the modules can import the bindings from another module or modules.

Within a given module, a name refers to at most one module binding. It is an error to create or import two or more different bindings with the same name in a single module. If a name does refer to a binding, the binding is said to be **accessible** from the module. Each binding is owned by exactly one module, but it can be accessible from many modules.

---

[*] This privacy can sometimes be circumvented through certain introspective operations.

Module bindings are created by definitions. **Explicit definitions** are created by `define constant`, `define variable`, `define generic`, `define macro` and the class name in `define class`. **Implicit definitions** are created by `define method` and the slot specifications of `define class`.

Within a library, a module binding may have no explicit definition or it may have one explicit definition. It may not have more than one explicit definition. If a module binding has no explicit definition, it must have one or more implicit definitions. If it does have an explicit definition, it can have zero or more implicit definitions.

A binding may be declared by the `create` clause of a module definition. This does not define the binding, but instead declares that it is owned by the module. Other modules may import the binding from that module. The binding must be defined by one of the modules that imports it.

If a binding is not declared by the `create` clause of a module definition, it is owned by the module in which its explicit definition appears. If it does not have an explicit definition, it is owned by one of the modules in which at least one of its implicit definitions appears; the exact owning module cannot be determined.

It is an error to reference a name for the purpose of getting or setting its value if the name does not designate either a local or module binding in the environment where the reference occurs.

Libraries

A library consists of the following parts:

- A library definition. This specifies a name for the library; a set of modules that are exported from the library for use by other libraries; a set of other libraries that are used by the library being defined; and a set of modules that are imported from the used libraries. To allow separate compilation, library-use relationships may not be circular. A complete description of library definitions is given on page 386.

- The association of source code with the library. The mechanism by which this association is made is controlled by the programming environment and is implementation-defined.

■ The association of executable code with the library. The mechanism by which this association is made is implementation-defined. The mechanism by which the compiler is invoked to produce the executable code is implementation-defined.

■ The export information of the library. The format of this information and the mechanism by which it is associated with the library is implementation-defined. The export information comprises the information required to process the source code of another library that imports the library.

The library export information is the only part of a Dylan library that is needed to allow some other library to import it. A library that exports some modules does not have any additional declarations providing information to the compiler when it is processing the code that imports those modules. Rather, any such information that is needed is obtained in some implementation-defined way while processing the source code of the exporting library and is retained in the library export information of the exporting library.

Exporting a module from a library makes all of the bindings exported by the module available for import by modules in other libraries.

Importing a module into a library allows the module to be used by modules defined within the library. This gives the library's modules access to the bindings of the module being imported.

Importing a module into a library does not allow source records in the importing library to be contained in the imported module.

Each implementation must provide a library named `dylan` that exports a module named `dylan`. That module must export exactly those bindings documented as being part of the Dylan language, and the values of those bindings must be as specified by the Dylan language. The `dylan` library is permitted to export additional implementation-defined modules.

Each library contains an implicitly defined module whose name is `dylan-user`. Within this module, all the bindings specified by the Dylan language are accessible using their specified names. Additional implementation-dependent bindings may also be accessible from this module.

Program Control

Contents

Overview   33
Function Calls   33
   General Syntax   33
   Slot Reference   34
   Element Reference   35
Operators   35
Assignment   38
Conditional Execution   39
   True and False   40
Iteration   40
   Iteration Statements   40
   Tail Recursion   41
Nonlocal Exits and Cleanup Clauses   41
Multiple Values   42
Order of Execution   43
   Execution Order Within Expressions   44

Overview

Dylan provides a number of program control constructs, implementing function calls, operators, assignment, conditional execution, iteration, and nonlocal flow of control.

This chapter also describes the multiple-value facility and the rules for order of execution of Dylan programs.

Function Calls

General Syntax

The general syntax for function calls is

function (*arg1* , *arg2* , ... *argn*)

function has the syntax of an operand and is the function to be called. The *args* have the syntax of expressions, and are the arguments to the function. The *function* will often be a named value reference, but it can be any other kind of operand as well.

In the following example, the function being called is the value of the binding `average`.

```
average(x, y)
```

In the following two examples, the function being called is the value of a `method` statement. The examples differ only in that the second example puts parentheses around the `method` statement, to make the code somewhat more readable.

```
method(x) x + 1 end (99)
```

```
(method(x) x + 1 end) (99)
```

In the following examples, the function being called is the result of another function call. `key-test` takes a collection as an argument, and returns a predicate function. The predicate function is then applied to the two keys. The following three program fragments will have the same effect.

```
key-test(collection)(key1, key2)
```

```
(key-test(collection))(key1, key2)
```

```
begin
  let fun = key-test(collection);
  fun(key1, key2);
end
```

Functions may accept keyword arguments. These are optional and order-independent. They may also accept a variable number of "rest" arguments.

A complete description of functions, parameter lists, and function calling is given in Chapter 6, "Functions."

Slot Reference

Dylan provides a shorthand syntax for functions that accept one argument. The syntax *argument . function* applies *function* to *argument*. This syntax is commonly used for slot reference, to access the *function* slot of *argument*.

Order of execution aside, the following pairs of function calls are equivalent:

```
america.capital
capital(america)
```

```
window.position
position(window)
```

Slot reference syntax can be cascaded and is left associative. Order of execution aside, the following pair of expressions are equivalent. Each returns the origin of the root-view of a window.

```
window.root-view.origin
origin(root-view(window))
```

Element Reference

Dylan provides a shorthand syntax for element reference. The syntax *sequence*`[i]` is equivalent to the function call `element`(*sequence*, `i`). The syntax *array*`[`i_1, i_2, ... i_n`]` is equivalent to the function call `aref`(*array*, i_1, i_2, ... i_n).

Order of execution aside, the following pairs of expressions are equivalent:

```
*all-windows*[0]
element(*all-windows*, 0)


*tic-tac-toe*[1, 2]
aref(*tic-tac-toe*, 1, 2)
```

The names `element` and `aref` are looked up in the environment of the element reference expression.

Operators

Dylan provides a small number of unary and binary operators. These are syntactic shorthand for function calls or function-macro calls.

Because of the possibility of token blending, operators and their operands must often be separated by whitespace. For example, `foo+bar` is a single named value reference, not an invocation of the addition operator. The complete rules of tokenization are given in the lexical syntax in Appendix A, "BNF."

All binary operators are left-associative, except for the assignment operator, `:=`, and the exponentiation operator, `^`, which are right-associative.

Each operator corresponds to a binding name, given in the table below. When an operator is called, the corresponding name is looked up in the environment of the call. (It is not looked up in the Dylan module, and will only refer to a binding in the Dylan module if that binding has been imported in the current module and has not been shadowed by a lexical binding.)

If the name given in the table has the same spelling as the operator, it must be escaped with \ to be used as a named value reference. For example, to add a method to + with `define method`, you use \+. To use < as an argument to `sort`, you write \<.

The operands of a binary operator call that is shorthand for a function call are executed in left to right order. The operands of a binary operator call which is shorthand for a function macro call are passed to the macro. Their order of execution depends on the definition of the macro. The built-in function macros are described in "Function Macros" on page 409.

The operators are listed in Table 4-1 in descending order of precedence. Operators within a group share the same precedence. When a function call using slot reference syntax appears as an operand, it has greater precedence than any of the binary operators.

Table 4-1   Operators

Operator	Unary/Binary	Description	Name
–	unary	arithmetic negation	negative
~	unary	logical negation	~
^	binary	exponentiation	^
*	binary	multiplication	*
/	binary	division	/
+	binary	addition	+
–	binary	subtraction	–
=	binary	equality	=
==	binary	identity	==
~=	binary	non-equality	~=
~==	binary	non-identity	~==
<	binary	less than	<
>	binary	greater than	>
<=	binary	less than or equals	<=
>=	binary	greater than or equals	>=
&	binary	logical and	&
|	binary	logical or	|
:=	binary	assignment	:=

Assignment

The operator := is used to set variables to new values and as an alternate syntax for calling setter functions and macros.

The assignment operator is described in detail on page 409.

The following examples show the use of : = to change the value of a module binding.

```
define variable *foo* = 10;
*foo*
  ⇒   10
*foo* := *foo* + 100;
  ⇒   110
*foo*
  ⇒   110
```

The following examples show the use of : = as shorthand for calling a setter function. In general, using this syntax to call a function *fun* is equivalent to calling the function *fun*-setter.

```
define variable *foo* = vector (10, 6, 8, 5);
element(*foo*, 2)
  ⇒   8
element(*foo*, 2) := "bar"
  ⇒   "bar"
*foo*
  ⇒   #[10, 6, "bar", 5]
```

The following examples show the use of : = as shorthand for calling a setter function using slot access notation.

```
window.position := point(100, 100)
vector.size := 50
```

The following examples show the use of : = as shorthand for calling element-setter or aref-setter.

```
my-vector[2] := #"two"
my-array[1,1] := #"top-left"
```

Conditional Execution

There are a number of statements and function macros that can be used to conditionally execute code. These are described in detail in Chapter 14, "The Built-In Macros and Special Definitions."

Table 4-2 Conditional Execution

Macro / Operator	Description	Page
if	Executes an implicit body if the value of a test is true or an alternate if the test is false.	395
unless	Executes an implicit body unless the value of a test is true.	396
case	Executes a number of tests until one is true, and then executes an implicit body associated with the true test.	397
select	Compares a target object to a series of potential matches, and executes an implicit body associated with the first match found.	398
|	Returns the value of the first of two operands that is true. This is a logical or operation.	412
&	If the value of a first operand is true, executes a second operand and returns its values. This is a logical and operation.	412

True and False

For the purposes of conditional execution, there is a single object that counts as false, and all other objects count as true.

The false object is the constant #f. There is a canonical true object, #t, which can be used for clarity of code. #t and #f are instances of the class <boolean>.

Because all values besides #f count as true, the term "true or false" is not equivalent to "#t or #f".

The operator ~ is used for logical negation. If its operand is true, it returns #f. If its operand is #f, it returns #t.

Iteration

Iteration is supported through a number of statements, as well as through recursive functions.

Iteration Statements

The statements supporting iteration are described in detail in Chapter 14, "The Built-In Macros and Special Definitions."

Table 4-3   Iteration Statements

Macro	Description	Page
while	Repeatedly executes a body until a test expression is false.	399
until	Repeatedly executes a body until a test expression is true.	400
for	Performs general iteration over a body, updating bindings and performing end tests on each iteration.	400

Tail Recursion

Implementations are encouraged to optimize tail recursive function calls whenever possible. Tail recursion occurs when a function F_1 returns the values of a call to another function F_2. In many cases, this can be used to create loops using self-recursive or mutually recursive functions. (Among the cases that cannot be optimized are those in which the return value types of F_1 and F_2 differ, requiring the F_1 to check the types of the values before returning them.)

The following example uses tail recursion to compute the name of the root volume on which a given file system object is stored.

```
define method root-volume-name (f :: <file-or-directory>)
  if ( root-volume?(f) )
    f.name
  else
    root-volume-name(f.container)
  end if;
end method;
```

The example above can execute with constant stack size, regardless of how deeply nested the file system hierarchy may be.

Nonlocal Exits and Cleanup Clauses

Nonlocal exits allow the direct transfer of control to a previous point in program execution. The normal chain of function returns is aborted.

Cleanup clauses are bodies that are guaranteed to execute, even if the program segment of which they are a part is aborted by a nonlocal exit.

Nonlocal exits and cleanup clauses are implemented by the `block` statement. A complete description of the `block` statement is given on page 404.

Multiple Values

The execution of an expression can yield one value, more than one value, or no values at all. This capability is called **multiple values**.

Multiple values are generated by the function `values`. They are received by the bindings of `let` declarations and `define constant` and `define variable` definitions.

Many statements will return multiple values if the last expression they execute returns multiple values. Similarly, a function will return all the values of the last subexpression it executes.

```
define method return-three-values (a, b, c)
  values(a, b, c)
end method return-three-values;

begin
  let (foo, bar, baz) = return-three-values (1, 2, 3);
  list (foo, bar, baz)
end
  => #(1, 2, 3)
```

Each expression in the argument list of a function call supplies only one argument to the function call. That argument is the first value returned by the expression. Additional values returned by the expressions are ignored.

```
list (return-three-values(1, 2, 3),
      return-three-values(1, 2, 3),
      return-three-values(1, 2, 3))
  ⇒ #(1, 1, 1)
```

Multiple values can be used to perform parallel binding:

```
begin
  let x = 10;
  let y = 20;
  let (x, y) = values (y, x);
  list (x, y);
end
  ⇒  #(20, 10)
```

The following rules apply when matching up an expression that returns multiple values with a binding declaration or definition that receives multiple values.

- If there are the same number of bindings and values, the bindings are initialized to the corresponding values.

- If there are more bindings than there are values, the extra bindings are initialized to #f. (If a binding is typed, #f must be an instance of its type or an error is signaled.)

- If there are more values returned than there are bindings, the excess values are placed in a sequence that is used as the initial value for rest-binding or discarded if there is no rest-binding.

```
begin
  let (one #rest nums) = return-three-values(1, 2, 3);
  nums;
end
  ⇒  #(2, 3)
```

- If there is a rest-binding but there are no excess values, rest-binding is initialized to an empty sequence.

Order of Execution

Order of execution is defined for the constituents within a body. With some exceptions noted below, this execution order is left-to-right.

Definitions form the overall structure of a program and are not said to execute. In particular, module bindings are not created in any order, but all exist when program execution commences. To the extent that these bindings must be initialized by the values of some expressions that cannot be analyzed at compile time, references to the bindings are constrained by the execution order of the expressions within the surrounding body.

Dylan implementations are encouraged to allow forward references to module bindings whenever possible.

The order of execution of the components of a call to a user-defined macro is determined by the macro.

Execution Order Within Expressions

In general, execution within an expression proceeds left-to-right. The chief exception to this rule is the assignment operator, which is executed right-to-left.

- In a standard function call, the function operand is executed first, followed by the argument expressions. (Remember, the function need not be a named value reference, but can be a more complex operand). After the function operand has been executed and each of the argument expressions has been executed, the function is applied to the arguments.

  ```
  one(two, three, four)
  ```

- In slot references, the object operand is executed first, followed by the function named value reference. Then the function is applied to the object.

  ```
  one.two
  ```

- In element references, the collection operand is executed first, followed by the key expressions in order. Then the element access is performed. The execution time of the binding `element` or `aref` is unspecified.

  ```
  one[two, three]
  ```

- In an operator call, the operands are executed left-to-right. The execution time of the binding specified by the operand (e.g. + or *) is unspecified.

  ```
  one + two - three
  ```

- In an assignment to a place that represents a function call, the order of execution is largely the same as it would be in a call to the corresponding setter function. The new-value expression is executed first, followed by the argument expressions. The execution time of the binding named by the setter function is undefined.

  ```
  function-setter(one, two, three)
  function(two, three) := one

  slot-setter(one, two)
  two.slot := one
  ```

```
element-setter(one, two, three)
two[three] := one

aref-setter(one, two, three, four)
two[three, four] := one
```

Types and Classes

Contents

Overview   49

The Type Protocol   49

   Base Types and Pseudosubtypes   50

   Type Disjointness   51

Classes   52

   Features of Classes   52

   Creating Classes   52

   Class Inheritance   53

   Computing the Class Precedence List   54

Slots   57

   Slot Inheritance   58

   Slot Specifications   58

Instance Creation and Initialization   64

   Overview   64

   Inherited Slot Specifications   67

   Initialization Argument Specifications   68

Singletons   71

Union Types   72

Limited Types   73

   Limited Type Constructor   74

   Limited Integer Types   74

   Limited Collection Types   75

Overview

The Dylan type system is used to categorize all objects. In concert with generic functions, types determine the behavior of objects. When an object is passed as an argument to a generic function, the generic function looks at the type of the object to determine which method should be run.

Dylan supports several kinds of types, including classes, singletons, union types, and limited types.

- Classes are used to define the structure, inheritance, and initialization of all objects. An object can be an instance of any number of types, but will always be a direct instance of exactly one class.

- Singletons are used to indicate individual objects.

- Union types are used to indicate objects that are instances of one of a set of specified types.

- Limited types are used to indicate objects that are instances of another type and have additional constraints. There are several kinds of limited types.

All types are first class objects, and are general instances of `<type>`. Implementations may add additional kinds of types. The language does not define any way for programmers to define new subclasses of `<type>`.

The Type Protocol

The type protocol comprises the following:

- All types may be used as specializers for method parameters, bindings, and slots.

- `instance?` (*object*, *type*) tests type membership.

- `subtype?` (*type1*, *type2*) tests type inclusion.

- `make` (*type* ...) makes an instance. This operation is only supported if the type is instantiable.

- Type objects are immutable.

- If two type objects are equivalent and are not classes, it is unspecified whether they are ==.

The following is an informal description of type relationships: The function subtype? defines a partial ordering of all types. Type t_1 is a subtype of type t_2 (i.e., subtype?(t_1, t_2) is true) if it is impossible to encounter an object that is an instance of t_1 but not an instance of t_2. It follows that every type is a subtype of itself. Two types t_1 and t_2 are said to be **equivalent types** if subtype?(t_1, t_2) and subtype?(t_2, t_1) are both true. t_1 is said to be a **proper subtype** of t_2 if t_1 is a subtype of t_2 and t_2 is not a subtype of t_1.

subtype? on classes is defined by inheritance. A class is a subtype of itself and of its general superclasses.

subtype? on singletons is defined by object type and identity. If x is an object and t is a type, subtype?(singleton(x), t) will be true only if instance?(x, t) is true.

subtype? rules for union types are given in "Union Types" on page 72. subtype? rules for limited integer types are given in "Limited Integer Types" on page 74. subtype? rules for limited collection types are given in "Limited Collection Types" on page 126.

<object> is the root of the type hierarchy. All objects are instances of <object>, and all types are subtypes of <object>.

A number of operations on types are described in "Reflective Operations on Types" on page 343.

Base Types and Pseudosubtypes

Every type has a **base type**. The base type for a class is the class itself. The base type of a singleton is the singleton itself. The base type of a union is the union of the base types of its component types. The base type of a limited type limited(C, ...) is C.

The type t_1 is a **pseudosubtype** of the type t_2 if t_1 is a subtype of the base type of t_2 and t_1 and t_2 are not disjoint.

Note that t_1 being a subtype of t_2 implies that t_1 is a pseudosubtype of t_2, but t_1 being a pseudosubtype of t_2 does not imply that t_1 is a subtype of t_2. Note also that if t_2 is not a limited type or some other nonstandard type, then pseudosubtype is the same as subtype.

Base types and pseudosubtypes are used in the rules for sealing, described in Chapter 9, "Sealing."

Type Disjointness

Informally, two types are disjoint if there can be no object that is an instance of both types. Formally, the disjointness of types is specified by the following set of rules. (Some of these rules reference definitions given in "Limited Integer Types" on page 74, "Element Types" on page 124 and "Limited Collection Types" on page 126.)

- Two classes are disjoint if they have no common subclasses.

- A union type is disjoint from another type if all of the union type's component types are disjoint from that other type.

- A singleton type is disjoint from another type if the singleton's object is not an instance of that other type.

- A limited collection type is disjoint from a class if their base types are disjoint, or the class is a subclass of `<collection>` and its element type is definite and not equivalent to the limited collection type's element type, or the class is a subclass of `<collection>` and its element type is indefinite and not a supertype of the limited collection type's element type.

- A limited collection type is disjoint from a limited integer type because the classes `<collection>` and `<integer>` are disjoint.

- Two limited collection types are disjoint if their base types are disjoint, or their element types are not equivalent, or their sizes are not compatible. Two sizes are compatible if either is `#f`, or they are = to each other, or one is a sequence of integers and the other is the product of those integers.

- Two limited integer types are disjoint if the minimum value of one is greater than the maximum value for the other.

- A limited integer type is disjoint from a class if their base types are disjoint or the class is a subclass of `<integer>` whose range is disjoint from the limited integer type's range.

Classes

Classes are used to define the inheritance, structure, and initialization of objects.

Every object is a **direct instance** of exactly one class, and a general instance of the **general superclasses** of that class.

A class determines which **slots** its instances have. Slots are the local storage available within instances. They are used to store the state of objects.

Classes determine how their instances are initialized by using the **initialization protocol**.

Features of Classes

There are four features of classes. These features relate to each other, but can be declared independently.

- A class can be **abstract** or **concrete**. If the class is concrete, it can have direct instances. If it is abstract, it cannot have direct instances, but only indirect instances.

- A class can be **instantiable** or **uninstantiable**. If the class is instantiable, it can be used as the first argument to `make`. If it is uninstantiable, it cannot be used as the first argument to `make`.

- A class can be **primary** or **free**. This controls how a class can be used for multiple inheritance. For a full description of this feature, see "Declaring Characteristics of Classes" on page 134.

- A class can be **sealed** or **open**. This controls whether a class can be subclassed outside the library where it is defined. For a full description of this feature, see "Declaring Characteristics of Classes" on page 134.

Creating Classes

New classes may be created by calling `make` on `<class>`, or with the definition `define class`. In most programs the latter is more commonly used.

When a class is created with `make`, it is instantiated and returned just like any other object. The options available when creating a class with `make` are described on page 191.

When a class is created with `define class` it is used to initialize a new module binding. `define class` allows the specification of superclasses, slots, initialization behavior, and options related to sealing. The complete syntax of `define class` is given on page 378.

The following simple class definition creates a class named by the module binding `<new>`. The class inherits from `<object>` and does not specify any slots.

```
define class <new> (<object>)
end class <new>;
```

The following class definition illustrates the creation of a class with multiple superclasses. Again, there are no slots defined by the class.

```
define class <color-window> (<palette>, <window>)
end class <color-window>;
```

Class Inheritance

When a class is created, its **direct superclasses** are specified. The new class directly inherits from these classes; it is a **direct subclass** of each of these classes. There can be no duplicates in the direct superclasses of a class.

The subclass relationship is transitive. If a class C is a direct subclass of C_1, C_1 is a direct subclass of C_2, and C_2 is a direct subclass of C_3, then C is an **indirect subclass** of C_2 and C_3. A **general subclass** is a direct or indirect subclass.

Inheritance cannot be circular. A class cannot be its own general subclass.

A class is a subtype of each of its general superclasses.

Every class is a general subclass of `<object>`.

Computing the Class Precedence List

The definition of a class specifies a total ordering on that class and its direct superclasses. This ordering is called the **local precedence order**. In the local precedence order:

- The class precedes its direct superclasses.

- Each direct superclass precedes all other direct superclasses that follow it in the sequence of direct superclasses given in the class definition.

The **class precedence list** for a class C is a total ordering on C and its superclasses that is consistent with the local precedence order of C and with the class precedence lists of its superclasses. (Two lists are consistent if for every A and B that are each members of both lists, either A precedes B in both or B precedes A in both.) The class precedence list is used in determining the order of specificity of methods based on the types they are specialized on when dispatching; for details, see "Method Dispatch" on page 95.

Sometimes there are several such consistent total orderings on C and its superclasses. Dylan uses a deterministic algorithm to compute the class precedence list, which chooses one of the consistent total orderings.

Sometimes there is no possible total ordering on C and its superclasses that is consistent with the local precedence orders for C and with the class precedence lists of its superclasses. In this case, the class precedence list cannot be computed, and an error is signaled.

Note that because the class precedence list for a class is consistent with the class precedence lists of its superclasses, inheritance in Dylan is **monotonic**. That is, if a generic function call using a direct instance of C dispatches to a method specialized in that parameter position on an indirect superclass of C, then there is a direct superclass of C that has the same behavior.

To compute the class precedence list for class C, merge the local precedence order of the class with the class precedence lists of the direct superclasses of the class. Computing the class precedence list for C requires computing the class precedence lists for its superclasses. This does not lead to infinite recursion because circular class inheritance is prohibited.

Note that because the class precedence lists of the direct superclasses are consistent with their local precedence orders and with the class precedence lists of their direct superclasses, and so on, the class precedence list for C is consistent with the local precedence orders and class precedence lists of all its superclasses and not just the direct superclasses.

The merge of several sequences is a sequence that contains each of the elements of the several input sequences. An element that appears in more than one of the input sequences appears only once in the output sequence. If two elements appear in the same input sequence, their order in the output sequence is the same as their order in that input sequence.

When there are several possible merges of the inputs, at each position in the output where there is a choice, pick the class that has a direct subclass closest to the end of the output sequence. (This is unambiguous because two candidates for a position cannot both be direct superclasses of the same class, since they would then be ordered by that class's local precedence order. This is easily computable because a class always follows its direct subclasses in the merge, therefore the most recently added direct subclass can be found by searching from the end to the beginning of the output sequence and the merge can be computed in one pass.)

This algorithm can be implemented with the following Dylan program:

```
define constant compute-class-linearization =
  method (c :: <class>) => (cpl :: <list>)
    local method merge-lists (reversed-partial-result :: <list>,
                              remaining-inputs :: <sequence>)

          if (every?(empty?, remaining-inputs))
            reverse!(reversed-partial-result)
          else
            local method candidate (c :: <class>)
                    // returns c if it can go in the result now,
                    // otherwise false

                    local method head? (l :: <list>)
                            c == head(l)
                          end method head?,

                    method tail? (l :: <list>)
                      member?(c, tail(l))
                    end method tail?;
```

Types and Classes

```
                    any?(head?, remaining-inputs)
                      & ~any?(tail?, remaining-inputs)
                      & c
                  end method candidate,

                method candidate-direct-superclass (c :: <class>)
                    any?(candidate, direct-superclasses(c))
                  end method candidate-direct-superclass;

            let next = any?(candidate-direct-superclass,
                            reversed-partial-result);

          if (next)
            local method remove-next (l :: <list>)
                    if (head(l) == next) tail(l) else l end
                  end method remove-next;
            merge-lists(pair(next, reversed-partial-result),
                        map(remove-next, remaining-inputs))
          else
            error("Inconsistent precedence graph");
          end if
        end if
      end method merge-lists;

  let c-direct-superclasses = direct-superclasses(c);
  local method cpl-list (c)
          as(<list>, all-superclasses(c))
        end method cpl-list;
  merge-lists(list(c),
              add(map(cpl-list, c-direct-superclasses),
                  as(<list>, c-direct-superclasses)));

end method; // compute-class-linearization
```

Note that the selection rule from above is enforced because any? uses the natural iteration order for sequences and returns the first true value it encounters when searching the reversed partially computed class precedence list.

Slots

Slots are the interface to information about instances. They correspond to the fields or instance variables of other object-oriented programming languages. By default, each instance of the class has private storage for each slot, so one instance can have one value in the slot and another instance can have another value. Some slots are shared among instances, as described in "Slot Allocation" on page 60.

All slot access is performed by function calls.[*] The method that returns the value of a slot is called the **getter method**, and the method that sets the value of a slot is called the **setter method**. The getter and setter methods are added to generic functions. When defining a class, you specify slots by specifying the generic functions to which the getter and setter methods should be added.

For example, the class definition for <point> might be

```
define class <point> (<object>)
  slot horizontal;
  slot vertical;
end class;
```

This definition indicates that instances of <point> should have two slots, horizontal and vertical. The getter method for the first slot is added to the generic function horizontal, and the getter method for the second slot is added to the generic function vertical. The setter method for the first slot is added to the generic function horizontal-setter, while the setter method for the second slot is added to the generic function vertical-setter.

The following two code fragments are equivalent. Each returns the horizontal coordinate of a point:

```
horizontal(a-point)
a-point.horizontal
```

The following three code fragments each set the horizontal coordinate of a point to 10:

---

[*] This is in contrast to some other languages where slots are accessed through named value references.

```
horizontal-setter(10, my-point)
horizontal(my-point) := 10
my-point.horizontal := 10
```

A slot setter method returns its new value argument.

Slot Inheritance

Slots are inherited from superclasses.

The collection of all the getter and setter generic functions for slots specified in a class or inherited from its superclasses must not contain any duplicates.

If a superclass is inherited through multiple paths, its slots are inherited once. For example, if class *A* has direct superclasses *B* and *C*, and both *B* and *C* have *D* as a direct superclass, *A* inherits from *D* both through *B* and through *C*, but the slots defined by *D* are only counted once. Because of this, multiple inheritance does not by itself create any duplicates among the getters and setters.

Note that two classes that specify a slot with the same getter or setter generic function are **disjoint** —they can never have a common subclass and no object can be an instance of both classes.

Slot Specifications

A slot specification describes a slot.

A slot specification must include the name of the getter of the slot (i.e., the name of the generic function to which the getter method will be added). This is how slots are identified. The specification may optionally include the name of the setter method. If it does not, a default name is generated by appending "-setter" to the name of the getter.

A number of other options are available in slot specifications:

- An initial value for the slot may be specified with an **init specification**.

- An init-keyword may be specified. This allows a value for the slot to be supplied when an instance is created.

- Slot allocation may be specified. This controls whether storage for the slot is allocated in each instance, or some other way.

- A slot may be specifed as constant. There will be no setter for the slot.

- A type may be specified. The value of the slot will be constrained to be an instance of that type.

- A sealing directive may be specified. See "Define Sealed Domain" on page 135 for a complete description of the sealing constraints imposed by this directive.

For the complete syntax of slot specifications, see the reference entry of `define class` on page 378.

The following example defines a class with three slots, using a variety of slot options.

```
define class <window> (<view>)
  slot title :: <string> = "untitled";
  slot position :: <point>, init-keyword: window-position:;
  slot color, init-keyword: color:, init-value: $blue-color;
end class <window>;
```

Init Specifications

An init specification provides a default initial value for a slot. It can do this directly (if it is an init specification of a slot) or it can do it indirectly by providing a default value for an init-keyword (if it is an init specification of an init-keyword).

There are three kinds of init specifications:

- An **init value** specifies a value that is used to initialize the slot. Each time the slot needs to be initialized, the identical value is used.

- An **init function** specifies a function to be called to generate a value that is used to initialize the slot. Each time the slot needs to be initialized, the function is called and its value is used. This allows slots to be initialized to fresh values, or to values computed from the current program state.

- An **init expression** specifies an expression to be executed to generate a value that is used to initialize the slot. Each time the slot needs to be initialized, the expression is executed and its value is used. This allows slots to be initialized to fresh values, or to values computed from the current program state.

Only one init specification may be supplied in a given slot specification, inherited slot specification, or initialization argument specification.

In general, an *init-function* will be called and an *init-expression* will be executed only if its value will actually be used.

Init-Keywords

An init-keyword allows the value of a slot to be specified by a keyword argument in the call to make when an instance is created. An init-keyword may be optional or required.

When the value of a slot is provided by a keyword in a call to make, it is called an **initialization argument**.

If an init-keyword is specified, the slot is said to be **keyword initializable**.

Slot Allocation

Options for slot allocation include instance, class, each-subclass, and virtual.

instance allocation specifies that each instance gets its own storage for the slot. This is the default.

class allocation specifies there is only one storage location used by all the general instances of the class. All the instances share a single value for the slot. If the value is changed in one instance, all the instances see the new value.

each-subclass allocation specifies that the class gets one storage location for the slot, to be used by all the direct instances of the class. In addition, every subclass of the class gets a storage location for the slot, for use by its direct instances.

virtual allocation specifies that no storage will be allocated for the slot. If allocation is virtual, then it is up to the programmer to define methods on the getter and setter generic functions to retrieve and store the value of the slot. Dylan will ensure the existence of generic functions for any specified getter and setter but will not add any methods to them. A virtual slot cannot specify an init specification or init-keyword. Any required initialization for the slot must be performed in a method on `initialize`.

Constant Slots

Specifying a slot as constant is equivalent to specifying `setter:` `#f`. If the constant adjective is supplied, it is an error to supply an explicit value for the `setter:` keyword in the slot specification. Such slots can only be given values at instance creation time (with an init specification or init-keyword).

```
define class <person> (<being>)
  constant slot birthplace, required-init-keyword: birthplace:;
end class <person>;

define class <astronaut> (<person>)
  constant class slot employer = #"NASA";
end class <astronaut>;

define class <hair-trigger> (<object>)
  constant slot error-if-touched;
end class <hair-trigger>;
```

Specializing Slots

Slots may be specialized by declaring the type of the slot when a class is created. Specializing a slot has the following effects on the getter and setter methods of the slot:

- The automatically defined slot getter method has its single parameter specialized on the class that specified the slot and has a return value declaration that indicates that it returns a single value of the type specified for the slot.

- The automatically defined slot setter method has its instance argument specialized on the class that specified the slot, has its new-value argument specialized on the type specified for the slot, and has a return value declaration that indicates that it returns a single value of the type specified for the slot.

The following example demonstrates how an explicitly defined setter method can be used to coerce a slot value of the wrong type (<sequence>) to the right type (<simple-object-vector>).

```
define class <person> (<object>)
  slot friends :: <simple-object-vector>, init-value: #[];
end class;

define method friends-setter (f :: <sequence>, p :: <person>)
  p.friends := as(<simple-object-vector>, f);
  f;                  // return new-value argument
end method

tom.friends := list(dick, harry);
```

The assignment expression invokes the method with the new-value parameter specialized on <sequence>, which reinvokes the function with a new-value argument that is a <simple-object-vector>, which invokes the slot setter method.

Overriding Slots in Subclasses

Some slot options related to instance initialization can be overridden in subclasses. The mechanisms for doing this are described in "Inherited Slot Specifications" on page 67 and in "Initialization Argument Specifications" on page 68.

Using Slots

Because slots are accessed through methods in generic functions, they appear to clients just like any other methods in generic functions. It is possible for a value to be stored in a slot in instances of one class, but computed from auxiliary values by instances of another class. It is possible to filter the value of a slot when it is retrieved or stored. In all of these cases, the interface to the value is a function call, thus hiding the implementation details from clients.

In the following example, the class <view> stores position directly, while <displaced-view> performs a transformation on the value of the slot when storing or retrieving it.

Types and Classes

```
define class <view> (<object>)
  instance slot position;
end class;

define class <displaced-view> (<view>)
end class;

define method position (v :: <displaced-view>)
  // call the  inherited method (the raw slot getter)
  // and transform the result
  displace-transform (next-method (v));
end method;

define method position-setter (new-position,
                               v :: <displaced-view>)
  // call the inherited method (the raw slot setter)
  // on the result of untransforming the position
  next-method (displace-untransform (new-position),
            v);
  new-position;  // return the new position '
end method;
```

In other situations, a programmer will want storage in an instance for a slot
value, but will want to perform some auxiliary action whenever the slot is
accessed. In this case, the programmer should define two slots: an instance slot
to provide the storage and a virtual slot to provide the interface. In general,
only the virtual slot will be documented. The instance slot will be an internal
implementation used by the virtual slot for storage. An example of such use
would be a slot that caches a value.

```
define class <shape> (<view>)
  virtual slot image;
  instance slot cached-image, init-value: #f;
  ...
end class;
```

```
define method image (shape :: <shape>)
  cached-image (shape)
    | (cached-image (shape) := compute-image (shape));
end method;

define method image-setter (new-image, shape :: <shape>)
  cached-image (shape) := new-image;
end method;
```

Instance Creation and Initialization

The creation and initialization of instances is controlled by the generic functions initialize and make, using initialization information supplied by the class definition and by keyword arguments in the call to make. Much of this behavior is supplied by the default make method defined on <class>.

Overview

Instance creation and initialization proceeds through the following steps:

- The program calls make specifying a class and a set of keyword arguments.

- Optionally, the default make method may be shadowed by a user-supplied method specialized with a singleton specializer. This enables the user method to get at all the arguments to make, and to provide actual instantiation and initializations based on them. For example, a singleton method on an abstract class can reinvoke make on a concrete subclass of the abstract class, passing along the same or augmented initialization arguments.

- The default make method examines its keyword arguments, which are known as the **supplied initialization arguments**. It then produces a set of **defaulted initialization arguments** by augmenting the supplied initialization arguments with any additional initialization arguments for which default values are defined by the class or any of its superclasses. If the supplied initialization arguments contains duplicate keywords, make will use the leftmost occurrence. This is consistent with keyword argument conventions used in function calls.

- The default `make` method signals an error if any required init-keyword is absent from the defaulted initialization arguments, or if any of the defaulted initialization arguments are not valid for initialization of that class. An initialization argument is valid if it is specified as an init-keyword in a slot specification or initialization argument specification, or if it is permitted by one or more of the `initialize` methods applicable to an instance of the class.

- The default `make` method allocates an instance and initializes all the slots for which it can provide values, as follows:

  □ If the slot is keyword initializable and its keyword is present in the defaulted initialization arguments, then the slot is initialized from the defaulted initialization arguments.

  □ If the slot is not initialized by a keyword but has an init specification, it is initialized from the init specification.

  □ In either case, an error of type `<type-error>` is signaled if the value is not of the type declared for the slot.

  □ Regardless of the source, the initial value is stored into the slot using an unspecified built-in mechanism. In particular, the setter generic function is not called to store the value into the slot.

- The default `make` method then calls `initialize` on the initialized instance and the defaulted initialization arguments. Methods on initialize can access these arguments by accepting them as keyword parameters or in a rest parameter. If they are accepted in a rest parameter and the defaulted initialization arguments contained duplicate keywords, it is undefined whether any entries other than the leftmost for that keyword will be present.

- Each `initialize` method typically calls `next-method`, and then performs its own initializations. (Note that it won't have to initialize slots that were initialized by the default `make` method.)

- The default `make` method ignores the value of the call to `initialize` and returns the instance.

The values of virtual slots are not automatically initialized when a new instance is created. The programmer must perform any necessary initialization. This would usually be done inside a method on `initialize`. Because the values of virtual slots are often computed from other values at run-time, many virtual slots will not require any explicit initialization.

Additional Behavior of Make and Initialize

The object returned by make is guaranteed to be a general instance of the first argument to make, but not necessarily a direct instance. This liberality allows make to be called on an abstract class; it can instantiate and return a direct instance of one of the concrete subclasses of the abstract class.

```
define abstract class <dog> (<object>)
end class

define class <yorkshire-terrier> (<dog>)
end class

define method make (the-class == <dog>, #rest init-args, #key)
  apply(make, <yorkshire-terrier>, init-args)
end
```

```
make(<dog>)
⇒   {instance of <yorkshire-terrier>}
```

make is not required to return a newly allocated instance. It may return a previously created instance if that is appropriate. If a new instance is allocated, make will call initialize on the instance before returning it.

The make method on <class> returns a newly allocated direct instance of its first argument.

Programmers may customize make for particular classes by defining methods specialized on singletons of classes. These methods may reinvoke make on a subtype of the class, or they may obtain the default make behavior by calling next-method.

The default make method signals an error if its first argument is an abstract class. An instantiable abstract class must override this method with its own method for make.

Initialization of Class Allocated Slots

The initalization of slots with allocation class or each-subclass is performed in the following way:

- If the slot is not keyword initializable and the class definition does not include an init specification for the slot, the slot remains uninitialized until it is explicitly assigned by the program.

- If the slot is not keyword initializable and the class definition does include an init specification for the slot, the slot is initialized from the init specification before or during the creation of the first instance of the class.

- If the slot is keyword initializable and the class definition also includes an init specification for the slot, the slot may be initialized or assigned by the default method of make whenever an instance is created, as follows:

  ☐ If the corresponding initialization argument is absent from the defaulted initialization arguments of the call to make and the slot has not yet been initialized, then the slot is initialized from the init specification. If the slot has already been initialized, no action is taken.

  ☐ If the corresponding initialization argument is present in the defaulted initialization arguments of the call to make, then the slot is set to the value of that initialization argument, regardless of whether the slot was previously initialized.

Testing the Initialization of a Slot

A program can test to see whether a slot has been initialized, using the slot-initialized? function, described on page 261. There is no portable mechanism for resetting a slot to the uninitialized state once it has been initialized.

To support the slot-initialized? protocol in a virtual slot, programmers must define a method for slot-initialized? that specializes on the getter of the slot and the class.

Inherited Slot Specifications

An inherited slot specification is used to provide an init specification for a slot inherited from a superclass. It can add an init specification if one was not already present, or it can override an existing init specification.

Inherited slot specifications identify the slot to be modified by the getter name. The inherited slot specification is only allowed if the class does indeed inherit a slot with that getter.

(An inherited slot specification is not required to include an init specification. If it does not, its only purpose is to ensure that the slot is present in a superclass. Because init specifications are not allowed for virtual slots, this is the only valid form of inherited slot specification for virtual slots.)

If an inherited slot specification supplies an init specification, it overrides any init specification inherited from a superclass. This allows the init specification of an inherited slot to be replaced in a subclass, thereby changing the default initial value of the slot.

```
define class <animal> (<object>)
  slot n-legs, init-value: 4;
end class;

define class <spider> (<animal>)
  inherited slot n-legs, init-value: 8;
end class;
```

Initialization Argument Specifications

Initialization argument specifications provide options for the handling of initialization arguments. They appear in `define class` forms, and have a syntax similar to that of slot specifications.

Initialization argument specifications allow the type of an initialization argument to be restricted, they allow an initialization argument to be declared to be required, and they allow the specification of a default value for an initialization argument.

Note that an initialization argument will only be used if it is specified to be the init-keyword of a slot, or if it is used as a keyword argument in an applicable method on `initialize`. An initialization argument specification can supply a default value for an initialization argument, and it can restrict the type of the argument or make it required, but it does not by itself cause the argument to be used when initializing an instance.

There are two kinds of initialization argument specifications: required initialization argument specifications, and optional initialization argument specifications.

A required initialization argument specification asserts that the initialization argument must be present in the defaulted initialization arguments. The default make method will signal an error if no such initialization argument is present.

An optional initialization argument specification can be used to specify a default value for the initialization argument, using an init specification. When a call to make does not specify the initialization argument, the default make method will add it to the defaulted initialization arguments with the value of the init specification.

The type argument has the same meaning in both kinds of initialization argument specification: it restricts the type of that initialization argument. Note that this is not the same thing as restricting the type of the slot.

The following example shows how initialization argument specifications can be used to override the behavior of a superclass:

```
define class <person> (<object>)
  slot favorite-beverage, init-value: #"milk",
                    init-keyword: favorite-beverage:;
  slot name required-init-keyword: name:;
end class <person>;

define class <astronaut> (<person>)
  keyword favorite-beverage: init-value: #"tang";
  keyword name: init-value: "Bud";
end class <astronaut>;
```

In this example, the <astronaut> class provides default values for the favorite-beverage: and name: init-keywords. In addition to indirectly supplying default values for these slots, this also has the effect of making the name: argument optional in calls to make on <astronaut>. If the call to make does not specify a name:, the name: will be added to the defaulted initialization arguments by the default make method before the defaulted initialization arguments are checked for completeness.

More than one keyword initializable slot may be initialized from the same initialization argument (that is, more than one keyword initializable slot may specify the same init-keyword). However, an error is signaled if a single define-class form has more than one initialization argument specification for the same keyword. An error will also be signaled if a single define-class form has a keyword initializable slot that includes an init specification and also includes an initialization argument specification for the same keyword that is either required or provides a default value. These error situations are all indications of code that can never be reached.

Initialization Argument Inheritance

The inheritance of initialization argument specifications is defined as follows.

- A slot specification that supplies an init-keyword *K* by using `required-init-keyword:` is treated as if the initialization argument specification `required keyword` *K* had been specified in the class definition.

- A slot specification that supplies both an init-keyword and also an init specification is not equivalent to an initialization argument specification that includes both the init-keyword and an init specification. In the former case the init specification is used to default the value of the slot directly, but does not affect the defaulted initialization arguments; in the latter case the init specification is used to default the value of the slot indirectly, by affecting the defaulted initialization arguments.

- If the initialization argument is being specified for the first time (it is not inherited from any superclass) there are three factors to consider:
  - The `type:` argument, which defaults to `<object>`, specifies the required type of the initialization argument. (This does not specify the type of the slot.)
  - If the initialization argument is specified with `required keyword` then it is required, otherwise it is optional.
  - If the initialization argument is specified with `keyword`, then it can provide an init specification that is used by the default `make` method to provide a default value for the initialization argument in the defaulted initialization arguments.

- If an initialization argument specification is being specified for an initialization argument that is inherited from a single superclass, the following factors hold:
  - The type must be a subtype of the type of the inherited initialization argument. This implies that the type must be specified unless the type of the inherited initialization argument is `<object>`.

☐ The initialization argument is required if the overriding initialization argument specification uses `required keyword`, or if the inherited initialization argument specification is required and the overriding initialization argument specification does not provide an init specification. When the overriding initialization argument specification uses `required keyword`, any init specification in the inherited initialization argument specification is discarded. This means that a subclass can make an initialization argument used by a superclass become required; it can also make a required initialization argument become optional by specifying a default value for it.

☐ Otherwise, the initialization argument is optional. If the overriding specification provides an init specification, then that is used to compute the defaulted initialization argument when the class is instantiated. Otherwise, the inherited initial value specification is used.

■ When an initialization argument specification is being inherited from multiple superclasses, if the superclasses have exactly the same definition for the initialization argument, then that definition can simply be inherited. If the definitions differ, then the class that combines these other classes must provide an initialization argument specification that is compatible with all of the inherited ones, as described above.

Singletons

Singleton types are used to indicate individual objects. When determining whether a singleton specializer matches a given object, the object must be == to the object used to create the singleton.

A singleton for an object is created by passing the object to the function `singleton`, or by calling the function `make` on the class `<singleton>`.

Singleton methods are considered more specific than methods defined on an object's class. Singletons are the most specific specializer.

```
define method double (thing :: singleton(#"cup"))
  #"pint"
end method
double (#"cup")
  ⇒  #"pint"
```

Dylan provides a concise syntax for singletons used as method specializers. The following definition is equivalent to the previous one; it generates a call to the binding of `singleton` in the current lexical environment.

```
define method double (thing == #"cup")
  #"pint"
end method
double (#"cup")
  ⇒  #"pint"
```

Union Types

Union types represent the union of the instances of two or more other types. Union types are created with the function `type-union`. They are not classes.

Union types are useful as slot specializers, and describe the return types of many common functions. For example, the return type of the collection method on `size` could be expressed as `type-union(<integer>, singleton(#f))`.

```
define constant <green-thing> = type-union(<frog>, <broccoli>);

define constant kermit = make(<frog>);

define method red? (x :: <green-thing>)
  #f
end method;

red?(kermit)
  ⇒  #f
```

The following rules govern `subtype?` and `instance?` for union types.

Given

- x is an object.

- $s_1...s_m$ and $t_1...t_n$ are nonunion types.

- The notation `type-union*`$(t_1...t_n)$ stands for any arrangement of nested calls to `type-union`, where none of the arguments is a subtype of any other, and none of the arguments forms an exhaustive partition of any other type.

Then

`type-union`$(t_1,\ t_1)$ is type equivalent to t_1.

`type-union`$(t_1,\ t_2)$ is type equivalent to `type-union`$(t_2,\ t_1)$.

`type-union`$(t_1,$ `type-union`$(t_2,\ t_3))$ is type equivalent to `type-union`(`type-union`$(t_1,\ t_2),\ t_3)$.

`type-union`$(t_1,\ t_2)$ is type equivalent to t_2 when `subtype?`$(t_1,\ t_2)$.

`instance?`$(x,$ `type-union*`$(t_1...t_n))$ will be true if and only if `instance?`$(x,\ t)$ is true for some t in $t_1...t_n$.

`subtype?`(`type-union*`$(t_1...t_n),\ s_1)$ will be true if and only if `subtype?`$(t,\ s_1)$ is true for every t in $t_1...t_n$.

`subtype?`$(s_1,$ `type-union*`$(t_1...t_n))$ will be true if and only if `subtype?`$(s_1,\ t)$ is true for some t in $t_1...t_n$.

`subtype?`(`type-union*`$(s_1...s_m)$ `type-union*`$(t_1...t_n))$ will be true if and only if every s in $s_1...s_m$ is a subtype of some t in $t_1...t_n$.

Limited Types

Limited types are subtypes of classes constrained by additional criteria. Limited types are created with the function `limited`. `limited`(`<integer>` `,min: 0 max: 255`) and `limited`(`<array>`, `of: <single-float>`) are examples of limited types that are useful both for error checking and for optimization of compiled code.

Limited types are not classes.

Limited Type Constructor

Limited types are created with the generic function `limited`. The first argument to limited is a class. Depending on the class, additional keyword arguments are allowed to specify the constraints of the limited type.

Not all classes support `limited`; the methods for `limited` are documented individually beginning on page 263.

Limited Integer Types

Limited integer types are subtypes of `<integer>` containing integers that fall within a specifed range. The range is specified by `min:` and `max:` keyword arguments to `limited`.

For example:

```
// accepts integers between -1000 and 1000 inclusive.
define method f (x :: limited(<integer>, min: -1000,
                                         max: 1000))
   ...
   end method f;

//accepts all strictly positive integers.
define method f (x :: limited(<integer>, min: 1))
   ...
   end method f;
```

Limited Integer Type Protocol

If w, x, y, and z are integers, the following equivalences hold:

- `instance?(x, limited(<integer>, min: y, max: z))` will be true if and only if `instance?(x, <integer>)`, $(y <= x)$, and $(x <= z)$ are all true.

- `instance?(x, limited(<integer>, min: y))` will be true if and only if `instance?(x, <integer>)` and $(y <= x)$ are both true.

- `instance?(x, limited(<integer>, max: z))` will be true if and only if `instance?(x, <integer>)` and $(x <= z)$ are both true.

- subtype?(limited(<integer>, min: w, max: x),
      limited(<integer>, min: y, max: z)) will be true if and only if (w >= y) and (x <= z) are both true.

- subtype?(limited(<integer>, min: w …),
      limited(<integer>, min: y …)) will be true if and only if (w >= y) is true.

- subtype?(limited(<integer>, … max: x),
      limited(<integer>, … max: z)) will be true if and only if (x <= z) is true.

Limited Collection Types

Limited collection types are subtypes of <collection> (and of subclasses of <collection>) that are constrained to be a specified size and/or to contain elements of a specified type.

A complete description of limited collection types is given in "Limited Collection Types" on page 126 in Chapter 8, "Collections."

Functions

Contents

Overview   79
  Generic Functions   79
  Methods   80
Parameter Lists   84
  Kinds of Parameters   85
  Kinds of Parameter Lists   86
  Specializing Required Parameters   88
  Keyword Parameters   89
  Return Value Declarations   91
  Parameter List Congruency   93
  Parameter Lists of Implicitly Defined Generic Functions   94
Method Dispatch   95
  Calling Less Specific Methods   98
Operations on Functions   100

Overview

All operations in Dylan are functions.

Functions accept zero or more arguments, and return zero or more values. The **parameter list** of the function describes the number and types of the arguments that the function accepts, and the number and types of the values it returns.

There are two kinds of functions, methods and generic functions. Both are invoked in the same way. The caller does not need to know whether the function it is calling is a method or a generic function.

A method is the basic unit of executable code. A method accepts a number of arguments, creates local bindings for them, executes an implicit body in the scope of these bindings, and then returns a number of values.

A generic function contains a number of methods. When a generic function is called, it compares the arguments it received with the parameter lists of the methods it contains. It selects the most appropriate method and invokes it on the arguments. This technique of **method dispatch** is the basic mechanism of polymorphism in Dylan.

All Dylan functions are objects, instances of `<function>`. Generic functions are instances of `<generic-function>` and methods are instances of `<method>`.

Generic Functions

Generic functions can be created with `define generic` or by calling `make` on the class `<generic-function>`. They are most often created with `define generic`.

Generic functions may also be created implicitly by `define method` or by slot specifications in class definitions.

A generic function definition includes a parameter list, which constrains the methods that can be added to the generic function; some aspects of the parameter must be matched by any method added. In addition, a generic function parameter list may specify that all keyword arguments are permitted in a call to the generic function.

Parameter list congruency is described on page 93. The complete syntax of `define generic` is given on page 376.

The following definition defines a generic function that accepts a single required argument. All methods added to this generic function must also accept a single required argument.

```
define generic double (thing)
```

The following definition defines a generic function that accepts two arguments of type <number>. All methods added to the generic function must accept two required arguments of type <number> or subtype of <number>.

```
define generic average (n1 :: <number>, n2 :: <number>)
```

Generic functions created with `define generic` may be sealed or open. For details of this option, see "Declaring Characteristics of Generic Functions" on page 135.

Methods

Methods can be created with `define method`, `local`, and `method` program constituents. `define method` is used to define a method and add it to a generic function in a module binding. `local` is used to create local bindings that contain self-recursive and mutually recursive methods. `method` is used to create and return methods for immediate application, for use as function arguments, or for storage in a variable or other data structure. Methods are also created for slot getters and setters when a class is created.

Methods cannot be created with `make`.

The parameters and return values of a method are described in its parameter list. The specializers in the parameter list declare the types of the arguments acceptable to the method. The method can be called only with arguments that match the specializers of the parameters. A complete description of parameter lists is given in "Parameter Lists" on page 84.

When the method is invoked, it executes its implicit body. Statements in the implicit body are executed in order, in an environment that contains the parameters bound to the arguments.

Methods may be invoked directly (used as functions), or indirectly through the invocation of a generic function.

Methods in Generic Functions

`define method` creates a method and adds it to a generic function in a module variable. If the module variable indicated is not already defined, it is defined as with `define generic`. Thus, `define method` will create a new generic function or extend an old one, as needed. Methods added to a generic function must have parameter lists that are congruent with the generic function's parameter list.

The following method accepts a single argument of type <number>, and returns the number doubled. The method will be added to the generic function in the module binding `double`.

```
define method double (thing :: <number>)
  => another-thing :: <number>;
  thing + thing;
end method;
```

`define method` allows the programmer to control aspects of the sealing of the generic function to which the method is added. For more details, see "Abbreviations for Define Sealed Domain" on page 138.

A generic function with no required parameters can contain a single method. Adding a new method has the effect of replacing the existing method.

The complete syntax of `define method` is given on page 377.

Local Methods

`local` is used for creating methods in local bindings. A single `local` declaration may create one or more such methods. These methods may be self-recursive and they may be mutually recursive with other methods created by the same `local` declaration.

`local` is similar to `let` in that it creates local bindings in the current body. The parameters and the bodies of the methods are within the scope of the bindings. In this way, the methods can refer to themselves and to other methods created by the same `local` declaration.

The complete syntax of `local` is given on page 391.

```
define method newtons-sqrt (x :: <number>)
   local method sqrt1 (guess)
          // note call to other local method
          if (close-enough? (guess))
             guess
          else
             sqrt1 (improve (guess))  // note self-recursive call
          end if
        end sqrt1,
        method close-enough? (guess)
          abs (guess * guess - x) < .0001
        end close-enough?,
        method improve (guess)
          (guess + (x / guess)) / 2
        end improve;
   sqrt1 (1)
end method newtons-sqrt;
```

Bare Methods

Methods can also be created and used directly with the method statement.

Methods created directly can be stored in module variables, passed as arguments to generic functions, stored in data structures, or immediately invoked.

The following example creates a method and stores it in the module variable square. It is appropriate to define a method in this way (rather than with define method) when the protocol of the function being defined does not require multiple methods.

```
define constant square = method (n :: <number>)
                  n * n;
                end method;
```

It is sometimes useful to create a method inline and pass it directly to another function that accepts a method as an argument, as in the following example.

```
// sort accepts a test argument, which defaults to \<
sort(person-list,
     test: method(person1, person2)
              person1.age < person2.age
          end method)
```

Methods created directly with the `method` statement may be called directly or they may be added to generic functions. Usually, however, when you want to add a method to a generic function, you create and add the method in a single declarative step, with `define method`.

Closures

Methods created with `method` or `local` can be passed to functions and returned from functions. In both cases, the methods retain access to the lexical context in which they were created. Such methods are called **closures**.

The following example defines a function that returns score-card methods. The method that is returned is **closed over** the `score` parameter. Each time this method is called, it updates the `score` parameter and returns its new value.

```
define method make-score (points :: <number>)
  method (increase :: <number>)
    points := points + increase;
  end method;
end method make-score;

define constant score-david = make-score(100)

define constant score-diane = make-score(400)

score-david(0)
  ⇒  100
score-david(10)
  ⇒  110
score-david(10)
  ⇒  120
score-diane(10)
```

⇒ 410

```
score-david(0)
```

⇒ 120

Each invocation of make-score creates a new binding for score, so each closure returned by make-score refers to a different binding. In this way, assignments to the variable made by one closure do not affect the value of the variable visible to other closures.

The following example defines a method for double that works on functions. When you double a function, you get back a method that accepts arguments and calls the function twice, passing the same arguments both times. The method that is returned is closed over the function that was passed in as an argument.

```
define method double (internal-method :: <function>)
  method (#rest args)
    apply (internal-method, args);
    apply (internal-method, args);
    #f
  end method
end method;

define constant double-david = double(score-david);

score-david(0)
  ⇒  120
double-david(10)
  ⇒  140
score-david(0)
  ⇒  140
```

Parameter Lists

The parameter list of a function describes the number and types of the arguments that the function accepts, and the number and types of the values it returns.

The parameter list of a generic function is used to define the overall protocol of the generic function. It constrains the methods that may be added to the generic function, through the parameter list congruency rules described on page 93. It may also specify that calls to the generic function may contain any keyword arguments.

The parameter list of a method specifies the types of arguments to which the method is applicable, and declares local bindings to which those arguments will be bound during the execution of the body of the method. It may also declare the return value types of the method.

Kinds of Parameters

Dylan parameter lists support **required parameters**, **rest parameters**, **keyword parameters**, and sometimes a **next-method parameter**. They also may include **return value declarations**.

The complete syntax of parameter lists is given in "Methods" on page 426.

Required parameters correspond to arguments that must be supplied when a function is called. The arguments are supplied in a fixed order and must appear before any other arguments.

Each required parameter may be a name or a name **specialized** by a type. Specifying a type declares that supplied argument must be a general instance of that type.

A rest parameter allows a function to accept an unlimited number of arguments.[*] After the required arguments of a function have been supplied, any additional arguments are collected in a sequence, which is passed as the value of the rest parameter. This sequence may be immutable, and it may or may not be freshly allocated. The types of rest parameters cannot be declared.

Keyword parameters correspond to arguments that are optional and may be given in any order. Symbols are used among the arguments to guide matching of arguments to parameters. These symbols are usually written in keyword syntax and so they are known as keywords. Keyword arguments can only be supplied after all required arguments are supplied. Keyword parameters may

---

[*] In practice, an implementation may place a reasonable limit on the number of arguments that may be passed to any function.

be specialized, restricting which values may be supplied for them. Keyword parameters may also be given default values to be used when the caller does not supply a value.

Required parameters come first in the parameter list, followed by the rest parameter, if any, and then the keyword parameters, if any. A rest parameter is indicated by the token `#rest` followed by the name of the parameter. Keyword parameters are indicated by the token `#key` followed by the keyword parameter specifiers, optionally followed by the token `#all-keys`.

If `#rest` and `#key` are used in the same parameter list, `#rest` must come first. The rest parameter will be bound to a sequence containing all the keyword arguments and their corresponding values.

A next-method parameter is indicated by the token `#next`, followed by the name of the parameter. It is not normally necessary to specify a next-method parameter explicitly. If a next-method parameter is not specified by the programmer, `define method` inserts one with the name `next-method`. If an explicit next-method parameter is given, it must come after the required parameters and before the rest and keyword parameters. Details of using next-method are given in "Calling Less Specific Methods" on page 98.

Kinds of Parameter Lists

Each function (generic function or method) has an argument passing protocol specified by its parameter list. The argument passing protocol for a method must be compatible with the argument passing protocol of any generic function to which it is added, as described in "Parameter List Congruency" on page 93.

The argument passing protocol of a function can be described in one of the following ways:

- A function is said to **require a fixed number of arguments** if its parameter list does not specify either `#rest` or `#key`.

- A function is said to **accept keyword arguments** if its parameter list specifies `#key`. The parameter list could also specify `#rest` if it is a method, but not if it is a generic function.

- A function is said to **accept all keyword arguments** if its parameter list specifies `#all-keys` in addition to `#key`.

Functions

- A function is said to **accept a variable number of arguments** if its parameter list specifies `#rest` but does not specify `#key`. (Note: If the parameter list specifies `#key` in addition to `#rest` it is not said to accept a variable number of arguments.)

A method that accepts keyword arguments is said to **recognize** the keywords mentioned in its parameter list. (A method may, of course, mention them in the parameter list and then ignore their values. It is still said to recognize them.) It is possible for a method to accept keyword arguments in general but not recognize any particular keywords; it does this by specifying `#key` without any subsequent keyword parameters.

If a generic function that accepts keyword arguments mentions any specific keyword arguments in its parameter list, these are the **mandatory keywords** of the generic function. Every method added to the generic function must recognize these keywords.

A function may accept all keyword arguments by specifying `#all-keys` in its parameter list.

When a function that accepts keyword arguments is called, it is said to **permit** a keyword argument in the call if one of the following is true:

- The function is a method that recognizes the keyword.

- The function is a generic function and the keyword is recognized by any of the applicable methods of the call.

- The function accepts all keyword arguments.

- The function is a generic function and any of the applicable methods of the call accepts all keyword arguments.

If a function that accepts keyword arguments is called, it will signal an error if called with a keyword argument that it does not permit, or if the arguments following the required arguments are not keyword/value pairs. This is true even if the function specifies `#rest`.

If a method is called via a generic function or via next-method (rather than directly), the method itself does not check whether it received any keyword arguments it does not permit, nor does it check that the arguments following the required arguments are keyword/value pairs. This check is performed by the generic function or next-method, and is made relative to the call as a whole, not relative to an individual method or the methods remaining to be called.

A call to a function may supply the same keyword argument more than once. When this is done, the leftmost keyword/value pair is used.

Specializing Required Parameters

When you define a generic function or method, you may specify the types of the arguments appropriate for the generic function or method. This is called **specializing** the generic function or method, or specializing the parameters of the generic function or method.

The following example defines a method specialized on <number>. The method will be applicable when double is called on a general instance of <number>.

```
define method double (thing :: <number>)
  thing + thing;
end method;
```

Specialization constrains the values that may be passed as the value of a parameter. The function can be called only with arguments that are instances of the specializers of the corresponding parameters.

Specialization is useful in three way:

- It makes the intent of the program clear. It indicates to the compiler and to anyone reading the code that an error is signaled if an argument is not of the specializer type.

- It allows the compiler to perform additional optimizations.

- It is used to control method dispatch. By defining methods on the same generic function with different specializers, you can define behavior applicable to different sets of types. A generic function chooses among its methods on the basis of the methods' specializers. The generic function chooses the method whose specializers most closely match the types of the arguments.

Syntactically, specializers are operands. These operands are executed once when the function is created. They are not re-executed each time the function is called. The value of the operand must be a type.

It is most common for specializers to be constant module bindings or calls to a built-in type constructor such as singleton, limited, or type-union.

There is a convenient syntax for singleton specializers, which is equivalent to explicitly calling `singleton` in the current lexical scope.

Keyword Parameters

The syntax of a keyword parameter is:

[*keyword*] *name* [: : *operand*] [= *expression*]

If *keyword* is not supplied, then *name* is used to indicate both the keyword and the name of the parameter. If the *keyword* and *name* are given independently, the *keyword* is used when calling the method, and the *name* is used as the name of the parameter inside the body of the method.

The *expression* supplies a default value for the parameter. It is used when the method is called and the keyword is not supplied. It is executed each time the method is called and the corresponding keyword argument is not supplied. If no *expression* is specified, the parameter corresponding to an unsupplied keyword argument is initialized to #f. The *expression* is executed in a scope that includes all the preceding parameters, including required parameters, the rest parameter (if any), the preceding keyword parameters, and the next-method parameter (if any).

In the following example, all three keyword parameters have default values, and all three use the same name for the keyword and the parameter.

```
define method percolate (#key brand = #"maxwell-house",
                               cups = 4,
                               strength = #"strong")
  make-coffee (brand, cups, strength);
end method;
```

The caller can choose which keyword arguments to supply and what order to supply them in:

```
percolate (brand: #"java", cups: 10);
percolate (strength: #"strong",
           brand: #"starbucks",
             cups: 1);
```

The following method has two keyword parameters. In each, the name of the keyword and the name of the parameter is specified separately. The first keyword parameter has a default value, the second does not.

```
define method layout (widget, #key position: the-pos = 0,
                                     size: the-size)
  let the-sibling = sibling (widget);
  unless (the-pos = position (the-sibling))
    align-objects (widget, the-sibling, the-pos, the-size);
end method;

layout(my-widget, position: 100, size: 500);
layout(my-widget, size: query-user-for-size() );
```

The keyword parameter syntax in which the keyword name and parameter name are given separately is needed to allow keyword names such as position: without forcing the method to use position as a local binding. If a method uses position as a local binding, it cannot access the module binding position (which contains a function). The local binding would shadow the module binding.

All required arguments must be supplied before any keyword arguments can be supplied. The following call to layout will signal an error:

```
layout(position: 100, size: 500);
```

Types for Keyword Parameters

When a type is indicated for a keyword parameter in a method, it is the same as establishing a type for a local binding. Specifically, the types of any keyword parameters are not used for method dispatch. Keyword parameter types are not allowed in generic function definitions, and do not figure into parameter list congruency.

The following two method definitions are equivalent:

```
method (#key X :: <integer>)
   ... X ...
end method;
```

```
method (#key X)
  let X :: <integer> = X;
  ... X ...
end method;
```

If a keyword parameter is given a type, if #f is not an instance of that type, and if the keyword parameter is not given a default value, then the keyword parameter is essentially required. An error of type <type-error> will be signaled if a call to the method does not include the keyword.

The following examples include keyword parameters that include both a type and a default value.

```
define method find-happiness (#key hint :: <symbol> =  #"here")
  ...
end method find-happiness;

define method find-food (#key hint :: <restaurant>
                              =  lookup-default-restaurant())
  ...
end method find-food;
```

Return Value Declarations

Parameter lists may include value declarations. Value declarations come at the end of the parameter list and are separated from the parameters by ->. For each return value, a value declaration can specify a name and an operand or just a name if the type is <object>. The complete syntax of value declarations is given in "Methods" on page 426.

The result of executing the operand at the time the function is defined is a type, called a **value type**. The name never comes into scope. It is included for documentation and for syntactic consistency with parameters. It is valid for the same name to be used in both one parameter and one value declaration in the same parameter list; this is useful as documentation that a function returns one of its arguments.

The last value declaration can be preceded by #rest to indicate a variable number of return values. A value declaration preceded by #rest is called a **rest value declaration**. A value declaration not preceded by #rest is called a **required value declaration**. The value type in a rest value declaration is the type of each one of the remaining individual values, not the type of a conceptual sequence of multiple values.

If a parameter-list does not contain a value declaration, it defaults to => #rest x :: <object>. That is, the function can return any number of values of any type.

A function will always return the number and types of values declared in its parameter-list. More precisely:

- Each value returned by a function must be an instance of the corresponding value type, or else an error of type <type-error> will be signaled.

- If fewer values are returned by the function's body (or by the applicable method if the function is a generic function) than the number of required value declarations in the function's parameter-list, the missing values are defaulted to #f and returned. If #f is not an instance of the corresponding value type, an error of type <type-error> is signaled.

- If a function does not have a rest value declaration, and more values are returned by the function's body (or by the applicable method if the function is a generic function) than the number of required value declarations in the function's parameter-list, the extra values are discarded and not returned.

Because of the parameter list congruency rules for value declarations (see "Parameter List Congruency" on page 93) the values returned by a generic function do not have to be checked by the generic function. The check inside a method will always be enough to verify that the return values are valid for the generic function.

```
define method average (x :: <number>, y :: <number>)
 => mean :: <number>;
 (x + y) / 2
end method;


// Returning multiple values
define method limits (center :: <number>, radius :: <number>)
 => (min :: <number>, max :: <number>);
 values(center - radius, center + radius);
end method;
```

```
// The same name used both as a parameter and as a value type
define method rotate (image :: <picture>, rotation-angle :: <number>)

 => (image :: <picture>);
 ...
end method;

// This method can return one, two, or three values
define method family (kid :: <person>)
  => (kid :: <person>, #rest parents);
  let mom = kid.mother;
  let dad = kid.father;
  case
    mom & dad => values(kid, mom, dad);
    mom => values(kid, mom);
    dad => values(kid, dad);
    otherwise => kid;
  end case
end method family;
```

Note that the following example does not declare a return value of type
<number>. It declares a return value of type <object>. To specify a type, both
the name and the type must be specified. If only one is given, it is taken as the
name.

```
define method average (x :: <number>, y :: <number>)
 => avg :: <number>;
 truncate/((x + y), 2);
end method;
```

Parameter List Congruency

For any given generic function, the generic function and all methods for that
function must have **congruent parameter lists**. Two parameter lists are
congruent if they satisfy the following conditions:

■ They have the same number of required arguments.

- Each of the method's parameter specializers is a subtype of the corresponding parameter specializer of the generic function.

- One of the following is true:
  - both accept keyword arguments
  - both accept a variable number of arguments
  - both require a fixed number of arguments

- If the generic function accepts keyword arguments, each method must recognize the mandatory keywords of the generic function.

In addition, the value declarations must be congruent, defined as follows:

- If the generic function's parameter list does not contain a rest value declaration, then
  - The method's parameter list must not contain a rest value declaration.
  - The two parameter lists must contain the same number of required value declarations.
  - Each value type in the method's parameter list must be a subtype of the corresponding value type in the generic function's parameter list.

- If the generic function's parameter list contains a rest value declaration, then:
  - The method's parameter list is permitted, but not required, to contain a rest value declaration.
  - The method's parameter list must contain at least as many required value declarations as the generic function's parameter list.
  - Each value type in the method's parameter list must be a subtype of the corresponding value type in the generic function's parameter list. If the method has a rest value type, it corresponds to the generic function's rest value type. If the method has more required value types than the generic function, the extra ones must be subtypes of the generic function's rest value type.

Parameter Lists of Implicitly Defined Generic Functions

As a general principle, the parameter list of an implicitly defined generic function will impose as few constraints as possible on the methods that may be added. If a more constrained generic function definition is desired, an explicit definition should be used.

The parameter list of an implicitly defined generic function is determined by its method definitions. These method definitions include both methods defined using `define method` and slot getter and setter methods defined using `define class`.

- The implicitly defined generic function has the same basic argument pattern as the methods. Either they must all require a fixed number of arguments, they must all accept a variable number of arguments, or they must all accept keyword arguments. A set of methods that includes members with more than one of these patterns violates the parameter list congruency requirement, and is an error.

- The implicitly defined generic function has the same number of required arguments as the methods. A set of methods that includes members with different numbers of required arguments violates the parameter list congruency requirement, and is an error.

- Each required argument of the implicitly defined generic function is specialized on `<object>`.

- If the implicitly defined generic function accepts keyword arguments, it does not have any mandatory keywords, nor does it accept all keyword arguments.

- The implicitly defined generic function has a rest value declaration of `<object>`.

Method Dispatch

When a generic function is called, the generic function uses the types of the arguments to determine which methods to call. This process is called **method dispatch**.

Method dispatch occurs in three phases. First, all the applicable methods are selected. Next, the applicable methods are sorted by specificity. Finally, the most specific method is called.

Method Specificity

For any two methods *A* and *B* that are applicable to a given generic function call, one method may be **more specific than** the other, or the methods may be **ambiguous methods**.

To order two methods *A* and *B* with respect to a particular set of arguments, compare each of *A*'s specializers with *B*'s specializer in the corresponding position using the argument that was supplied for that position. The comparison works in the following way.

- If the specializers are type equivalent, then *A* and *B* are unordered at the current argument position. That is, this argument position provides no information about the order of the two methods.

- Otherwise, if the specializer of *A* is a subtype of the specializer of *B*, then *A* precedes *B* at the current argument position.

- Otherwise, if both specializers are classes, then their order in the class precedence list of the argument's class is used to determine which is more specific. If *A*'s specializer precedes *B*'s specializer in the class precedence list of the argument's class, then *A* precedes *B* at the current argument position.

- Otherwise, the methods are unordered in the current argument position.

The method *A* is more specific than the method *B* if and only if *A* precedes *B* in at least one argument position, and *B* does not precede *A* in any argument position. Similarly, *B* is more specific than *A* if and only if *B* precedes *A* in at least one argument position, and *A* does not precede *B* in any argument position. If neither of these cases apply then *A* and *B* are ambiguous methods.

When the applicable methods are sorted by specificity, the sorted list is divided into two parts, each possibly empty. The first part contains methods that are more specific than every method that follows them. The second part (which cannot itself be sorted) begins at the first point of ambiguity; there are at least two methods that could equally well go first in the second part. When a generic function is called, if the first part of the sorted applicable methods is empty then an error is signaled. Similarly, if the last method in the first part attempts to call next-method, an error is signaled.

Consider the following class definitions:

```
define class <sentient> (<life-form>) end class;

define class <bipedal> (<life-form>) end class;

define class <intelligent> (<sentient>) end class;

define class <humanoid> (<bipedal>) end class;

define class <vulcan> (<intelligent>, <humanoid>) end class;
```

Computing the class precedence list for <vulcan> yields

```
#(<vulcan>,<intelligent>,<sentient>,<humanoid>,<bipedal>,<life-form>)
```

The class precedence lists computed for two different classes may have different precedence orders for some intermediate superclasses. This is not a problem as long as there is no class that inherits from both classes. For example, we could define a class <human> as follows:

```
define class <human> (<humanoid>, <intelligent>) end class;
```

For the class <human> defined as above, the class precedence list would be

```
#(<human>,<humanoid>,<bipedal>,<intelligent>,<sentient>,<life-form>)
```

It is not a problem that the two class precedence lists give different orders to some of the intermediate superclasses such as <bipedal> and <sentient> as long as no class is added that inherits from both <vulcan> and <human>.

When sorting the applicable methods, each specializer needs to be viewed with respect to the class precedence list for the class of the argument passed to the generic function in that argument position. For example, given the following definitions

```
define method psychoanalyze (being :: <intelligent>)
    …
end method;
```

```
define method psychoanalyze (being :: <humanoid>)
   ...
end method;
```

calling the generic function psychoanalyze on a being of type <human> would cause the method for <humanoid> to be called first, while calling the generic function on a being of type <vulcan> would cause the method for <intelligent> to be called first.

The order of arguments is not significant when computing method specificity. Given the above class definitions, the following methods are unambiguous when their generic function is called on two beings of type <vulcan> or two beings of type <human>, but the methods are ambiguous when the call includes one being of type <vulcan> and one of type <human>.

```
define method superior-being (a :: <intelligent>,
                              b :: <intelligent>)
  most-intelligent-being (a, b)
  end method;

define method superior-being (a :: <humanoid>,
                              b :: <humanoid>)
  best-looking-being (a, b)
  end method;
```

Calling Less Specific Methods

In many situations, a subtype wants to modify the behavior of a method, rather than replace it completely; it wants to perform some work but also use the inherited behavior. This can be accomplished with **next-method**. Next-method is a function that, when called, invokes the next most specific method applicable in the generic function. The next-method is the value of the #next parameter. Normally this parameter is named next-method, though it can have other names at the programmer's discretion.

One can think of next-method as invoking the method that would have been called if the current method did not exist.

If there are no more methods available, the next-method parameter will be bound to the value #f instead of to a method.

Passing Different Arguments to Next-Method

In the usual case, next-method is called with no arguments. This indicates that the next-method should be passed the same arguments that were supplied to the current method.

It is valid to supply arguments, including different arguments, when calling next-method. However, if you pass different arguments, the new arguments must result in the same ordered sequence of applicable methods as the original arguments. Otherwise, the program behavior is undefined.

In some cases, the methods in a generic function accept different keyword arguments. In such cases, it's convenient for the methods also to accept a rest parameter. That way, all the keyword/value pairs passed to the generic function are captured in the rest parameter. By using `apply`, the next-method can be invoked with the complete set of arguments. (This technique is only necessary, of course, when the method calls next-method and passes arguments explicitly.)

As usual, if there are duplicates of a given keyword argument, the leftmost occurrence is used. This allows keyword arguments to be easily overridden.

The Next-Method Parameter

The value of the next-method parameter is supplied by the generic function dispatch mechanism. When a method is called by its generic function, the generic function dispatch mechanism automatically passes the appropriate value for next-method. There is no way for a user program to specify the next-method argument when calling a method.

If you create a method directly (i.e., with `method` rather than with `define method`) and you want this method to accept a next-method parameter, then you should insert a `#next` into the parameter list explicitly. You would do this if you are creating a method that you plan to add to a generic function, and you want this method to be able to call next-method. You can also supply the next-method parameter when using `define method`, in cases where you want to give the parameter a different name.

Operations on Functions

The Dylan language defines a number of functions that operate on other functions.

There are two broad categories of these functions:

- Introspective functions take a function as an argument and return information about it. These are described in "Reflective Operations on Functions" on page 351.

- Higher order functions take one or more functions as arguments and return a new function. These are described in "Functional Operations" on page 346.

Conditions

Contents

Background   103
Overview   105
Signalers, Conditions, and Handlers   105
Exception Handling   107
   Stack Model   107
   Recovery and Exits   108
   Restarts   111
   Recovery Protocols   111
Condition Messages   112
Introspective Operations   114

Background

A long-standing problem of software engineering is the need to develop an organized way to deal with exceptions, situations that must be handled gracefully but that are not conceptually part of the normal operation of the program.

Of course it is possible to program exception handling without using special linguistic features. For example, all functions could return an extra result that indicates whether they succeeded or failed, functions could take an extra argument that they consult if an exception occurs, or a designated exception-handling function could be called whenever a problem arises. All of these approaches have been used in one real-life system or another, but they are deficient in two ways. First, they are too informal and don't provide enough structure to allow an organized, systematic approach to exception handling. Second, and more importantly, the first two approaches do not provide textual separation between "normal code" and "code for dealing with exceptions"; exception-related code is sprinkled throughout the program. This leads to two problems: one is the well-known mistake of forgetting to test error codes and thus failing to detect an exception (perhaps because the programmer believed the error could never occur); the other is that program clarity is lost because it isn't easy to think about the main flow of the program while temporarily ignoring exceptions.

All exception systems involve the concept of "signal" (sometimes with a different name, such as "raise" or "throw") and the concept of "handle" (sometimes with a different name such as "on-unit" or "catch"). Most exception systems dynamically match signalers with handlers, first invoking the most recently established matching handler still active, and then, if that matching handler declines to handle the exception, invoking the next most recent matching handler, and so on.

In addition, it is necessary to have a way to clean up when execution of a function is terminated by a nonlocal exit initiated either by the function itself or by something it explicitly or implicitly called.

Exception systems may be name-based or object-based, they may be exiting or calling, and they may or may not provide formal recovery mechanisms.

Conditions

In a name-based exception system a program signals a name, and a handler matches if it handles the same name or "any." The name is a constant in the source text of the program, not the result of an expression.

In an object-based exception system a program signals an object, and a handler matches if it handles a type that object belongs to. Object-based exceptions are more powerful, because the object can communicate additional information from the signaler to the handler, because the object to be signaled can be chosen at run-time rather than signaling a fixed name, and because type inheritance in the handler matching adds abstraction and provides an organizing framework.

In an exiting exception system, all dynamic state between the handler and the signaler is unwound before the handler receives control, as if signaling were a nonlocal goto from the signaler to the handler.

In a calling exception system the signaler is still active when a handler receives control. Control can be returned to the signaler, as if signaling were a function call from the signaler to the handler.

Exiting exception systems are acceptable for errors. However, they do not work for an exception that is not an error and doesn't require an exit, either because there is a default way to handle it and recover or because it can safely be ignored by applications that don't care about it. Non-error exceptions are quite common in networked environments, in computers with gradually expiring resources (such as batteries), in complex user interfaces, and as one approach for reflecting hardware exceptions such as page protection violations or floating-point overflow to the application.

Most languages have not formalized how to recover from exceptions, leaving programmers to invent ad hoc mechanisms. However, a formal recovery mechanism is useful for several reasons: it ensures that recovery is implemented correctly; it allows options for recovery to be categorized just as exceptions are categorized; and it allows introspection on the options for recovery, for example, by a debugger.

The Dylan exception facility is object-based. It uses calling semantics but also provides exiting handlers. It provides formal recovery.

Overview

The Dylan exception system is built on top of an underlying signal system. Together, the signal system and the exception system comprise the Dylan condition system.

At the signal layer, the condition system provides a way of establishing a run-time connection between a **signaler** and a **handler** through a **condition**. This is essentially a run-time analog to the more usual fixed connection between a caller and a callee established through function-name matching. This layer of the condition system is little more than a way to locate and call a function. The function call does not necessarily involve any exceptional situation or nonlocal flow of control.

At the exception layer, the condition system specifies a set of protocols for categorizing and handling exceptional situations through **recovery** or **exit**. This higher layer provides overall structure, eliminates the possibility of failing to notice an exceptional situation, and provides a clean separation between "normal code" and "code for dealing with exceptions."

The nonlocal exit and clean-up features of the `block` statement are often used in conjunction with the facilities described in this chapter. `block` is described on page 404.

Signalers, Conditions, and Handlers

A condition is an object used to locate and provide information to a handler. A condition represents a situation that needs to be handled. Examples are errors, warnings, and attempts to recover from errors. All conditions are instances of `<condition>`. Several subclasses of `<condition>` are provided for additional behavior. These are described in "Conditions" on page 244.

A handler is a function for handling conditions of a particular type. Handlers may be installed dynamically with the local declaration `let handler`, and with the `exception` clause of the `block` statement. Dynamically installed handlers are active for the duration of the execution of a body. More recently installed handlers take precedence over less recently installed handlers. If no dynamically installed handler handles a condition, the generic function `default-handler` is called. `default-handler` has predefined methods and may also have program-defined methods.

Signaling is the mechanism for locating the most recently installed handler for a condition. The basic mechanism for signaling is the function `signal`. Several functions built on `signal` are provided for additional behavior. These are described in "Signaling Conditions" on page 357.

When a condition is signaled, the condition facility locates the most recently installed applicable handler and calls it. An applicable handler is one that matches the signaled condition by type and by an optional test function associated with the handler. The condition system is simply a way for a signaler and a handler to be introduced to each other. Once they have met, they communicate through an ordinary function call. The condition object is the argument to that call.

Like any function, the called handler either returns some values or takes a nonlocal exit. Either way, the handler has handled the condition, and the act of signaling is completed.

A handler also has the option of declining to handle the condition by passing control to the next applicable handler. It does this by tail recursively calling a next-handler function which it received as an argument. The next-handler function calls the next most recently installed applicable handler with appropriate arguments. This is analogous to the next-method function used in methods of generic functions.

(The call to next-handler is described as tail-recursive to ensure that all values returned by the call are returned by the handler. Not returning all the values could interfere with the condition's recovery protocol. A handler that really knows what it is doing could use a non-tail-recursive call, but anything that knows what it's doing in this situation is probably unmodular. Note that a handler might not know the full recovery protocol, because the condition might be a subtype of the handler's expected type.)

Every signaled condition is handled, because the system ensures that there is always an applicable default handler that does not decline.

If a handler handles a condition by returning (rather than by taking a nonlocal exit) the values it returns are returned by `signal`.

Exception Handling

A set of classes, functions, and associated conventions extend the underlying condition handling capabilities to provide a complete exception handling facility.

The classes are described in "Conditions" on page 244, and the functions are described in "Signaling Conditions" on page 357.

Stack Model

Condition handlers are installed dynamically, with more recent handlers shadowing previously installed handlers. In addition, exception handling often involves the use of nonlocal exits. For these reasons it is useful to describe the behavior of the exception system using the following terms from the stack model of function calling.

- **outside stack**
  The state existing just before the handler was established.

- **signaling unit**
  The conceptual program component that includes the expression that signaled the condition and does not include the expression that established the handler. This informal concept provides a notion of where the interface boundary between the signaler and the handler lies.

- **middle stack**
  The state existing just before the signaling unit was called, minus the outside stack. In other words, the state between the handler and the signaling unit.

- **inside stack**
  The state existing just before signaling occurred, minus the middle stack and outside stack. In other words, the portion of the signaling unit prior to the call to `signal`.

Figure 7-1   The Stack Model

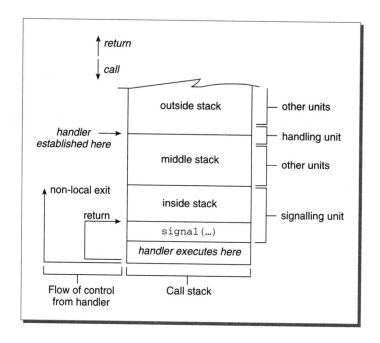

The handler in Figure 7-1 may either return normally, in which case execution resumes as the call to `signal` returns normally, or the handler may make a nonlocal exit, such as calling the exit function from a dynamically active `block` statement.

Recovery and Exits

There are two ways to handle an exception: by recovery or by exit. Recovery involves making some repair to the program state and leaving control in the signaling unit. Exit involves transferring control outside of the signaling unit through the use of a nonlocal exit.

The simplest way to handle an exception is to exit the signaling unit by taking a nonlocal exit to a target established in the outside stack. The `exception` clause of the `block` statement provides a convenient mechanism for accomplishing this.

A less common handling style is to exit the signaling unit by taking a nonlocal exit to a target established in the middle stack, thus leaving the handler in force.

Instead of exiting, a handler can recover by returning control to the signaling unit. This can be done either by returning values that the signaling unit will understand or by taking a nonlocal exit to a target established in the inside stack.

The following examples show three ways of handling a copy-protection violation while copying a series of files. Note that the signaling code does not need to know how the condition will be handled. The only changes are in the code that handles the condition.

```
// Assume there is a class for file-system errors.
// We are interested in a special kind of file-system error
// that occurs when attempting to copy a copy-protected file,
// so we define a new class to indicate such errors.
define class <copy-protection-violation> (<file-system-error>)
   slot file, init-keyword: file:;    // Store the file name
end class;

// Define a function to copy a single file. This
// function signals a <copy-protection-violation> if
// the file is copy-protected.
define method copy-file (source, destination)
   if ( copy-protected?(source) )
     signal(make(<copy-protection-violation>, file: source));
   else
     // copy normally
     notify-user("Copying %s to %s.", source, destination);
   end if;
end method;

// The following function copies a sequence of files.
// If one of the files is copy-protected, the user is
// notified, and the remaining files are copied.
define method backup-all-possible (volume, archive)
```

```
    let handler <copy-protection-violation>
        = method (condition, next)
            // The handler just notifies the user and continues
            notify-user("The file %s could not be copied.",
                        condition.file);
          end method;
    // start copying files, with the handler in effect
    for (each-file in volume)
      copy-file(each-file, archive)
    end for;
end method;


// The following function stops copying as soon as it
// hits a copy-protected file
define method backup-exit (volume, archive)
  // set up a block so we can do a nonlocal exit
  block (exit)
    let handler <copy-protection-violation>
        = method (condition, next)
            // Notify the user and abort the backup
            notify-user(
      "Backup interrupted: the file %s could not be copied.",
                        condition.file);
            exit(#f);
          end method;
    // start copying files, with the handler in effect
      for (each-file in volume)
        copy-file(each-file, archive)
      end for;
    end block;
end method;


// The following function uses the convenient exception clause of
// the block statement to achieve essentially the same effect as
// as backup-exit.
define method backup-block (volume, archive)
  // get ready to do backups
  block ()
```

```
    // start copying files
    for (each-file in volume)
      copy-file(each-file, archive)
    end for;
  exception (condition :: <copy-protection-violation>)
    notify-user(
    "Backup interrupted: the file %s could not be copied.",
              condition.file);
  end block;
end method;
```

Restarts

Recovering or exiting can be accomplished directly, or a more formal
mechanism called **restarting** can be used. Using restarts provides more
assurance that the handler and the signaling unit agree on the meaning of what
they are doing and provides some isolation of the handler from names and
data representations internal to the signaling unit.

A handler restarts by signaling a restart. All restarts are instances of
<restart>. Any values needed for recovery are passed in the restart (that is,
in initialization arguments that the restart remembers, typically in slots). The
restart is handled by a restart handler that either returns or takes a nonlocal
exit. If the restart handler returns some values, signal returns those values
and the handler that called signal also returns them. The call to signal from
the signaling unit that signaled the original condition returns the same values,
and the signaling unit recovers as directed by those values.

Recovery Protocols

For every condition class there should be a **recovery protocol** that defines the
meaning of handling by returning, the meaning of the values returned, and
which restart handlers are supposed to be established by the signaling unit.
The recovery protocol tells the handler what to expect from the signaler. For
many condition classes, this is the empty protocol: handling by returning isn't
allowed, and no particular restart handlers are provided. In this case only
handling by exiting is possible. (Exiting might be accomplished by signaling a
restart whose handler was established in the outside or middle stack and does

a nonlocal exit back to where it was established, or by an ordinary nonlocal exit.) The recovery protocol for a subclass should be compatible with the recovery protocol of a superclass. That is, a handler that applies a class's recovery protocol should operate correctly when the condition is an instance of some subclass of that class.

An example recovery protocol for a hypothetical <unbound-slot> condition could include the following:

- Returning is allowed. Returning a value uses that value as if it had been the contents of the slot.

- A restart handler for <new-value> is available. <new-value> has initialization arguments value:, the value to use, and permanent:, which indicates whether to store the value into the slot or leave the slot unbound.

No formal mechanism is provided for describing recovery protocols; they are left to the documentation of a condition class. Introspective functions are provided for discovering which recovery facilities are actually available, but this is different from (and sometimes is a superset of) the recovery facilities guaranteed by a recovery protocol always to be available.

The debugger is the condition handler of last resort. It receives control if no program-provided handler handles a serious condition. (This is true even if the debugger provided cannot analyze or intervene in the execution of programs but can only abort or restart them. The debugger might be merely a "core dumper," a "bomb box," or something similar.) An interactive debugger ought to offer the user the ability to signal any restart for which a restart handler is applicable and to return if the condition's recovery protocol allows it. This could, for example, be done with a menu titled "Recovery."

Condition Messages

Some condition classes provide a message to communicate the meaning of the condition to the program user.

Condition messages are constructed using **format strings**. A format string is a string template into which values can be inserted to construct a message. The two-character **format directives** %d, %b, %o, %x, %c, %s, and %= are replaced by the corresponding element of the associated sequence of **format arguments**.

Upper and lower case letters are equivalent in these format directives. The inserted value is formatted according to the following table:[*]

Table 7-1   Format Directives

Directive	Argument Type	Textual Format
%d	<integer>	decimal number
%b	<integer>	binary number
%o	<integer>	octal number
%x	<integer>	hexadecimal number
%c	<character>	character (with no quotes)
%s	<string>	string (with no quotes)
%s	<condition>	condition message (with no quotes)
%=	<object>	unspecified, but works with any object
%%	none	literal %

The text printed by the %= format directive for any given object is implementation-defined. The behavior when a format argument is not of the type specified in the table above is implementation-defined. The behavior when too many or too few format arguments are supplied is implementation-defined.

The two-character sequence %% does not consume a format argument, but inserts a % character.

All other uses of the % character in a format string are implementation-defined.

There is no standard way to get the message from a condition (although it can be inserted into another message). Debuggers get the message using implementation-dependent mechanisms. A streams library or other implementation-dependent feature might include a function to get the message from a condition. However, in some implementations, the message might only exist in the debugger, not in the program runtime.

---

[*] These format directives are designed for compatibility with C's printf, with some omissions and with the addition of %=.

There is no standard way for a user-defined condition class to supply a message. Individual implementations and libraries can specify such a mechanism that is appropriate to their needs.

Introspective Operations

The function `do-handlers` allows introspection of all the dynamically active handlers. For each handler, it provides the type, test, function, and init-arguments that were declared when the handler was installed. `do-handlers` is typically used by the debugger or other error-recovery system to discover what restart handlers are available before signaling a restart.

Additional operations support introspection on conditions. See "Introspection on Conditions" on page 362 for a complete description of these introspective functions.

CHAPTER 8

Collections

Contents

Overview   117
   The Iteration Protocol   117
Collection Keys   118
Iteration Stability and Natural Order   118
Mutability   119
Collection Alteration and Allocation   119
Collection Alignment   120
Defining a New Collection Class   121
Tables   122
Element Types   124
Limited Collection Types   126
   Creating Limited Collection Types   128

Overview

Collections are aggregate data structures that map from **keys** to **elements**. All collections are instances of the class <collection>.

<collection> has two covering subclasses: <sequence> and <explicit-key-collection>. Every concrete subclass of <collection> must also be a subclass of <sequence> or <explicit-key-collection>. **Sequences** use successive non-negative integers as keys; **explicit key collections** may use any object as a key. Both of these classes have predefined subclasses and may be additionally subclassed by programmers. See "Collections" on page 206 for a complete description of these classes.

A large number of functions are available on collections, including functions for iteration, mapping, random access of elements, sorting, filtering, etc. See "Collection Operations" on page 294 for a complete description of these functions.

The Iteration Protocol

All collections implement an **iteration protocol** that allows iteration to be specified abstractly. Many higher level operations on collections can be defined in terms of only the iteration protocol. For many programs these higher level operations are sufficient; they will not need to use the iteration protocol directly. The iteration protocol is used by programs defining new collection types, and for certain types of iteration that cannot be handled by the built-in higher level operations.

The iteration protocol centers on the notion of a "state" object for an iteration. Each collection class chooses its own most appropriate representation for an iteration state, and only the functions of the iteration protocol are affected by this choice.

Use of the iteration protocol is based on the assumption that the collection over which iteration occurs remains static for the duration of the iteration. That is, arbitrary changes to a mutable collection while an iteration is in progress may cause the iteration to produce unpredictable results.

With notable exceptions, two or more iterations over the same collection are not guaranteed to produce the same values in the same order, even if the collection is unaltered. For details, see "Iteration Stability and Natural Order" as follows.

The built-in collection functions are implemented in terms of the iteration protocol. When defining a new collection class, a programmer need only define the iteration protocol for the class. Once this is done, instances of the class can be used with all the built-in collection functions. Of course, in some cases it will be more efficient to define methods on these functions optimized for the new class, rather than relying on the default implementation based on the iteration protocol.

Collection Keys

All collections in Dylan are keyed. That is, all collections can be viewed abstractly as partial functions that map keys to elements. (This choice precludes pure sets from being considered collections, although it is straightforward simply to ignore the keys for a collection and consider it simply as a set of elements.) The element function implements this partial mapping of keys to elements.

Every collection has a **key test**, which is the test used for determining whether a given key matches a key in the collection. The key test of a collection can be accessed using the key-test function.

Iteration Stability and Natural Order

A collection is **stable under iteration** if any two iterations over the collection are guaranteed to produce the same values in the same order in the absence of modifications to the table. If this guarantee does not hold, the collection is **unstable under iteration**.

Sequences are required to be stable under iteration. Explicit key collections may or may not be stable under iteration.

The order in which elements and keys are enumerated by the iteration protocol for a particular iteration is known as the **natural order** for that iteration over the collection. If a collection is stable under iteration, then every iteration over that collection will have the same natural order, and we may speak of the natural order of the collection itself. Most of the operations on collections are required to operate in natural order, usually for the purpose of understanding interactions among side effects.

Mutability

Some collections can be modified after they have been created while others cannot. The <mutable-collection> and <stretchy-collection> mixin classes are provided to allow methods to distinguish between mutable and immutable collections. Instances of <mutable-collection> can have their elements changed after they are created. Instances of <stretchy-collection> can have keys added and removed after they are created.

An element of a mutable collection is set to a new value with element-setter. If the collection is not stretchy, then the key specified must already be present in the collection; its value will be changed. If the collection is stretchy, then the key will be added if it is not already present. If the collection is a stretchy sequence and the key is not already present, then the size of the sequence will first be set to the new key plus 1, and then the value of the new key will be set.

A key and its corresponding value can be removed from an explicit key collection with the function remove-key!.

Collection Alteration and Allocation

The contents of a collection are the key/value pairs stored in the collection. The contents are said to be **altered** when:

- Keys are added or removed (according to the collection's key test).

- The value of a key (according to the key test) changes (as tested by ==).

- The ordering of the key/value pairs changes. This type of alteration is only possible for explicit key collections that are stable under iteration.

A function **destructively modifies** its argument collection if calling the function could alter the contents of the argument collection. Unless explicitly documented to do so, functions do not destructively modify their arguments.

The ! convention, described on page 24, is used to indicate some destructive operations.

Unless explicity noted, destructive operations are not required to leave their arguments in a well-defined state. More particularly, a destructive operation does not in general turn the argument into the result. It may reuse components of the argument or alter the argument in some unpredictable way in order to produce the result. As a general rule, the return value of the function should be used.

A collection C is **fresh** if modification of any pre-existing collection's contents can never modify the contents of C and if modifications to C can never modify the contents of any pre-existing collection. Immutable collections cannot be modified, so a fresh immutable collection can share structure with other immutable collections.

For example, given that <pair> is mutable and the result of a call to list is a fresh instance of <pair>, we can guarantee that the following expression is always false:

```
list(1) == list(1)
```

Collection Alignment

Some operations on collections are defined to allow the use of more than a single collection. For example, some looping functions accept any number of collections and operate on these collections in parallel. Each pass through the loop uses one element from each collection. The presence of collections that are unstable under iteration can create problems for multi-collection operations unless special care is taken. If iteration is effectively performed in random order, then naively performing parallel iterations over two different collections would randomly combine values from the two collections. This would presumably have no meaning.

To prevent such random combinations, operations on more than one collection must in general align the collections. **Collection alignment** consists of effectively computing the intersection of the collections' key sequences and then using the random-access operations (`element` and `element-setter`) to operate on the collections themselves.

If implemented naively, this definition of alignment has the potential for extreme inefficiency because of its dependence on `element` and the potential loops implied by the calls to `key-sequence`. However, an important special case of this problem is that of iterating over multiple sequences. In this case, the intersection of key sequences will always be the non-negative integers up to the length of the shortest sequence. Further, unlike collections in general, sequences are required to exhibit stability so the explicit computation of key sequences is not actually required. It is correct simply to iterate until one or more of the sequences is exhausted.

Iteration operations that store results in a target collection must generally include the target collection during alignment. This alignment requirement is relaxed if the target collection is a `<stretchy-collection>`. In this case, the target collection is not considered during alignment. Rather, only the source collections are aligned. New keys may be added to the target collection during the course of the iteration, and keys may be given new values. Other keys are left undisturbed.

It is only possible to align collections that have identical key tests.

Defining a New Collection Class

Every collection class must provide an implementation of the iteration protocol. A method on `forward-iteration-protocol` is required. A method on `backward-iteration-protocol` is optional.

Every collection must provide or inherit methods for `element` and `key-test`. If the collection is also a `<mutable-collection>`, it must provide or inherit a method for `element-setter`. A collection that is not a `<mutable-collection>` must provide an implementation of `type-for-copy`.

Individual collection classes may impose further requirements on their subclasses. For example, concrete subclasses of `<table>` must provide or inherit a method for `table-protocol`.

For efficiency, it may be desirable to provide specialized implementations for certain generic functions. Collections that can implement functions such as `size` or `member?` more efficiently should do so. Sequences that can reuse storage to implement functions such as `reverse!` and `sort!` should do so.

Tables

Tables map arbitrary keys to elements. Table keys may be any object, including complex objects such as strings. All tables are instances of `<table>`. `<table>` is the only instantiable subclass of `<explicit-key-collection>` defined by Dylan. Tables are unstable under iteration.

The iteration protocol for tables is implemented in terms of the function `table-protocol`. Every concrete subclass of `<table>` must provide or inherit a method for `table-protocol`. This function accepts a table as an argument, and returns an equivalence predicate and hash-function, as described below.

The **equivalence predicate** of a table is used to compare keys. (It is the table's key test.) The table maps keys that are equivalent under the predicate to the same table element. An equivalence predicate is a boolean function of two arguments that returns true if and only if the arguments are considered to be the same according to some specified criteria. For a function to be used as an equivalence predicate, it must be reflexive, commutative, and transitive. That is, for a function F and any arguments X, Y, and Z in the domain of F, the following must be true:

- $F(X, X)$ must be true.

- $F(X, Y)$ must be true if and only if $F(Y, X)$ is true.

- If both $F(X, Y)$ and $F(Y, Z)$ are true then $F(X, Z)$ must be true.

An **equivalence class** (for an equivalence predicate) is a set of objects, or potential objects, that are all the same under the specified equivalence predicate and different from all objects not in the class. (This use of the term "class" does not refer to Dylan classes.)

An object is said to be **visibly modified** with respect to an equivalence predicate if the modification changes the equivalence class of the object. The modifications that are visible to an equivalence predicate are determined by the definition of the predicate. (For example, changing a character in a string would be a visible modification with respect to an equivalence predicate that compared strings character by character, but it would not be a visible modification with respect to an equivalence predicate that compared objects by identity, without regard for their contents.)

If an object X is a key in a table T and is visibly modified with regard to the test function of T, then the consequences are unspecified if any of the following objects are used as a key in any subsequent operations on T:

- The original object, X.

- Some object Y that is in the same equivalence class (as determined by the test function) as X prior to the modification of X.

- Some object Z that is in the same equivalence class (as determined by the test function) as X after the modification of X.

Each table also has an associated **hash function**, which is a function that relates table keys and table elements by computing **hash codes**. A hash code is a conceptual object consisting of a **hash id** and its associated **hash state**. (It is not an actual Dylan object.) A hash id is an integer encoding of an object. A hash state is an object of implementation-dependent type that is associated with a particular hash id and can be used by the implementation to determine whether the hash id has been invalidated. A hash function accepts one argument, a key, and returns two values, a hash id and a hash state, which together represent the hash code.

Each hash function is associated with a specific equivalence predicate, and must obey the following constraints:

- The domain of the hash function must include the domain of valid arguments to the corresponding equivalence predicate. A hash function need not be defined for all Dylan objects, only those that are acceptable as arguments to the equivalence predicate.

- All objects in a given equivalence class have the same (=) valid hash id, where validity is determined from the associated hash state.

In addition, a hash function should have the property that the hash ids computed by it are well distributed over the range of possible values. That is, it should be unlikely that two randomly chosen equivalence classes have the same valid hash id.

Element Types

Each instance X of <collection> has a conceptual **element type** that is an instance of <type>. If the element type of X is T, X stores elements of type T. The element method will always return an instance of T and the element-setter method (if X is mutable) will accept any instance of T. The analogous functions returned by the iteration protocol also return/accept any instance of T.

Each subclass C of <collection> has a conceptual element type that is either T_1 or indefinite $\Leftarrow T_1$, where T_1 is a type. (The symbol "$\Leftarrow$" in the "indefinite $\Leftarrow$ T_1" notation is an abbreviation for "subtype.")

If the element type of C is T_1, each general instance of C must have an element type T_2 that is type equivalent to T_1. Each subclass of C must have an element type T_3 that is type equivalent to T_1.

If the element type of C is indefinite $\Leftarrow T_1$, each general instance of C must have an element type T_2 that is a subtype of T_1. Therefore, element called on that instance will return an instance of T_1 (and will not return all possible instances of T_1 if T_2 is a proper subtype of T_1). It is not determined by C what the applicable element-setter method will accept (thus C's element type is said to be "indefinite"). Each subclass of C must have element type T_3 or indefinite $\Leftarrow T_3$, where T_3 is a subtype of T_1.

User-defined collection classes must also follow these rules.

Note: the above statements about the value returned by element only apply when no default: keyword argument is specified.

Table 8-1   Element Types of Built-in Collections

Collection	Element Type
<collection>	indefinite $\Leftarrow$ <object>
<explicit-key-collection>	indefinite $\Leftarrow$ <object>
<mutable-collection>	indefinite $\Leftarrow$ <object>
<stretchy-collection>	indefinite $\Leftarrow$ <object>

Table 8-1   Element Types of Built-in Collections (continued)

Collection	Element Type
`<sequence>`	indefinite $\Leftarrow$ `<object>`
`<mutable-explicit-key-collection>`	indefinite $\Leftarrow$ `<object>`
`<mutable-sequence>`	indefinite $\Leftarrow$ `<object>`
`<table>`	indefinite $\Leftarrow$ `<object>`
`<object-table>`	indefinite $\Leftarrow$ `<object>`
`<array>`	indefinite $\Leftarrow$ `<object>`
`<vector>`	indefinite $\Leftarrow$ `<object>`
`<simple-vector>`	indefinite $\Leftarrow$ `<object>`
`<stretchy-vector>`	indefinite $\Leftarrow$ `<object>`
`<deque>`	indefinite $\Leftarrow$ `<object>`
`<string>`	indefinite $\Leftarrow$ `<character>`
`<range>`	indefinite $\Leftarrow$ `<real>`
`<simple-object-vector>`	`<object>`
`<unicode-string>`	K_1 (see note below)
`<byte-string>`	K_2 (see note below)
`<list>`	`<object>`
`<pair>`	`<object>`
`<empty-list>`	`<object>`

Note: K_1 and K_2 are subtypes of `<character>` that have not been given standardized names.

By convention, if C is an instantiable subtype of `<collection>` and C's element-type is indefinite $\Leftarrow$ `<object>`, then instantiating C produces a collection whose element type is `<object>`.

Instantiating `<range>` produces a collection whose element-type is unspecified except that it is a subtype of `<real>` and every element of the range is an instance of the element type.

The preceding section describes the element type of every object that is created by make of an instantiable built-in collection class. The element type of an instance of a user-defined collection class is unspecified, but should follow the rules given here in order to preserve the property that any operation that works on an instance of a supertype must work on an instance of a subtype.

Limited Collection Types

Limited collections are subtypes of `<collection>` that are constrained to have a particular size or dimensions and that are constrained to hold elements of a particular type.

If C is a subclass of `<collection>` whose element type is indefinite $\Leftarrow T_1$, then it is possible to create any number of limited collection types that can be described as `limited(C, of: $T_2$, size: $S$)`.

Like a collection class, a limited collection type has a conceptual element type. The element type of `limited(C, of: $T_2$, size: $S$)` is T_2. T_2 must be an instance of `<type>` and a subtype of T_1. C is the base class of the new limited collection type.

S limits the size of instances of a limited collection type. S can be `#f`, which means no limitation, or a non-negative integer, which means that every instance of the limited collection type has exactly that many elements.

S must be `#f` if C is stretchy (e.g. `<table>`, `<stretchy-vector>`, or `<deque>`).

If C is `<array>` then it is also possible to create any number of limited collection types, which can be described as `limited(<array>, of: $T$, dimensions: $D$)`. D must be a sequence of non-negative integers; the rank of each instance is `size(D)` and the dimensions of each instance are the elements of D. You cannot specify both `size:` and `dimensions:` in the same type.

Some limited collection types are instantiable. `make(limited(C, ...), ...)` returns a direct instance of some subclass of C. Typically this class is not standardized and its name is not exported, but it is valid for this class to be C itself. There is nothing special about this class; it is simply a class known to the applicable `limited` method and its creation is subject to all the usual sealing restrictions.

An object X is an instance of a limited collection type `limited(C, of: `T_2`, size: `S`)` if and only if all of the following are true:

- `object-class(X)` is a subclass of C.

- X's size matches S, as described above.

- If X is an instance of `<stretchy-collection>` then S must be `#f`.

- The element type of X is equivalent to T_2.

An object X is an instance of a type `limited(C, of: `T_2`, dimensions: `D`)` if and only if all of the following are true:

- `object-class(X)` is a subclass of C.

- `dimensions(X)` = D.

- X is not an instance of `<stretchy-collection>`.

- The element type of X is equivalent to T_2.

Each element of an instance of a limited collection type must be an instance of the element type. Fetching an element of the collection is guaranteed to return an instance of the element type. Setting or initializing an element will check that the new element is an instance of the element type and signal an error of type `<type-error>` if it is not.

If L_1 is a subtype of L_2 and L_2 is a limited collection type, then L_1 is either a singleton of an instance of L_2 or a limited collection type that satisfies one of the following sets of rules:

1. If neither L_1 nor L_2 specifies a `dimensions:` attribute, let L_1 be `limited(`C_1`, of: `T_1`, size: `S_1`)`, and L_2 be `limited(`C_2`, of: `T_2`, size: `S_2`)`. All of the following must be true:

   - C_1 is a subclass of C_2.
   - If S_2 is not `#f`, $S_1 = S_2$.
   - T_1 and T_2 are equivalent types.

2. If either L_1 or L_2, specifies a `dimensions:` attribute, then all of the following must be true. Let L_1 be `limited(`C_1`, of: `T_1`, dimensions: `D_1`)`, and L_2 be either `limited(`C_2`, of: `T_2`, dimensions: `D_2`)` or `limited(`C_2`, of: `T_2`, size: `S_2`)`.

   - C_1 is a subclass of C_2.
   - D_1 is present (i.e. L_1 must specify a dimensions attribute).

- If D_2 is present, $D_1 = D_2$.
- If S_2 is not #f, `reduce1(\*, `D_1`)` $= S_2$.
- T_1 and T_2 are equivalent types.

The limited collection type `limited(C, of: T, size: S)` is a subtype of C. The limited collection type `limited(C, of: T, dimensions: D)` is a subtype of C.

Element Type Subclassing

The element type subclassing rules are generalized to limited collection types as follows (this is implied by the preceding and is included here for explanatory purposes only):

If the element type of a limited collection type L_1 is T_1, each instance of L_1 stores elements of type T_1. The `element` method will always return an instance of T_1 and the `element-setter` method will accept any instance of T_1. Each limited collection type that is a subtype of L_1 must have an element type T_2 that is equivalent to T_1.

If the element type of a class C_1 is indefinite $\Leftarrow T_1$, each limited collection type that is a subtype of C_1 has an element type T_2 and T_2 must be a subtype of T_1. Thus `element` on any instance of C_1 will return an instance of T_1 (and will not return all possible instances of T_1 if T_2 is a proper subtype of T_1), and it is not determined by C_1 what the applicable `element-setter` method will accept (hence the term "indefinite").

The above statements about the value returned by `element` only apply when no `default:` keyword argument is specified.

Creating Limited Collection Types

You obtain a type object for a limited collection type by calling the `limited` generic function on a collection class. There are several built-in methods for `limited` specialized for specific subclasses of `<collection>`. Each of these methods accepts a required keyword argument `of:` and also accepts an optional keyword argument `size:` if the class is not stretchy. If the class is `<array>` the optional keyword argument `dimensions:` is also accepted. Each method returns a type. The returned type is never a class. If the `size:` keyword argument is accepted but not supplied, it defaults to #f.

Users cannot write portable methods for `limited`. There are no built-in methods for `limited` applicable to user-defined classes.

Uninstantiable Limited Collection Types

Methods on `limited` support the creation of uninstantiable limited types for the following classes:

- `<collection>`
- `<explicit-key-collection>`
- `<mutable-collection>`
- `<stretchy-collection>`
- `<mutable-explicit-key-collection>`
- `<sequence>`
- `<mutable-sequence>`

Although limited types created from these classes cannot be instantiated, they are still useful as specializers.

Instantiable Limited Collection Types

Methods on `limited` support the creation of instantiable limited types for the following classes:

- `<table>`
- `<object-table>`
- `<array>`
- `<vector>`
- `<simple-vector>`
- `<stretchy-vector>`
- `<string>`
- `<range>`

These methods are described in Chapter 12, "The Built-In Functions," on page 263.

Sealing

Contents

Overview   133
Explicitly Known Objects   133
Declaring Characteristics of Classes   134
Declaring Characteristics of Generic Functions   135
Define Sealed Domain   135
   Rationale   136
   Pseudosubtype Examples   138
   Abbreviations for Define Sealed Domain   138
   Implied Restrictions on Method Definitions   139

Overview

This chapter describes techniques for **sealing** portions of a Dylan program by declaring that classes or functions will never be used in particular ways, or will never be extended in particular ways. These **sealing directives** enable a range of compiler optimizations, and also clarify the programmer's intent.

The sealing directives include:

- Declaring a class to be `sealed` or `open`. This controls whether a class can be directly subclassed outside the library in which it is defined.

- Declaring a class to be `abstract` or `concrete`. This controls whether a class can have direct instances.

- Declaring a class to be `primary` or `free`. This controls how a class can be used for multiple inheritance.

- Declaring a generic function to be `sealed` or `open`. This controls whether methods can be added to the generic function from outside the library in which the generic function is defined.

- Using `define sealed domain`, or using the abbreviations `define sealed method` and `sealed slot`. These disallow the addition of some methods from outside the library in which the generic function is defined.

With the exception of `define sealed domain`, these directives are expressed as adjectives on the generic function definition, class definition, method definition, or slot specification.

Explicitly Known Objects

A class, generic function, or method may or may not be **explicitly known** to a given library. A sealing restriction may limit the set of classes, generic functions, and methods to those that are explicitly known; others cannot be added.

- A class C is explicitly known in a library L if it is defined by `define class` in L or in a library used by L.

- A generic function G is explicitly known in a library L if G is defined by `define generic` in the library or in one of the libraries L uses, or if G is implicitly defined by the definition of a method explicitly known in L or if G is implicitly defined by a slot specification for a class explicitly known in L.

- A method M is explicitly known in a library L if M is defined by `define method` in L or in one of the libraries L uses, or if M is defined by a slot specification for a class explicitly known in L.

Declaring Characteristics of Classes

A class definition may include the adjectives `sealed`, `open`, `primary`, `free`, `abstract`, or `concrete`. These adjectives declare characteristics of the class.

Additional restrictions on the ability to subclass classes may be imposed by `define sealed domain`.

- An explicitly defined class can be declared to be either sealed or open. If a class is sealed then no additional direct subclasses other than those explicitly known in the same library may be created. Thus, it is an error to define a direct subclass of a sealed class in some library other than the one that defined the sealed class, or to use `make` of `<class>` with a sealed class included in the direct superclasses specified by the `superclasses:` initialization argument. An open class does not prohibit such operations. When explicitly defining a class, the default is for the class to be sealed. This may be overriden by explicitly specifying that it is open. A class created using `make` of `<class>` is open. There is no specified way to create a sealed class using `make`.

- An explicitly defined class may be declared to be either primary or free. The default is free. Each primary superclass of a class must be either a subclass or a superclass of all the other primary superclasses of the class. (This essentially restricts primary classes to forming a single inheritance chain.) Slots defined in a primary class may be accessed more efficiently than slots defined in a free class.

- An explicitly defined class may be defined to be either abstract or concrete. The default is concrete. The superclasses of an abstract class must be abstract. The default method on `make` will signal an error if passed an

abstract class. For an abstract class to be instantiable, it must define a
method on `make` that delegates to a concrete subclass.

Declaring Characteristics of Generic Functions

A generic function definition may include either the adjective `sealed` or the
adjective `open`. These adjectives declare whether the generic function is sealed.

If a generic function is sealed then no additional methods other than those
explicitly known in the same library may be added to the generic function and
no methods may be removed from it. Thus, it is an error to define a method for
a sealed generic function in some library other than the one which defined the
sealed generic function, or to apply `add-method` or `remove-method` to a
sealed generic function. An open generic function does not prohibit these
operations.

When explicitly defining a generic function, the default is for the generic
function to be sealed. It can be declared to be open by using the `open` adjective
in the generic function definition. A generic function that has no explicit
definition but has an implicit definition provided by explicit definitions of
generic function methods or slot accessors is also sealed. A generic function
created using `make` of `<generic-function>` is open. There is no specified
way to create a sealed generic function using `make`.

Additional restrictions on the ability to add methods to a generic function may
be imposed by `define sealed domain`.

Define Sealed Domain

`define sealed domain` is used to make specific portions of a generic
function and of the class hierarchy invariant without disallowing all future
changes. The arguments to `define sealed domain` are an explicitly known
generic function and a series of types, one for each required argument of the
generic function.

The complete syntax of `define sealed domain` is given on page 388.

A define sealed domain definition in a library L for a generic function G with types $T_1...T_n$ imposes the following constraints on programs:

1. A method M that is congruent to G and that is not an explicitly known method in L may be added to G only if at least one of the specializers for M is disjoint from the corresponding T.

2. A method M may be removed from G only if at least one of the specializers for M is disjoint from the corresponding T.

3. A class C (with direct superclasses $D_1...D_m$) that is not explicitly known in L may be created only if no method in G actually blocks C.

   □ A method M (with specializers $S_1...S_n$) in G potentially blocks C at argument position i if there exist j and k such that D_j is a pseudosubtype of S_i, D_k is a pseudosubtype of T_i, and D_k is not a pseudosubtype of S_i.

   □ A method M actually blocks C if M potentially blocks C at some argument position, and for every argument position i where S_i and T_i are disjoint, M potentially blocks C at i.

The third constraint is illustrated by the following example:

```
define generic m (x);
define class <t> (<object>) end class <t>;
define class <s> (<object>) end class <s>;
define method m (s :: <s>) end method m;
define sealed domain m (<t>);

define class <c> (<s>, <t>) end class <c>;
```

The definition of class `<c>` would be valid if it appeared in the same library as the preceding definitions or in a library used by them, but invalid if it appeared in a different library. The reason is that without the definition of `<c>`, the method defined on m is not within the domain declared by the define sealed domain, but with the definition of `<c>` the method is within that domain.

Rationale

define sealed domain permits the compiler to assume certain properties of the program that can be computed based on explicitly known classes and methods, with a guarantee that an attempt to violate any of those assumptions will be detected.

The goal of rule 3 is that the creation of the class C must not make any method M applicable to a part of the sealed domain to which it was not previously applicable.

The "potentially blocks" concept describes the mechanism for testing whether the set of objects that are instances of both S_i and T_i (i.e., to which the method is applicable at the ith argument position and that are within the sealed domain at that argument position) would change as a result of creating C. By specifying what valid programs are allowed to do, rule 3 implicitly specifies the assumptions a compiler can make. A define sealed domain definition accomplishes this by permitting the compiler to eliminate some of the known methods on a generic function from the set of methods that might be applicable to a particular call at runtime. For example, if this leaves exactly one applicable method, the compiler can eliminate a run-time method dispatch and consider additional optimizations such as inlining.

Specifically, suppose the compiler is compiling a call to G and has determined that the argument at position i is an instance of some type U (where U is not necessarily a standard Dylan type, but could instead be a compiler-internal extension to the type system, such as a difference of two types). For the compiler to be able to rely on the define sealed domain definition, U must be a subtype of T_i. For the compiler to determine that M is not applicable, U must be disjoint with S_i. Creating C can't change whether U is a subtype of T_i, but it can change whether U is disjoint with S_i. If there could be an object that is simultaneously an instance of U, C, and S_i, it would violate the compiler's assumption that M is not applicable in the call to G, and therefore creating C would be a sealing violation. If there can't be such an object, then creating C is allowed.

This maps onto rule 3 as follows (ignoring for the moment the added complication of limited types that lead to the use of the pseudosubtype relationship rather than subtype):

U is a subtype of D_k and therefore is a subtype of T_i, because subtype is transitive.

D_k is not a subtype of S_i, because if it were then U could not be disjoint from S_i.

D_j is a subtype of S_i.

If U and C would have a nonempty intersection, then the creation of C must be prevented, else U would no longer be disjoint from S_i. One possible U is the set of all general instances of D_k that are not also general instances of any of the explicitly known direct subclasses of D_k. That U would indeed have a non-empty intersection with C. The existence of this U makes the proposed rule 3 necessary.

Rule 3 does not need to address the possibility of multiple inheritance being used to combine classes involved in the element types of limited collection classes. Changes to the disjointness relationships between element types does not affect the relationships between collection types with those element types.

Pseudosubtype Examples

Suppose A and B are disjoint subclasses of `<collection>`, S_i is `limited(A, of: T)`, and T_i is `limited(B, of: T)`. Thus, S_i and T_i are disjoint and M is outside the sealed domain. If C inherits from A and B it should be potentially blocked by M, because an instance of `limited(C, of: T)` would be an instance of both S_i and T_i. Since B is not a subtype of T_i, there would be no blockage if the constraints in rule 3 were defined in terms of `subtype`. However, B is a pseudosubtype of T_i, so specifying rule 3 using the pseudosubtype relationship correctly causes M to potentially block C.

Suppose S_i is `limited(<stretchy-vector>, of: <integer>)` and T_i is `limited(<sequence>, of: <integer>)`. It should be possible to create `<stretchy-string>`, a direct subclass of `<stretchy-vector>` and `<string>`. The element-type of `<stretchy-string>` must be a subtype of `<character>`, therefore, assuming `<integer>` and `<character>` are disjoint, `<stretchy-string>` is disjoint from both S_i and T_i, and so is not blocked. This example shows the need for the non-disjointness requirement in the definition of pseudosubtype.

Abbreviations for Define Sealed Domain

`define sealed method` defines a method on a generic function and also seals the generic function for the types that are the specializers of the method.

The following two program fragments are equivalent:

Sealing

```
define sealed method insert (source :: <list>, i :: <object>)
  => (result :: <list>)
  ...
end method insert;
```

and

```
define method insert (source :: <list>, i :: <object>)
  => (result :: <list>)

  ...
end method insert;
define sealed domain insert (<list>, <object>);
```

The `sealed slot` option to `define class` defines a slot and also makes the getter generic function sealed over the class, and the setter generic function, if there is one, sealed over the type of the slot and the class.

The following two program fragments are equivalent:

```
define class <polygon> (<shape>)
  sealed slot sides :: <integer>, required-init-keyword: sides:;
end class <polygon>;
```

and

```
define class <polygon> (<shape>)
  slot sides :: <integer>, required-init-keyword: sides:;
end class <polygon>;
define sealed domain sides (<polygon>);
define sealed domain sides-setter (<integer>, <polygon>);
```

Implied Restrictions on Method Definitions

To avoid potential sealing violations among separately developed libraries, one of the following conditions should be true for every method *M* defined in a library *L*:

- Either the generic function to which *M* is added should be defined in the library *L*, or

- One of the specializers of M should be a subtype of a class defined in library L.

The following example illustrates why this condition is necessary.

Library L_1 defines and exports the following:

```
define generic g (x)
define class <c1> (<object>) end class <c1>;
```

Library L_2 uses L_1 and defines the following

```
define class <c2> (<c1>) end class <c2>;
define method g (x :: <c2>) end method;
define sealed domain g (<c2>)
```

Library L_3 uses L_1 and defines the following

```
define method g (x :: <c>) end method;
```

Libraries L_2 and L_3 are developed independently, and have no knowledge of each other. An application that attempts to use both L_2 and L_3 contains a sealing violation. L_2 is clearly valid. Therefore, L_3 is at fault for the sealing violation. Because the compiler cannot prove that use of L_3 will lead to an error (and indeed, it will only lead to an error in the presence of L_2), it is appropriate to issue a warning but not disallow the compilation of L_3.

Macros

Contents

Overview   143
   Compilation and Macro Processing   143
Extensible Grammar   147
   Definition Macros   147
   Statement Macros   148
   Function Macros   148
Macro Names   148
Rewrite Rules   150
Patterns   151
   Special Rules for Definitions   155
   Special Rules for Statements   156
   Special Rules for Function Macros   156
Pattern Variable Constraints   157
   Intermediate Words   158
Templates   159
Auxiliary Rule Sets   161
Hygiene   161
   Intentional Hygiene Violation   163
   Hygiene Versus Module Encapsulation   163
Rewrite Rule Examples   165
   Statement Macros   166
   Definition Macros   173
   Operator Function Macros   177
   Additional Examples   177

Overview

A macro is an extension to the core language that can be defined by the user, by the implementation, or as part of the Dylan language specification. Much of the grammatical structure of Dylan is built with macros. A macro defines the meaning of one construct in terms of another construct. The compiler substitutes the new construct for the original. The purpose of macros is to allow programmers to extend the Dylan language, for example by creating new control structures or new definitions. Unlike C, Dylan does not intend macros to be used to optimize code by inlining. Other parts of the language, such as sealing and `define constant`, address that need.

Throughout this chapter, *italic font* and SMALL CAPS are used to indicate references to the formal grammar given in Appendix A, "BNF."

Compilation and Macro Processing

Compilation consists of six conceptual phases:

1. Parsing a stream of characters into tokens, according to the lexical grammar in Appendix A, "BNF."

2. Parsing a stream of tokens into a program, according to the phrase grammar in Appendix A, "BNF."

3. Macro expansion, which translates the program to a core language.

4. Definition processing, which recognizes special and built-in definitions and builds a compile-time model of the static structure of the program.

5. Optimization, which rewrites the program for improved performance.

6. Code generation, which translates the program to executable form.

Portions of a program can be macro calls. Macro expansion replaces a macro call with another construct, which can itself be a macro call or contain macro calls. This expansion process repeats until there are no macro calls remaining in the program, thus macros have no space or speed cost at run time. Of course, expanding macros affects the speed and space cost of compilation.

Macros

A macro definition describes both the syntax of a macro call and the process for creating a new construct to replace the macro call. Typically the new construct contains portions of the old one, which can be regarded as arguments to the macro. A macro definition consists of a sequence of rewrite rules. The left-hand side of each rule is a pattern that matches a macro call. The right-hand side is a template for the expansion of a matching call. Pattern variables appearing in the left-hand side act as names for macro arguments. Pattern variables appearing in the right-hand side substitute arguments into the expansion. Macro arguments can be constrained to match specified elements of the Dylan grammar. Auxiliary rule sets enhance the rewrite rule notation with named subrules.

Some implementations and a future version of the Dylan language specification might allow macro expansions to be produced by compile-time computation using the full Dylan language and an object-oriented representation for programs. Such a "procedural macro" facility is not part of Dylan at this time.

The input to, and output from, macro expansion is a fragment, which is a sequence of elementary fragments. An elementary fragment is one of the following:

- A token: the output of the lexical grammar. The bracket tokens (,), [,], {, }, #(, and #[are not allowed. Core reserved words (except otherwise), BEGIN-WORDS, and FUNCTION-WORDS are not allowed unless quoted with backslash.

- A bracketed fragment: balanced brackets ((), [], or {}) enclosing a fragment.

- A macro call fragment: a macro call.

- A parsed fragment: a single unit that is not decomposable into its component tokens. It has been fully parsed by the phrase grammar. A parsed fragment is either a function call, a list constant, a vector constant, a definition, or a local declaration.

The second and third phases of compilation (parsing and macro expansion) are interleaved, not sequential. The parsing phase of the compiler parses a macro call just enough to find its end. See *definition-macro-call, statement, function-macro-call, body-fragment, list-fragment,* and *basic-fragment* in Appendix A, "BNF." This process of parsing a macro call also parses any macro calls nested inside it. The result is a macro call fragment.

This loose grammar for macro calls gives users a lot of flexibility to choose the grammar that their macros will accept. For example, the grammar of macro calls doesn't care whether a bracketed fragment will be interpreted as an argument list, a parameter list, a set of `for` clauses, or a module import list.

The compiler delays computing the expansion of a macro call fragment until it is needed. If an argument to a macro is a macro call, the outer macro call is always expanded first. When the compiler computes the expansion of a macro call fragment, it obeys the macro's definition. Constraints on pattern variables can cause reparsing of portions of the macro call.

A *constituent, operand,* or *leaf* that is a macro call expands the macro during or before the definition processing and optimization phases. The compiler brackets the expansion in `begin ... end`, using the standard binding of `begin` in the Dylan module, and then reparses it as a *statement*. This reparsing may discover more macro calls. A parse error while reparsing a macro expansion could indicate an invalid macro definition or an incorrect call to the macro that was not detected during pattern matching. Once the cycle of macro expansion and reparsing has been completed, no tokens, bracketed fragments, or macro call fragments remain and the entire source record has become one parsed fragment.

This `begin ... end` bracketing ensures that the expansion of a macro call will not be broken apart by operator precedence rules when the macro call is a subexpression. Similarly, it ensures that the scopes of local declarations introduced by a macro will not extend outside that macro expansion when the macro call is a statement in a body.

The fragment produced by parsing a macro call, which is the input to macro expansion, is as follows:

- Local declarations and special definitions are parsed fragments.

- Calls to macros are macro call fragments.

- List constants and vector constants are parsed fragments.

- Anything in brackets is a bracketed fragment.

- If the macro call was not the result of macro expansion, everything else is represented as sequences of tokens. There are a few restrictions on the tokens, for example semicolons must appear in certain places and bare brackets cannot appear; for details see the definition of *body-fragment* and *list-fragment* in Appendix A, "BNF."

Macros

- In a macro call that is the result of macro expansion, additional items can be parsed fragments, due to pattern-variable substitution.
- Many built-in macros expand into implementation-specific parsed fragments.

The fragment produced by parsing an expression is as follows:

- An expression consisting of a single token returns a one-token fragment. This will be a variable-name, noncollection literal, or SYMBOL.
- An expression consisting of just a string literal returns a one-token fragment. If the string literal consists of multiple STRING tokens, they are concatenated into a single STRING token.
- An expression consisting of just a list constant or a vector constant returns a list constant or vector constant fragment.
- An expression consisting of just a statement or function-macro-call returns a macro call fragment.
- An operator call, slot reference, or element reference that calls a function macro returns a macro call fragment.
- A function call, operator call, slot reference, or element reference that calls something other than a function macro returns a function call fragment.
- Enclosing an expression in parentheses does not change how it parses.

The term "parsed expression fragment" refers to any of the above.

The parser recognizes parsed fragments as well as raw tokens. The nonterminals *definition* and *local-declaration* in the phrase grammar accept parsed fragments of the same kind. The nonterminal *operand* accepts parsed function call fragments and macro call fragments. The nonterminal *literal* accepts list constant and vector constant fragments. The nonterminal *simple-fragment* accepts parsed function call fragments and macro call fragments. The nonterminal *macro* accepts macro call fragments. The parser expands bracketed fragments into their constituent tokens before parsing them.

Extensible Grammar

There are three kinds of macros: definition macros, which extend the available set of definitions; statement macros, which extend the available set of statements; and function macros, which syntactically resemble function calls but are more flexible. Named value references and local declarations cannot be macro calls. Only statements, function calls, and definitions are extensible.

Definition Macros

A definition macro extends the *definition-macro-call* production of the Dylan phrase grammar to recognize additional constructs as valid definitions, by creating a new DEFINE-BODY-WORD that is recognized by the following grammar line:

definition-macro-call:
    define *modifiers*$_{opt}$ DEFINE-BODY-WORD *body-fragment*$_{opt}$ *definition-tail*

or by creating a new DEFINE-LIST-WORD that is recognized by the following grammar line:

definition-macro-call:
    define *modifiers*$_{opt}$ DEFINE-LIST-WORD *list-fragment*$_{opt}$

This allows programmers to extend Dylan by defining new kinds of definitions. The syntax of the definition must be parseable by one of these two predefined grammar rules. The first handles body-style definitions like `define class`, `define method`, and `define module`, while the second handles list-style definitions like `define constant`. See Appendix A, "BNF," for the details.

The new DEFINE-BODY-WORD or DEFINE-LIST-WORD becomes a partially reserved word in each module where the macro definition is visible. In particular a DEFINE-BODY-WORD or DEFINE-LIST-WORD cannot be used as a modifier in a definition. It can still be used as a variable-name.

Statement Macros

A statement macro extends the *statement* production of the Dylan phrase grammar to recognize additional constructs as valid statements by creating a new BEGIN-WORD that is recognized by the following grammar line:

statement:
    BEGIN-WORD *body-fragment*$_{opt}$ *end-clause*

The new BEGIN-WORD becomes a reserved word in each module where the macro definition is visible. It can only be used at the beginning and end of this new statement.

Function Macros

A function macro extends the *function-macro-call* production of the Dylan phrase grammar to recognize additional constructs by creating a new FUNCTION-WORD that is recognized by the following grammar line:

function-macro-call:
    FUNCTION-WORD (*body-fragment*$_{opt}$)

In addition, a function macro can be invoked by any of the shorthand syntax constructs available for invoking functions. In this case, the arguments are always parsed expression fragments, as described on page 146.

The new FUNCTION-WORD becomes a reserved word in each module where the macro definition is visible. It can only be used at the beginning of a macro call.

Macro Names

A macro is named by a constant module binding. The macro is available to be called in any scope where this binding is accessible. Macro names can be exported and can be renamed during module importing just like any other module binding. Macro bindings are constant and cannot be changed by the assignment operator : =.

The name bound to a definition macro is the macro's DEFINE-BODY-WORD or DEFINE-LIST-WORD suffixed by "-definer". This suffixing convention is

analogous to the naming convention for setters and allows the
DEFINE-BODY-WORD or DEFINE-LIST-WORD to be used for another purpose. The
name bound to a statement macro is the macro's BEGIN-WORD. The name bound
to a function macro is the macro's FUNCTION-WORD.

A named value reference is not allowed when the value of the binding is a
macro, because macros are not run-time objects.

A macro cannot be named by a local binding. Macro definitions are always
scoped to modules.

Attempting to create a local binding that shadows a binding to a macro is an
error.

Reserved words created by a macro definition are reserved in any module
where the binding that names the macro is accessible. In other modules, the
same words are ordinary names. Each module has an associated syntax table
used when parsing code associated with that module. The syntax table controls
the lexical analyzer's assignment of names to the DEFINE-BODY-WORD,
DEFINE-LIST-WORD, BEGIN-WORD, and FUNCTION-WORD categories. Importing a
macro into a module makes the same modifications to that module's syntax
table that would be made by defining that macro in the module. If a definition
macro is renamed when it is imported, the DEFINE-BODY-WORD or
DEFINE-LIST-WORD derives from the new name. If the new name does not end in
"-definer", the imported macro cannot be called.

A NAME or UNRESERVED-NAME in the lexical grammar can be a backslash ('\')
character followed by a word. This prevents the word from being recognized as
a reserved word during parsing, but does not change which binding the word
names. Quoting the name of a statement or function macro with a backslash
allows the name to be mentioned without calling the macro, for example to
export it from a module.

When a binding that names a macro is exported from a module that is exported
from a library, clients of that library can call the macro. Information derived
from the macro definition goes into the library export information part of the
library description.

Rewrite Rules

The grammar of a macro definition is **define macro** *macro-definition*. For details see Appendix A, "BNF."

If the optional NAME at the end of a *macro-definition* is present, it must be the same NAME that appears at the beginning of the *macro-definition*.

The kind of macro being defined, and thus the Dylan grammar production that this macro extends, is determined by which kind of rules appear in the macro's *main-rule-set*.

The NAME preceding the *main-rule-set* is the name of the binding whose value is this macro. It must be consistent with each left-hand side of the *main-rule-set*. It can be any name, even a reserved word or backslash followed by an operator. For statement and function macros this NAME must be the same as the NAME that appears as the first token in each *main-rule-set* pattern. For definition macros this NAME must be the same as the NAME in the *xxx-style-definition-rule* with the suffix "-definer" added.

A NAME can belong to more than one of the lexical categories BEGIN-WORD, FUNCTION-WORD, DEFINE-BODY-WORD, and DEFINE-LIST-WORD. A NAME cannot belong to both BEGIN-WORD and FUNCTION-WORD. A NAME cannot belong to both DEFINE-BODY-WORD and DEFINE-LIST-WORD.

For simplicity of documentation, the *xxx-style-definition-rule* productions are written ambiguously. The NAME in the left-hand side of the rule must be the NAME immediately following define macro with the "-definer" suffix removed, not an arbitrary NAME, which would be ambiguous with *modifier*.

The general idea is that the *main-rule-set* is an ordered sequence of rewrite rules. Macro expansion tests the macro call against each left-hand side in turn until one matches. The corresponding right-hand side supplies the new construct to replace the macro call. The left- and right-hand sides can contain pattern variables. The portion of the macro call that matches a particular pattern variable on the left replaces each occurrence of that pattern variable on the right. It is an error for the right-hand side of a rule to contain a pattern variable that does not appear on the left-hand side of the same rule.

If none of the left-hand sides match, the macro call is invalid. If more than one left-hand side matches, the first matching rule is used. Note that (as described in the next section) a pattern variable with a wildcard constraint can match an empty portion of the macro call. A comma or a semicolon followed by a pattern variable with a wildcard constraint also can match an empty portion of the macro call. Do not assume that only an empty pattern can match an empty input. In general when writing recursive rewrite rules it is better to put the base case first, before the inductive cases, in case an inductive case rewrite rule might match a base case input.

The punctuation marks `?`, `??`, and `?=` used in patterns and templates are customarily written without any whitespace following them.

Patterns

Approximately speaking, a pattern looks like the construct that it matches, but contains pattern variables that bind to portions of the construct. Hence, a left-hand side in the *main-rule-set* looks like a macro call. However, the grammar of patterns is not the same as the grammar of programs, but contains just what is required to match the portions of the Dylan grammar that are extensible by macros. Patterns have a simple nested grammar, with semicolons, commas, and brackets used to indicate levels of nesting. See the definition of *pattern* in Appendix A, "BNF."

A pattern matches a fragment (a sequence of elementary fragments) by executing the following algorithm from left to right. It is easy to create patterns that are ambiguous when considered as grammars. This ambiguity is resolved by the left to right processing order and the specified try-shortest-first order for matching wildcards. Pattern matching succeeds only if all sub-patterns match. If pattern matching fails, the current rule fails and control passes to the next rule in the current rule set. If all patterns in a rule set fail to match, the macro call is invalid.

Multiple occurrences of the same pattern variable name in a single rule's left-hand side are not valid.

A *pattern* matches a fragment as follows:

■ If the pattern consists of just one pattern-list, go to the next step. Otherwise, divide the pattern into subpatterns and the fragment into subfragments at semicolons, and match subpatterns to subfragments individually in order. The subpatterns and subfragments do not include the semicolons that separate them. Suppose the pattern consists of N + 1 pattern-lists separated by N semicolons. Locate the first N semicolons in the fragment (without looking inside of elementary fragments) and divide up the fragment into subfragments accordingly. The match fails if the fragment contains fewer than N - 1 semicolons. As a special case, if the fragment contains N - 1 semicolons, the match still succeeds and the last subfragment is empty. If the fragment contains more than N semicolons, the extra semicolons will be in the last subfragment.

A *pattern-list* matches a fragment as follows:

- If the pattern-list consists of just a pattern-sequence, go to the next step. If the pattern-list consists of just a property-list-pattern, go to that step. Otherwise divide the pattern-list into subpatterns and the fragment into subfragments at commas, and match subpatterns to subfragments individually in order. The subpatterns and subfragments do not include the commas that separate them. Suppose the pattern consists of N + 1 subpatterns separated by N commas. Locate the first N commas in the fragment (without looking inside of elementary fragments) and divide up the fragment into subfragments accordingly. The match fails if the fragment contains fewer than N - 1 commas. As a special case, if the fragment contains N - 1 commas, the match still succeeds and the last subfragment is empty. If the fragment contains more than N commas, the extra commas will be in the last subfragment. Note that the subdivision algorithms for commas and semicolons are identical.

A *pattern-sequence* matches a fragment as follows:

- Consider each simple-pattern in the pattern-sequence in turn from left to right. Each simple-pattern matches an initial subsequence of the fragment and consumes that subsequence, or fails. The entire pattern match fails if any simple-pattern fails, if the fragment is empty and the simple-pattern requires one or more elementary fragments, or if the fragment is not entirely consumed after all simple-patterns have been matched. There is a special backup and retry rule for wildcards, described below.

A *simple-pattern* matches a fragment as follows:

- A NAME or => consumes one elementary fragment, which must be identical to the *simple-pattern*. A NAME matches a name that is spelled the same, independent of modules, lexical scoping issues, alphabetic case, and backslash quoting. As a special case, after the word `otherwise`, an => is optional in both the pattern and the fragment. Presence or absence of the arrow in either place makes no difference to matching.

- A *bracketed-pattern* matches and consumes a *bracketed-fragment*. If the enclosed *pattern* is omitted, the enclosed *body-fragment* must be empty, otherwise the enclosed *pattern* must match the enclosed *body-fragment* (which can be empty). The type of brackets ((), [], or {}) in the *bracketed-fragment* must be the same as the type of brackets in the *bracketed-pattern*.

A *binding-pattern* matches a fragment as follows:

- *pattern-variable* :: *pattern-variable* consumes as much of the fragment as can be parsed by the grammar for *variable*. It matches the first pattern-variable to the *variable-name* and the second to the *type*, a parsed expression fragment. If no specializer is present, it matches the second pattern-variable to a parsed expression fragment that is a named value reference to <object> in the Dylan module. This matching checks the constraints on the pattern variable, fails if the constraint is not satisfied, and binds the pattern variable to the fragment.

- *pattern-variable* = *pattern-variable* consumes as much of the fragment as can be parsed by the grammar for *variable* = *expression*. It matches the first pattern-variable to the *variable*, a fragment, and the second to the *expression*, a parsed expression fragment.

- *pattern-variable* :: *pattern-variable* = *pattern-variable* consumes as much of the fragment as can be parsed by the grammar for *variable* = *expression*. It matches the first two pattern-variables the same as the first kind of *binding-pattern* and it matches the third pattern-variable the same as the second kind of *binding-pattern.*

A *pattern-variable* matches a fragment as follows:

- When the constraint is a wildcard constraint (see "Pattern Variable Constraints" on page 157), the pattern variable consumes some initial subsequence of the fragment, using a backup and retry algorithm. First, the wildcard consumes no elementary fragments, and matching continues with the next *simple-pattern* in the *pattern-sequence*. If any *simple-pattern* in the current *pattern-sequence* fails to match, back up to the wildcard, consume one more elementary fragment than before, and retry matching the rest of the *pattern-sequence*, starting one elementary fragment to the right of the previous start point. Once the entire *pattern-sequence* has successfully matched, the pattern variable binds to a fragment consisting of the sequence of elementary fragments that it consumed.

- It is an error for more than one of the *simple-patterns* directly contained in a *pattern-sequence* to be a wildcard.

- When the constraint is other than a wildcard constraint, the pattern variable consumes as much of the fragment as can be parsed by the grammar specified for the constraint in "Pattern Variable Constraints" on page 157. If the parsing fails, the pattern match fails. The pattern variable binds to the fragment specified in "Pattern Variable Constraints." This can be a parsed fragment rather than the original sequence of elementary fragments.

- The ellipsis *pattern-variable*, . . . , can only be used in an auxiliary rule set. It represents a pattern variable with the same name as the current rule set and a wildcard constraint.

A *property-list-pattern* matches a fragment as follows:

- Parse the fragment using the grammar for *property-list*$_{opt}$. If the parsing fails or does not consume the entire fragment, the pattern match fails.

- If the *property-list-pattern* contains #key and does not contain #all-keys, the match fails if the SYMBOL part of any property is not the NAME in some *pattern-keyword* in the *property-list-pattern*. Comparison of a SYMBOL to a NAME is case-insensitive, ignores backslash quoting, and is unaffected by the lexical context of the NAME.

- If the *property-list-pattern* contains #rest, bind the pattern variable immediately following #rest to the entire fragment. If the pattern variable has a non-wildcard constraint, parse the *value* part of each property according to this constraint, fail if the parsing fails or does not consume the entire *value* part, and substitute the fragment specified in "Pattern Variable Constraints" on page 157 for the *value* part.

- Each *pattern-keyword* in the *property-list-pattern* binds a pattern variable as follows:
  - A single question mark finds the first property whose SYMBOL is the NAME of the *pattern-keyword*. Comparison of a SYMBOL to a NAME is case-insensitive, ignores backslash quoting, and is unaffected by the lexical context of the NAME. If the *pattern-keyword* has a non-wildcard constraint, parse the property's *value* according to this constraint, fail if the parsing fails or does not consume the entire *value* , and bind the pattern variable to the fragment specified in "Pattern Variable

Constraints" on page 157. If the *pattern-keyword* has a wildcard constraint, bind the pattern variable to the property's *value*.

☐ A double question mark finds every property with a matching SYMBOL, processes each property's *value* as for a single question mark, and binds the pattern variable to a sequence of the values, preserving the order of properties in the input fragment. This sequence can only be used with double question mark in a template. Constraint-directed parsing applies to each property *value* individually.

■ If a single question mark *pattern-keyword* does not find any matching property, then if a *default* is present, the pattern variable binds to the default expression, otherwise the property is required so the pattern match fails.

■ If a double question mark *pattern-keyword* does not find any matching property, then if a *default* is present, the pattern variable binds to a sequence of one element, the default expression, otherwise the pattern variable binds to an empty sequence.

■ Note: the default expression in a *pattern-keyword* is not evaluated during macro expansion; it is a parsed expression fragment that is used instead of a fragment from the macro call. The default is not subject to a pattern variable constraint.

Special Rules for Definitions

A list-style definition parses as the core reserved word `define`, an optional sequence of modifiers, a DEFINE-LIST-WORD, and a possibly-empty *list-fragment*. The left-hand side of a *list-style-definition-rule* matches this by treating the *definition-head* as a *pattern-sequence* and matching it to the sequence of modifiers, and then matching the *pattern* to the *list-fragment*. If no *definition-head* is present, the sequence of modifiers must be empty. If no *pattern* is present, the *list-fragment* must be empty. The word `define` and the DEFINE-LIST-WORD do not participate in the pattern match because they were already used to identify the macro being called and because the spelling of the DEFINE-LIST-WORD might have been changed by renaming the macro during module importing.

A body-style definition parses as the core reserved word `define`, an optional sequence of modifiers, a DEFINE-BODY-WORD, a possibly-empty *body-fragment*, the core reserved word `end`, and optional repetitions of the DEFINE-BODY-WORD and the NAME (if any) that is the first token of the *body-fragment*. The left-hand side of a *body-style-definition-rule* matches this by treating the *definition-head* as a *pattern-sequence* and matching it to the sequence of modifiers, and then matching the *pattern* to the *body-fragment*. If no *definition-head* is present, the sequence of modifiers must be empty. If no *pattern* is present, the *body-fragment* must be empty. If the *body-fragment* ends in a semicolon, this semicolon is removed before matching. The optional semicolon in the rule is just decoration and does not participate in the pattern match. The word define and the DEFINE-BODY-WORD do not participate in the pattern match because they were already used to identify the macro being called and because the spelling of the DEFINE-BODY-WORD might have been changed by renaming the macro during module importing. The word end and the two optional items following it in the macro call are checked during parsing, and so do not participate in the pattern match.

It is an error for a *definition-head* to contain more than one wildcard.

Special Rules for Statements

A statement parses as a BEGIN-WORD, a possibly-empty *body-fragment*, the core reserved word end, and an optional repetition of the BEGIN-WORD. The left-hand side of a *statement-rule* matches this by matching the *pattern* to the *body-fragment*. If the rule does not contain a *pattern*, the *body-fragment* must be empty. If the *body-fragment* ends in a semicolon, this semicolon is removed before matching. The optional semicolon in the rule is just decoration and does not participate in the pattern match. The BEGIN-WORD does not participate in the pattern match because it was already used to identify the macro being called and because its spelling might have been changed by renaming the macro during module importing. The word end and the optional item following it in the macro call are checked during parsing, and so do not participate in the pattern match.

Special Rules for Function Macros

A call to a function macro parses as a FUNCTION-WORD followed by a parenthesized, possibly-empty *body-fragment*. The left-hand side of a *function-rule* matches this by matching the *pattern* to the *body-fragment*. If the rule does not contain a *pattern*, the *body-fragment* must be empty. The FUNCTION-WORD does not participate in the pattern match because it was already used to identify the macro being called and because its spelling might have been changed by renaming the macro during module importing. The parentheses in the rule are just decoration and do not participate in the pattern match.

A function macro can also be invoked by any of the shorthand syntax constructs available for invoking functions. In this case, the arguments are always parsed expression fragments, as described on page 146. However, the left-hand side of a function-rule has to use function-macro-call syntax even if the macro is intended to be called by operator, slot reference, or element reference syntax.

Pattern Variable Constraints

Each *pattern-variable* in the left-hand side of a rule in a macro definition has a constraint associated with it. This prevents the pattern from matching unless the fragment matched to the pattern-variable satisfies the constraint. In most cases it also controls how the matching fragment is parsed.

You specify a constraint in a *pattern-variable* by suffixing a colon and the constraint name to the pattern variable name. Intervening whitespace is not allowed. As an abbreviation, if a pattern variable has the same name as its constraint, the *pattern-variable* can be written ?:*the-name* instead of ?*the-name*:*the-name*.

The available constraints are listed in Table 10-1.

Table 10-1   Available constraints

Constraint name	Grammar accepted	Binds pattern variable to
expression	*expression*	parsed expression fragment(1)
variable	*variable*	fragment(2)
name	NAME	one-token fragment
token	TOKEN	one-token fragment
body	*body*$_{opt}$ (3)	parsed expression fragment (4)

continued

Table 10-1   Available constraints (continued)

Constraint name	Grammar accepted	Binds pattern variable to
case-body	*case-body*$_{opt}$ (3)	fragment(2)
macro	*macro*	fragment(5)
*	(wildcard)	fragment

Notes:

1. Parsed expression fragments are described on page 146.

2. Where *expression, operand, constituents* or *body* appears in the grammar that this constraint accepts, the bound fragment contains a parsed expression fragment, not the original elementary fragments.

3. Parsing stops at an intermediate word.

4. The body is wrapped in begin … end to make it an expression, using the standard binding of begin in the Dylan module. An empty body defaults to #f.

5. A pattern-variable with a macro constraint accepts exactly one elementary fragment, which must be a macro call fragment. It binds the pattern variable to the expansion of the macro.

Some implementations and a future version of the Dylan language specification might add more constraint choices to this table.

When a pattern variable has the same name as an auxiliary rule-set, its constraint defaults to wildcard and can be omitted. Otherwise a constraint must be specified in every *pattern-variable* and *pattern-keyword*.

A constraint applies only to the specific pattern variable occurrence to which it is attached. It does not constrain other pattern variable occurrences with the same name.

Intermediate Words

When a *pattern-variable* has a constraint of body or case-body, its parsing of the fragment stops before any token that is an intermediate word. This allows intermediate words to delimit clauses that have separate bodies, like else and `elseif` in an `if` statement. The intermediate words of a macro are identified as follows:

- Define a body-variable to be a pattern variable that either has a constraint of `body` or `case-body`, or names an auxiliary rule-set where some left-hand side in that rule-set ends in a body-variable. This is a least fixed point, so a recursive auxiliary rule-set does not automatically make its name into a body-variable. Note that an ellipsis that stands for a pattern variable is a body-variable when that pattern variable is one.

- Define an intermediate-variable to be a pattern variable that either immediately follows a body-variable in a left-hand side, or appears at the beginning of a left-hand side in an auxiliary rule-set named by an intermediate-variable.

- An intermediate word is a NAME that either immediately follows a body-variable in a left-hand side, or occurs at the beginning of a left-hand side in an auxiliary rule-set named by an intermediate-variable. Intermediate words are not reserved, they are just used as delimiters during the parsing for a *pattern-variable* with a `body` or `case-body` constraint.

Templates

Approximately speaking, a template has the same structure as what it constructs, but contains pattern variables that will be replaced by fragments extracted from the macro call. Thus a template in the *main-rule-set* looks like the macro expansion.

However, templates do not have a full grammar. A template is essentially any sequence of tokens and *substitutions* in which all of Dylan's brackets are balanced: `()`, `[]`, `{}`, `#()`, and `#[]`. Substitution for pattern variables produces a sequence of tokens and other elementary fragments.

Note that using unparsed token sequences as templates allows a macro expansion to contain macro calls without creating any inter-dependencies between macros. Since the template is not parsed at macro definition time, any macros called in the template do not have to be defined first, and macros can be compiled independently of each other. This simplifies the implementation at the minor cost of deferring some error checking from when a macro is defined until the time when the macro is called.

The grammar for templates is the definition of *template* in "Templates" on page 429.

All *template-elements* other than *substitution* are copied directly into the macro expansion. The various kinds of *substitution* insert something else into the macro expansion, as follows:

? NAME The fragment bound to the pattern variable named NAME.

name-prefix$_{opt}$? *name-string-or-symbol name-suffix*$_{opt}$

> The fragment bound to the pattern variable named *name-string-or-symbol*, converted to a STRING or SYMBOL and/or concatenated with a prefix and/or suffix. Note that this rule applies only when the first rule does not. The fragment must be a NAME. Concatenate the prefix, if any, the characters of the fragment, and the suffix, if any. The alphabetic case of the characters of the fragment is unspecified. Convert this to the same grammatical type (NAME, STRING, or SYMBOL) as *name-string-or-symbol*. When the result is a NAME, its hygiene context is the same as that of the fragment.

?? NAME *separator*$_{opt}$ . . .

> The sequence of fragments bound to the pattern variable named NAME, with *separator* inserted between each pair of fragments. The pattern variable must have been bound by a ?? *pattern-keyword*. *Separator* can be a binary operator, comma, or semicolon. If the size of the sequence is 1 or *separator* is omitted, no separator is inserted. If the sequence is empty, nothing is inserted.

. . . The fragment bound to the pattern variable that names this rule set; this is only valid in an auxiliary rule set.

?= NAME A reference to NAME, in the lexical context where the macro was called.

It is an error for a single question-mark *substitution* to use a pattern variable that was bound by a double question-mark *pattern-keyword*.

It is an error for a double question-mark *substitution* to use a pattern variable that was bound by a single question-mark *pattern-variable* or *pattern-keyword*.

It is an error for a *substitution* to use a pattern variable that does not appear on the left-hand side of the same rule.

When a template contains a *separator* immediately followed by a *substitution*, and the fragment inserted into the macro expansion by the *substitution* is empty, the separator is removed from the macro expansion.

Auxiliary Rule Sets

Auxiliary rule sets are like subroutines for rewrite rules. An auxiliary rule set rewrites the value of a pattern variable after it is bound by a pattern and before it is substituted into a template. Auxiliary rule sets only come into play after a pattern has matched; the failure of all patterns in an auxiliary rule set to match causes the entire macro call to be declared invalid, rather than back-tracking and trying the next pattern in the calling rule set.

See the definition of *aux-rule-sets* in "Auxiliary Rule Sets" on page 430.

A SYMBOL flags the beginning of an auxiliary rule set. For readability it is generally written as name: rather than #"name". The name of the symbol is the same as the name of the pattern variable that is rewritten by this auxiliary rule set. All occurrences of this pattern variable in all rule sets are rewritten. A pattern variable can occur in the very auxiliary rule set that rewrites that pattern variable; this is how you write recursive rewrite rules, which greatly expand the power of pattern-matching.

When an auxiliary rule set's pattern variable occurs in a double question-mark *pattern-keyword*, the auxiliary rule set rewrites each property value in the sequence individually.

The order of auxiliary rule sets in a macro definition is immaterial.

The ellipsis . . . in patterns and templates of an auxiliary rule set means exactly the same thing as the pattern variable that is rewritten by this auxiliary rule set. Using ellipsis instead of the pattern variable can make recursive rewrite rules more readable.

Hygiene

Dylan macros are always **hygienic**. The basic idea is that each named value reference in a macro expansion means the same thing as it meant at the place in the original source code from which it was copied into the macro expansion. This is true whether that place was in the macro definition or in the macro call. Because a macro expansion can include macro calls that need further expansion, named value references in one final expansion can come from several different macro definitions and can come from several different macro calls, either to different macros or—in the case of recursion—distinct calls to the same macro.

(Sometimes the property that variable references copied from a macro call mean the same thing in the expansion is called "hygiene" and the property that variable references copied from a macro definition mean the same thing in the expansion is called "referential transparency." We include both properties in the term "hygiene.")

Specifically, a macro can bind temporary variables in its expansion without the risk of accidentally capturing references in the macro call to another binding with the same name. Furthermore, a macro can reference module bindings in its expansion without the risk of those references accidentally being captured by bindings of other variables with the same name that surround the macro call. A macro can reference module bindings in its expansion without worrying that the intended bindings might have different names in a module where the macro is called.

One way to implement this is for each *template-element* that is a NAME, UNARY-OPERATOR, or BINARY-OPERATOR to be replaced in the macro expansion by a special token that plays the same grammatical role as the NAME, UNARY-OPERATOR, or BINARY-OPERATOR but remembers three pieces of information:

- The original NAME. For an operator, this is the name listed in Table 4-1 on page 37.

- The lexical context where the macro was defined, which is just a module since macro definitions are only allowed at top level, not inside of bindings.

- The specific macro call occurrence. This could be an integer that is incremented each time a macro expansion occurs.

In general one cannot know until all macros are expanded whether a NAME is a bound variable reference, a module binding reference, a variable that is being bound, or something that is not a binding name at all, such as a definition *modifier* or an intermediate word. Similarly, one cannot know until all macros are expanded whether a UNARY-OPERATOR or BINARY-OPERATOR refers to a local binding or a module binding. Thus the information for each of those cases is retained in the special token. A named value reference and a binding connect if and only if the original NAMES and the specific macro call occurrences are both the same. (In that case, the lexical contexts will also be the same, but this need not be checked.) A named value reference and a binding never connect if one originated in a template and the other originated in a macro call.

References in a macro expansion to `element` or `aref` created by using element reference syntax must receive similar treatment so the NAME `element` or `aref` gets looked up in the environment of the macro definition, not the environment of the macro call.

For purposes of hygiene, a *pattern-keyword default* is treated like part of a template, even though it is actually part of a pattern.

The mapping from getters to setters done by the `:=` operator is hygienic. In all cases the setter name is looked up in the same lexical context and macro call occurrence as the getter name.

Intentional Hygiene Violation

Sometimes it is necessary for a macro to violate the hygienic property, for example to include in a macro expansion a named value reference to be executed in the lexical context where the macro was called, not the lexical context where the macro was defined. Another example is creating a local binding in a macro expansion that will be visible to the body of the macro. This feature should be used sparingly, as it can be confusing to users of the macro, but sometimes it is indispensable.

The construct `?=` NAME in a template inserts into the expansion a reference to NAME, in the lexical context where the macro was called. It is as if NAME came from the macro call rather than from the template.

Hygiene Versus Module Encapsulation

A named value reference in a macro expansion that was produced by a *template-element* that is a NAME, UNARY-OPERATOR, BINARY-OPERATOR, or [*template$_{opt}$*] and that does not refer to a local binding created by the macro expansion must have the same meaning as would a named value reference with the same name adjacent to the macro definition. This is true even if the macro call is in a different module or a different library from the one in which the macro definition occurs, even if the binding is not exported.

This allows exported macros to make use of private bindings without requiring these bindings to be exported for general use. The module that calls the macro does not need to import the private bindings used by the expansion.

If one of the following template-element sequences appears in the right-hand side of a rewrite rule, it may introduce named value references to the indicated name in an expansion of the macro. If such a named value reference does not refer to a local binding created by the macro expansion then it must have the same meaning as would a named value reference with the same name adjacent to the macro definition.

- *variable-name*

  Reference to *variable-name*

- *getter-name* (*template*$_{opt}$) *assignment-operator*
  assignment-operator-name (*template*$_{opt}$ *getter-name* (*template*$_{opt}$))

  Reference to *getter-name* `##` `"-setter"`

- [*template*$_{opt}$] *assignment-operator*
  assignment-operator-name (*template*$_{opt}$ [*template*$_{opt}$])

  Reference to either `element-setter` and `aref-setter`

- . *getter-name assignment-operator*
  assignment-operator-name (*template*$_{opt}$. *getter-name*)

  Reference to *getter-name* `##` `"-setter"`

- `define` *definition-head*$_{opt}$ *definer-name*

  Reference to *definer-name* `##` `"-definer"`

Items in the preceding template-element sequences have the following meanings:

  ☐ *assignment-operator-name* is a NAME, and the value of the binding with that name (in the module containing the macro definition in which the template occurs) is the assignment macro that is the value of the binding named \ := exported by the Dylan module of the Dylan library.

□ *assignment-operator* is a binary-operator whose associated binding is an *assignment-operator-name*.)

□ *definer-name* is a DEFINE-BODY-WORD or DEFINE-LIST-WORD.

□ *variable-name* and *getter-name* are NAMEs.

□ *template* is defined in Appendix A, "BNF," on page 429.

□ *definition-head* is defined in Appendix A, "BNF," on page 427.

□ The notation *foo* `##` `"string"` indicates a new token composed of the text of *foo* concatenated with the string.

Note that these template-element sequences can overlap in a template. For example { `foo` (`bar`) `:=` } is a potential reference to `foo`, to `foo-setter`, and to `bar`.

Implementations must use some automatic mechanism for noting the bindings associated with the named value references in macro expansions produced by the template-element sequences described above, and must make such bindings available to any library where the macro is accessible. In general, the set of bindings that must be made available to other libraries cannot be computed precisely because the right-hand sides of rewrite rules are not fully parsed until after a macro is called and expanded, making it impossible to determine whether an occurrence of one of the described sequences of template elements will actually produce a named variable reference in the expansion. However, an upper bound on this set of bindings can be computed by assuming that all occurrences of the described template-element sequences might introduce the indicated named value reference if there is a binding for that name accessible from the module in which the macro definition appears.

Rewrite Rule Examples

The following definitions of all of the built-in macros are provided as examples. This section is not intended to be a tutorial on how to write macros, just a collection of demonstrations of some of the tricks.

The built-in macros cannot really be implemented this way; for example `if` and `case` cannot really both be implemented by expanding to the other. Certain built-in macros cannot be implemented with rewrite rules or necessarily rewrite into implementation-dependent code; in these cases the right-hand sides are shown as *id*.

Statement Macros

Begin

```
define macro begin
  { begin ?:body end } => { ?body }
end;
```

Block

```
define macro block
  { block () ?ebody end }
   => { ?ebody }
  { block (?:name) ?ebody end }
   => { with-exit(method(?name) ?ebody end) }

 // Left-recursive so leftmost clause is innermost
 ebody:
  { ... exception (?type:expression, ?eoptions) ?:body }
   => { with-handler(method() ... end,
                     method(ignore) ?body end,
                  ?type, ?eoptions) }
  { ... exception (?:name :: ?type:expression, ?eoptions) ?:body }
   => { with-handler(method() ... end,
                     method(?name) ?body end,
                  ?type, ?eoptions) }
  { ?abody cleanup ?cleanup:body}
   => { with-cleanup(method() ?abody end, method () ?cleanup end) }
  { ?abody }
   => { ?abody }

 abody:
  { ?main:body }
   => { ?main }
  { ?main:body afterwards ?after:body }
   => { with-afterwards(method() ?main end, method () ?after end) }
```

Macros

```
eoptions:
  { #rest ?options:expression,
    #key ?test:expression = always(#t),
    ?init-arguments:expression = #() }
   => { ?options }
end;
```

Case

```
define macro case
  { case ?:case-body end }              => { ?case-body }
 case-body:
  { }                                   => { #f }
  { otherwise ?:body }                  => { ?body }
  { ?test:expression => ?:body; ... } => { if (?test) ?body
                                            else ... end if }
end;
```

For

```
// This macro has three auxiliary macros, whose definitions follow
define macro for
  { for (?header) ?fbody end }         => { for-aux ?fbody, ?header end }

// pass main body and finally body as two expressions
fbody:
  { ?main:body }                        => { ?main, #f }
  { ?main:body finally ?val:body }    => { ?main, ?val }

// convert iteration clauses to property list via for-clause macro
header:
  { ?v:variable in ?c:expression, ... }
   => { for-clause(?v in ?c) ... }
  { ?v:variable = ?e1:expression then ?e2:expression, ... }
   => { for-clause(?v = ?e1 then ?e2) ... }
  { ?v:variable from ?e1:expression ?to, ... }
```

Macros

```
  => { for-clause(?v from ?e1 ?to) ... }
  { }                                  => { }
  { #key ?while:expression }           => { for-clause(~?while stop) }
  { #key ?until:expression }           => { for-clause(?until stop) }

// parse the various forms of numeric iteration clause
to:
  { to ?limit:expression by ?step:expression }
                                       => { hard ?limit ?step }
  { to ?limit:expression }             => { easy ?limit 1   > }
  { above ?limit:expression ?by }      => { easy ?limit ?by <= }
  { below ?limit:expression ?by }      => { easy ?limit ?by >= }
  { ?by }                              => { loop ?by }

by:
  { }                                  => { 1 }
  { by ?step:expression }              => { ?step }
end;

// Auxiliary macro to make the property list for an iteration clause.
// Each iteration clause is a separate call to this macro so the
// hygiene rules will keep the temporary variables for each clause
// distinct.
// The properties are:
//   init0: - constituents for start of body, outside the loop
//   var1:  - a variable to bind on each iteration
//   init1: - initial value for that variable
//   next1: - value for that variable on iterations after the first
//   stop1: - test expression, stop if true, after binding var1's
//   var2:  - a variable to bind on each iteration, after stop1 tests
//   next2: - value for that variable on every iteration
//   stop2: - test expression, stop if true, after binding var2's
define macro for-clause

  // while:/until: clause
  { for-clause(?e:expression stop) }
    => { , stop2: ?e }
```

Macros

```
// Explicit step clause
{ for-clause(?v:variable = ?e1:expression then ?e2:expression) }
 => { , var1: ?v, init1: ?e1, next1: ?e2 }


// Collection clause
{ for-clause(?v:variable in ?c:expression) }
 => { , init0: [ let collection = ?c;
                 let (initial-state, limit,
                      next-state, finished-state?,
                      current-key, current-element)
                     = forward-iteration-protocol(collection); ]
      , var1: state, init1: initial-state
      , next1: next-state(collection, state)
      , stop1: finished-state?(collection, state, limit)
      , var2: ?v, next2: current-element(collection, state) }


// Numeric clause (three cases depending on ?to right-hand side)
{ for-clause(?v:name :: ?t:expression from ?e1:expression
             loop ?by:expression) }
 => { , init0: [ let init = ?e1;
                 let by = ?by; ]
      , var1: ?v :: ?t, init1: init, next1: ?v + by }


{ for-clause(?v:name :: ?t:expression from ?e1:expression
             easy ?limit:expression ?by:expression ?test:token) }
 => { , init0: [ let init = ?e1;
                 let limit = ?limit;
                 let by = ?by; ]
      , var1: ?v :: ?t, init1: init, next1: ?v + by
      , stop1: ?v ?test limit }


{ for-clause(?v:name :: ?t:expression from ?e1:expression
             hard ?limit:expression ?by:expression) }
 => { , init0: [ let init = ?e1;
                 let limit = ?limit;
                 let by = ?by; ]
```

Rewrite Rule Examples   **169**

```
          , var1: ?v :: ?t, init1: init, next1: ?v + by
          , stop1: if (by >= 0) ?v > limit else ?v < limit end if }
end;
```

```
// Auxiliary macro to expand multiple for-clause macros and
// concatenate their expansions into a single property list.
define macro for-aux
  { for-aux ?main:expression, ?value:expression, ?clauses:* end }
    => { for-aux2 ?main, ?value ?clauses end }

 clauses:
  { } => { }
  { ?clause:macro ... } => { ?clause ... }
end;
```

```
// Auxiliary macro to assemble collected stuff into a loop.
// Tricky points:
// loop iterates by tail-calling itself.
// return puts the finally clause into the correct lexical scope.
// ??init0 needs an auxiliary rule set to strip off the shielding
// brackets that make it possible to stash local declarations in
// a property list.
// ??var2 and ??next2 need a default because let doesn't allow
// an empty variable list.
// ??stop1 and ??stop2 need a default because if () is invalid.
define macro for-aux2
  { for-aux2 ?main:expression, ?value:expression,
             #key ??init0:*, ??var1:variable,
                  ??init1:expression, ??next1:expression,
                  ??stop1:expression = #f,
                  ??var2:variable = x, ??next2:expression = 0,
                  ??stop2:expression = #f
    end }
  => { ??init0 ...
       local method loop(??var1, ...)
               let return = method() ?value end method;
               if (??stop1 | ...) return()
               else let (??var2, ...) = values(??next2, ...);
```

Macros

```
                    if(??stop2 | ...) return()
                    else ?main; loop(??next1, ...)
                    end if;
                end if;
            end method;
        loop(??init1, ...) }

 // strip off brackets used only for grouping
 init0:
   { [ ?stuff:* ] } => { ?stuff }
 end;
```

If

```
define macro if
  { if (?test:expression) ?:body ?elses end }
                                    => { case ?test => ?body;
                                            otherwise ?elses end }
 elses:
  { }                               => { #f }
  { else ?:body }                   => { ?body }
  { elseif (?test:expression) ?:body ... }
                                    => { case ?test => ?body;
                                            otherwise ... end }
 end;
```

Method

```
define macro method
  { method (?parameters:*) => (?results:*) ; ?:body end }      => id
  { method (?parameters:*) => (?results:*) ?:body end }        => id
  { method (?parameters:*) => ?result:variable ; ?:body end } => id
  { method (?parameters:*) ; ?:body end }                     => id
  { method (?parameters:*) ?:body end }                       => id
 end;
```

Select

```
define macro select
   { select (?what) ?:case-body end } => { ?what; ?case-body }

what:
   { ?object:expression by ?compare:expression }
                                    => { let object = ?object;
                                         let compare = ?compare }
   { ?object:expression }           => { let object = ?object;
                                         let compare = \== }

case-body:
   { }
    => { error("select error, %= doesn't match any key", object) }
   { otherwise ?:body }              => { ?body }
   { ?keys => ?:body; ... }          => { if (?keys) ?body
                                          else ... end if }

keys:
   { ?key:expression }               => { compare(object, ?key) }
   { (?keys2) }                      => { ?keys2 }
   { ?keys2 }                        => { ?keys2 }

keys2:
   { ?key:expression }               => { compare(object, ?key) }
   { ?key:expression, ... }          => { compare(object, ?key) | ... }
end;
```

Unless

```
define macro unless
   { unless (?test:expression) ?:body end }
    => { if (~ ?test) ?body end }
end;
```

Macros

Until

```
define macro until
  { until (?test:expression) ?:body end }
   => { local method loop ()
                if (~ ?test)
                   ?body;
                   loop()
                end if;
             end method;
        loop() }
end;
```

While

```
define macro while
  { while (?test:expression) ?:body end }
   => { local method loop ()
                if (?test)
                   ?body;
                   loop()
                end if;
             end method;
        loop() }
end;
```

Definition Macros

Define Class

```
define macro class-definer
  { define ?mods:* class ?:name (?supers) ?slots end }  =>  id
```

```
supers:
  { }                                                      =>  id
  { ?super:expression, ... }                               =>  id

slots:
  { }                                                      =>  id
  { inherited slot ?:name, #rest ?options:*; ... }         =>  id
  { inherited slot ?:name = ?init:expression,
    #rest ?options:*; ... }                                =>  id
  { ?mods:* slot ?:name, #rest ?options:*; ... }           =>  id
  { ?mods:* slot ?:name = ?init:expression,
    #rest ?options:*; ... }                                =>  id
  { ?mods:* slot ?:name :: ?type:expression,
    #rest ?options:*; ... }                                =>  id
  { ?mods:* slot ?:name :: ?type:expression = ?init:expression,
    #rest ?options:*; ... }                                =>  id
  { required keyword ?key:expression,
    #rest ?options:*; ... }                                =>  id
  { required keyword ?key:expression ?equals:token ?init:expression,
    #rest ?options:*; ... }                                =>  id
  { keyword ?key:expression, #rest ?options:*; ... }       =>  id
  { keyword ?key:expression ?equals:token ?init:expression,
    #rest ?options:*; ... }                                =>  id
end;
```

Define Constant

```
define macro constant-definer
  { define ?modifiers:* constant
    ?:name :: ?type:expression = ?init:expression }        =>  id
  { define ?modifiers:* constant
    (?variables:*) ?equals:token ?init:expression }        =>  id
end;
```

Macros

Define Domain

```
define macro domain-definer
  { define sealed domain ?:name ( ?types ) }              =>  id

 types:
  { } => { }
  { ?type:expression, ... } => { ?type, ... }
end;
```

Define Generic

```
define macro generic-definer
  { define ?mods:* generic ?:name ?rest:* }               =>  id

 rest:
  { ( ?parameters:* ), #key }                             =>  id
  { ( ?parameters:* ) => ?:variable, #key }               =>  id
  { ( ?parameters:* ) => (?variables:*), #key }           =>  id
end;
```

Define Library

```
define macro library-definer
  { define library ?:name ?items end }                    =>  id

 items:
  { }                                                     =>  id
  { use ?:name, #rest ?options:*; ... }                   =>  id
  { export ?names; ... }                                  =>  id

 names:
  { ?:name }                                              =>  id
  { ?:name, ... }                                         =>  id
end;
```

Define Method

```
define macro method-definer
  { define ?mods:* method ?:name ?rest end }          =>  id
 rest:
  { (?parameters:*) => (?results:*) ; ?:body }         =>  id
  { (?parameters:*) => (?results:*) ?:body }           =>  id
  { (?parameters:*) => ?result:variable ; ?:body }     =>  id
  { (?parameters:*) ; ?:body }                         =>  id
  { (?parameters:*) ?:body }                           =>  id
end;
```

Define Module

```
define macro module-definer
  { define module ?:name ?items end }                 =>  id

 items:
  { }                                                 =>  id
  { use ?:name, #rest ?options:*; ... }               =>  id
  { export ?names; ... }                              =>  id
  { create ?names; ... }                              =>  id

 names:
  { ?:name }                                          =>  id
  { ?:name, ... }                                     =>  id
end;
```

Define Variable

```
define macro variable-definer
  { define ?modifiers:* variable
    ?:name :: ?type:expression = ?init:expression }   =>  id
  { define ?modifiers:* variable
    (?variables:*) ?equals:token ?init:expression }   =>  id
end;
```

Operator Function Macros

&

```
define macro \&
  { \&(?first:expression, ?second:expression) }
   => { if (?first) ?second else #f end }
end;
```

|

```
define macro \|
  { \|(?first:expression, ?second:expression) }
   => { let temp = ?first;
        if (temp) temp else ?second end }
end;
```

:=

```
define macro \:=
  { \:=(?place:macro, ?value:expression) }                =>   id
  { \:=(?place:expression, ?value:expression) }          =>   id
end;
```

Additional Examples

The following macros are not built-in, but are simply supplied as examples.
Each is shown as a definition followed by a sample call.

Macros

Test and Test-setter

```
define macro test
  { test(?object:expression) }
   => { frame-slot-getter(?object, #"test") }
end macro;

define macro test-setter
  { test-setter(?value:expression, ?object:expression) }
   => { frame-slot-setter(?value, ?object, #"test") }
end macro;

test(foo.bar) := foo.baz;
```

Transform!

```
define macro transform!
 // base case
 { transform!(?xform:expression) } => { ?xform }
 // the main recursive rule
 { transform!(?xform:expression, ?x:expression, ?y:expression,
             ?more:*) }
  => { let xform = ?xform;
      let (nx, ny) = transform(xform, ?x, ?y);
      ?x := nx; ?y := ny;
      transform!(xform, ?more) }
end macro;

transform!(w.transformation, xvar, yvar, w.pos.x, w.pos.y);
```

Formatting-table

```
define macro formatting-table
  { formatting-table (?:expression,
                      #rest ?options:expression,
                      #key ?x-spacing:expression = 0,
```

Macros

```
                              ?y-spacing:expression = 0)
      ?:body end }
  => { do-formatting-table(?expression, method() ?body end,
                           ?options) }
end macro;

formatting-table (stream, x-spacing: 10, y-spacing: 12)
  foobar(stream)
end;
```

With-input-context

```
define macro with-input-context
  { with-input-context (?context-type:expression,
                        #key ?override:expression = #f)
    ?bbody end }
  => { do-with-input-context(?context-type, ?bbody,
                             override: ?override) }

 bbody:
  { ?:body ?clauses }  => { list(?clauses), method() ?body end }

 clauses:
  { }                  => { }
  { on (?:name :: ?spec:expression, ?type:variable) ?:body ... }
   => { pair(?spec, method (?name :: ?spec, ?type) ?body end),
        ... }
end macro;

with-input-context (context-type, override: #t)
      // the body that reads from the user
      read-command-or-form (stream);
    // the clauses that dispatch on the type
    on (object :: <command>, type) execute-command (object);
    on (object :: <form>, type) evaluate-form (object, type);
end;
```

Define Command

```
define macro command-definer
  { define command ?:name (?arguments:*) (#rest ?options:expression)
      ?:body end }
  => { define-command-1 ?name (?arguments) ?body end;
       define-command-2 ?name (?arguments) (?options) end }
end macro;

// define the method that implements a command
// throws away the "stuff" in each argument used by the command parser
define macro define-command-1
  { define-command-1 ?:name (?arguments) ?:body end }
  => { define method ?name (?arguments) ?body end }

  // map over ?arguments, reducing each to a parameter-list entry
  // but when we get to the first argument that has a default, put
  // in #key and switch to the key-arguments loop
  arguments:
    { } => { }
    { ?:variable = ?default:expression ?stuff:*, ?key-arguments }
      => { #key ?variable = ?default, ?key-arguments }
    { ?argument, ... } => { ?argument, ... }

  // map over keyword arguments the same way, each must
  // have a default
  key-arguments:
    { } => { }
    { ?key-argument, ... } => { ?key-argument, ... }

  // reduce one required argument spec to a parameter-list entry
  argument:
    { ?:variable ?stuff:* } => { ?variable }
```

```
// reduce one keyword argument spec to a parameter-list entry
key-argument:
  { ?:variable = ?default:expression ?stuff:* }
   => { ?variable = ?default }
end macro;

// generate the datum that describes a command and install it
define macro define-command-2
 { define-command-2 ?:name (?arguments) (#rest ?options:*) end }
  => { install-command(?name, list(?arguments), ?options) }

 // map over ?arguments, reducing each to a data structure
 arguments:
  { } => { }
  { ?argument, ... } => { ?argument, ... }

 // reduce one argument specification to a data structure
 argument:
  { ?:name :: ?type:expression = ?default:expression ?details }
   => { make(<argument-info>, name: ?"name", type: ?type,
           default: ?default, ?details) }
  { ?:name :: ?type:expression ?details }
   => { make(<argument-info>, name: ?"name", type: ?type, ?details) }

 // translate argument specification to <argument-info> init keywords
 details:
  { } => { }
  { ?key:name ?value:expression ... } => { ?#"key" ?value, ... }
end macro;

define command com-show-home-directory
      (directory :: <type> provide-default #t,
       before :: <time> = #() prompt "date",
       after  :: <time> = #() prompt "date")
      // Options
      (command-table: directories,
```

```
      name: "Show Home Directory")
   body()
end command com-show-home-directory;
```

Get-resource

```
// The idea is that in this application each library has its own
// variable named $library, which is accessible to modules in that
// library. Get-resource gets a resource associated with the library
// containing the call to it. Get-resource-from-library is a function.
// The get-resource macro is a device to make programs more concise.
define macro get-resource
  { get-resource(?type:expression, ?id:expression) }
   => { get-resource-from-library(?=$library, ?type, ?id) }
end macro;

show-icon(get-resource(ResType("ICON"), 1044));
```

Completing-from-suggestions

```
// The completing-from-suggestions macro defines a lexically visible
// helper function called "suggest," which is only meaningful inside
// of calls to the completer. The "suggest" function is passed as an
// argument to the method passed to complete-input; alternatively it
// could have been defined in a local declaration wrapped around the
// method.
define macro completing-from-suggestions
  { completing-from-suggestions (?stream:expression,
                                     #rest ?options:expression)
     ?:body end }
  =>{ complete-input(?stream,
                     method (?=suggest) ?body end,
                     ?options) }
end macro;
```

```
completing-from-suggestions (stream, partial-completers: #(' ', '-'))
  for (command in commands)
    suggest (command, command-name (command))
  end for;
end completing-from-suggestions;
```

Define Jump-instruction

```
define macro jump-instruction-definer
  { define jump-instruction ?:name ?options:* end }
  => { register-instruction("j" ## ?#"name",
                            make(<instruction>,
                                 debug-name: "j" ## ?"name",
                                 ?options)) }
end macro;

define jump-instruction eq cr-bit: 2, commutative?: #t end;
```

The Built-In Classes

Contents

Overview   187
Objects   187
Types   189
  General Types   190
  Classes   191
  Singletons   194
Simple Objects   195
  Characters   195
  Symbols   196
  Booleans   197
Numbers   197
  General Numbers   198
  Complex Numbers   199
  Reals   200
  Floats   202
  Rationals   203
  Integers   204
Collections   206
  General Collections   208
  Explicit Key Collections   210
  Sequences   211
  Mutable Collections   214
  Stretchy Collections   217
  Arrays   218
  Vectors   221
  Deques   225

Lists   226
Ranges   230
Strings   232
Tables   235
Functions   238
    General Functions   238
    Generic Functions   241
    Methods   243
Conditions   244
    General Conditions   245
    Serious Conditions   247
    Errors   247
    Warnings   249
    Restarts   251
    Aborts   253

Overview

This chapter contains an entry for every class defined by Dylan.

The superclasses listed for a class C are those classes defined by the Dylan language from which C most directly inherits. They are not required to be the direct superclasses of C, because implementations are free to insert implementation-defined classes in the class hierarchy. However, any classes defined by Dylan that appear in the class precedence list of C must appear in the same order in which they would appear if the specified superclasses were the direct superclasses of C, in the order given.

All classes are specified as open or sealed. A class may be specifed as abstract; if it is not, then it is concrete. A class may be specified as primary; if it is not, than it is free. A class may be specified as instantiable. If it is not, then it is uninstantiable. Chapter 9, "Sealing," contains a complete description of these characteristics.

An implementation may choose to impose fewer restrictions than specified. For example, a class specified as sealed may be left open, and a class specified as primary may be left free. However, any program that takes advantage of this liberality will not be portable.

Each class entry includes tables of operations defined on the class. These tables are cross references to Chapter 12, "The Built-In Functions," and represent redundant information. A function, generic function, or method is listed under a class if one of its arguments is specialized on the class. In addition, constructors are listed. Not all generic functions that specialize on <object> are listed.

Objects

<object>   [Open Abstract Class]

The class of all Dylan objects.

Superclasses: None. `<object>` is the root of the Dylan class hierarchy.

Init-keywords: None.

Description: The class `<object>` is the root of the type system. All objects are general instances of `<object>`, all types are subtypes of `<object>`, and all classes are subclasses of `<object>`.

Operations: The class `<object>` provides the following operations:

Table 11-1   Functions on `<object>`

Function	Description	Page
identity	Returns its argument.	287
always	Returns a function that always returns a particular object.	350
instance?	Tests whether an object is an instance of a type.	343
object-class	Returns the class of an object.	344
==	Compares two objects for identity.	268
~==	Compares two objects for nonidentity.	269
~	Returns true if its argument is false; otherwise returns false.	268
object-hash	The hash function for the equivalence predicate ==.	342

Table 11-2   Generic functions on <object>

Function	Description	Page
initialize	Performs instance initialization that cannot be specified declaratively by a class definition.	260
as	Coerces an object to a type.	288
shallow-copy	Returns a copy of its argument.	292
type-for-copy	Returns an appropriate type for creating mutable copies of its argument.	292
size	Returns the size of its argument.	295
empty?	Returns true if its argument is empty.	294

Table 11-3   Methods on <object>

Function	Description	Page
initialize	Performs instance initialization that cannot be specified declaratively by a class definition.	260
type-for-copy	Returns an appropriate type for creating mutable copies of its argument.	292
=	Compares two objects for equality.	269

Types

Types are used to categorize objects. Figure 11-1 shows the built-in classes of types and some of their characteristics.

Figure 11-1   The Type Classes

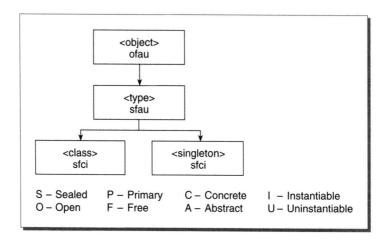

S – Sealed   P – Primary   C – Concrete   I – Instantiable
O – Open   F – Free   A – Abstract   U – Uninstantiable

General Types

<type>   **[Sealed Abstract Class]**

The class of all types, including classes and other types.

Superclasses: <object>

Init-keywords: None.

Description: The class of all types. All types (including <type> and <class>) are instances
of <type>.

Operations: The class <type> provides the following operations:

Table 11-4   Functions on <type>

Function	Description	Page
instance?	Tests whether an object is an instance of a type.	343
subtype?	Tests whether a type is a subtype of another type.	343
type-union	Returns the union of two or more types.	266

Table 11-5   Generic Functions on <type>

Function	Description	Page
make	Returns a general instance of its first argument.	258

Classes

<class>   **[Sealed Instantiable Class]**

The class of all Dylan classes.

Superclasses: <type>

Init-keywords: The class <class> supports the following init-keywords:

superclasses:
    An instance of <class> or <sequence> specifying the direct
    superclasses of the class. If it is a sequence, the elements of the
    sequence must be instances of <class>. The default value is
    <object>. The meaning of the order of the superclasses is the
    same as in define class.

abstract?: An instance of <boolean> specifying whether the class is
    abstract or concrete. The default value is #f.

slots: An instance of <sequence> containing slot specs, where each
           slot-spec is a sequence of keyword/value pairs.

           The following keywords and corresponding values are accepted
           by all implementations. Implementations may also define
           additional keywords and values for use within slot specs.

   getter: A generic function of one argument. Unless the
                allocation of the slot is virtual, the getter method
                for the slot will be added to this generic function.
                This option is required.

   setter: A generic function of two arguments, or #f
                indicating "no setter." Unless the allocation of
                the slot is virtual, the setter method for the slot
                will be added to this generic function. The
                default value is #f.

   type: A type. Values stored in the slot are restricted to
                be of this type. The default value is <object>.

   deferred-type:
                A function of no arguments, which returns a
                type, and is called once to compute the type of
                the slot, within the call to make that constructs
                the first instance of that class. For a given slot
                spec, either type: or deferred-type: may be
                specified, but not both.

   init-value: A default initial value for the slot. This option
                cannot be specified along with
                init-function: or
                required-init-keyword: and it cannot be
                specified for a virtual slot. There is no default.

   init-function:
                A function of no arguments. This function will be
                called to generate an initial value for the slot
                when a new instances is created. This option
                cannot be specified along with init-value: or
                required-init-keyword: and it cannot be
                specified for a virtual slot. There is no default

   init-keyword:
                A keyword. This option permits an initial value
                for the slot to be passed to make, as a keyword

argument using this keyword. This option cannot be specified for a virtual slot. There is no default. This option cannot be specified along with `required-init-keyword:`.

`required-init-keyword:`
A keyword. This option is like `init-keyword:`, except it indicates an init-keyword that must be provided when the class is instantiated. If `make` is called on the class and a required init-keyword is not provided in the defaulted initialization arguments, an error is signaled. There is no default. This option cannot be specified if `init-keyword:`, `init-value:`, or `init-function:` is specified, or for a virtual slot.

`allocation:` One of the keywords `instance:`, `class:`, `each-subclass:`, or `virtual:`, or an implementation defined keyword. The meaning of this option is the same as adding the corresponding adjective to a `define class` form.

Description: The class of all classes. All classes (including `<class>`) are general instances of `<class>`.

In most programs the majority of classes are created with `define class`. However, there is nothing to prevent programmers from creating classes by calling `make`, for example, if they want to create a class without storing it in a module binding, or if they want to create new classes at runtime.

If `make` is used to create a new class and creating the new class would violate any restrictions specified by sealing directives, then an error of type `<sealed-object-error>` is signaled.

Operations: The class <class> provides the following operations:

Table 11-6   Functions on <class>

Function	Description	Page
all-superclasses	Returns the class precedence list a class.	344
direct-superclasses	Returns the direct superclasses of a class.	345
direct-subclasses	Returns the direct subclasses of a class.	345
limited	Returns a limited subtype of a class.	263

Table 11-7   Methods on <class>

Function	Description	Page
make	Returns a general instance of its first argument.	259

Singletons

<singleton>   **[Sealed Instantiable Class]**

The class of types that indicate a single object.

Superclasses: <type>

Init-keywords: The class <singleton> supports the following init-keyword:

object: An instance of <object>. The object that the singleton indicates. There is no default for this argument. If it is not supplied, an error will be signaled.

Description: The class of singletons.

If a singleton for the specified object already exists, implementations may return it rather than allocating a new singleton.

Operations: None.

Simple Objects

Simple objects are sealed, uninstantiable, and concrete. They are often represented by program literals. Figure 11-2 shows the built-in classes of simple objects.

Figure 11-2   The Simple Object Classes

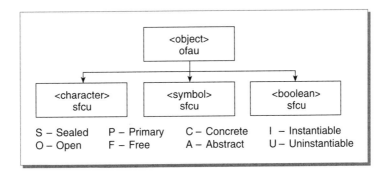

Characters

<character>   **[Sealed Class]**

The class of characters.

Superclasses: <object>

Init-keywords: None.

Description: The class of characters. All characters are instances of <character>.

Operations: The class <character> provides the following operations:

Table 11-8   Methods on <character>

Function	Description	Page
<	Returns true if its first operand is less than its second operand.	271
as-uppercase	Coerces an object to uppercase.	290
as-lowercase	Coerces an object to lowercase.	291
as	Coerces an object to a type.	288

Symbols

<symbol>   **[Sealed Class]**

The class of symbols.

Superclasses: <object>

Init-keywords: None.

Description: The <symbol> class provides a built-in, non-case-sensitive dictionary that associates a string with a unique immutable object that can be compared with == (which should be faster than calling a string-comparison routine). This dictionary is accessed through the as function: as(<symbol>, *string*) and as(<string>, *symbol*). Any string can be used.

Operations: The class <symbol> provides the following operation:

Table 11-9   Methods on <symbol>

Function	Description	Page
as	Coerces an object to a type.	288

Booleans

`<boolean>`   **[Sealed Class]**

The class of boolean values.

Superclasses: `<object>`

Init-keywords: None.

Operations: None.

Description: The class of boolean values. The literal constants #t and #f are general instances of `<boolean>`. Note that for the purposes of conditional expressions, all objects besides #f count as true. (This does not imply any other objects are instances of `<boolean>`.)

Numbers

Dylan provides a variety of numeric classes. Classes under `<complex>` are sealed, so that numeric operations on them can be highly optimized. User defined numeric classes will be subclasses of `<number>`.

Figure 11-3 shows the built-in number classes and some of their characteristics.

Figure 11-3   The Number Classes

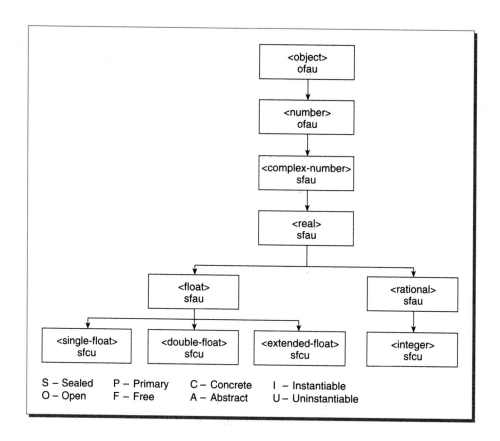

General Numbers

<number>   **[Open Abstract Class]**

The class of all numbers.

Superclasses: <object>

Init-keywords: None.

Operations: None.

Description: The class of all numbers.

The class <number> is open, to allow programmers to create additional numeric classes. The built-in numeric operations do not provide default implementations for <number>, but for <complex>, a sealed subclass of <number>.

Complex Numbers

<complex>   **[Sealed Abstract Class]**

The class of complex numbers.

Superclasses: <number>

Init-keywords: None.

Description: The sealed superclass of all built-in numbers, including real numbers. There are no non-real subclasses of <complex> defined by the language, but implementations may define such subclasses. Because <complex> and all its defined subclasses are sealed, implementation-defined subclasses may be added efficiently.

Many built-in functions are defined to have methods on <complex>. This means that the function is defined on all built-in subclasses of <complex>. It does not imply that there is a single method specialized on the <complex> class.

Operations: The class <complex> provides implementations for the following functions:

Table 11-10   Methods on <complex>

Function	Description	Page
=	Compares two objects for equality.	269
zero?	Tests for the property of being equal to zero.	275
+	Returns the sum of its arguments.	277
*	Returns the product of its arguments.	277
−	Returns the difference of its arguments.	278
/	Returns the quotient of its arguments.	278
^	Raises an object to a specified power.	283

Reals

<real>   **[Sealed Abstract Class]**

The class of real numbers.

Superclasses: <complex>

Init-keywords: None.

Description: The class of real numbers.

Operations: The class `<real>` provides implementations for the following functions:

Table 11-11   Functions on <real>

Function	Description	Page
floor	Truncates a real number toward negative infinity.	279
ceiling	Truncates a real number toward positive infinity.	280
round	Rounds a real number toward the nearest mathematical integer.	280
truncate	Truncates a real number toward zero.	280
floor/	Returns the floor of the quotient of two numbers.	281
ceiling/	Returns the ceiling of the quotient of two numbers.	281
round/	Rounds off the quotient of two numbers.	282
truncate/	Returns the truncated quotient of two numbers.	282
modulo	Returns the second value of `floor/`.	282
remainder	Returns the second value of `truncate/`.	283

Table 11-12   Methods on <real>

Function	Description	Page
<	Returns true if its first operand is less than its second operand.	271
abs	Returns the absolute value of its argument.	284
positive?	Tests for the property of being positive.	276

continued

Table 11-12   Methods on <real> (continued)

Function	Description	Page
negative?	Tests for the property of being negative.	276
integral?	Tests for the property of being integral.	276
negative	Returns the negation of an object.	279

Floats

The classes <single-float> and <double-float> are intended but not required to be the corresponding IEEE types. The class <extended-float> is intended but not required to have more range and/or precision than <double-float>.

If an implementation has fewer than three floating point classes, the names <single-float>, <double-float> and <extended-float> may all refer to the same object.

<float>   **[Sealed Abstract Class]**

The class of floating-point numbers.

Superclasses: <real>

Init-keywords: None.

Description: The class of all floating-point numbers. This class is abstract. All floating point numbers will be instances of some concrete subclass of this class.

Operations: None.

<single-float>   **[Sealed Class]**

The class of single-precision floating-point numbers.

Superclasses: <float>

Init-keywords: None.

Description: The class of single-precision floating-point numbers. This class is intended but not required to correspond to IEEE single-precision.

Operations: None.

`<double-float>`   **[Sealed Class]**

The class of double-precision floating-point numbers.

Superclasses: `<float>`

Init-keywords: None.

Description: The class of double-precision floating-point numbers. This class is intended but not required to correspond to IEEE double-precision.

Operations: None.

`<extended-float>`   **[Sealed Class]**

The class of extended-precision floating-point numbers.

Superclasses: `<float>`

Init-keywords: None.

Description: The class of extended-precision floating-point numbers. This class is intended but not required to provide more precision that `<double-float>`.

Operations: None.

Rationals

`<rational>`   **[Sealed Abstract Class]**

The class of rational numbers.

Superclasses: `<real>`

Init-keywords: None.

Description: The class of rational numbers.

Operations: None.

Integers

<integer>   **[Sealed Class]**

The class of integers.

Superclasses: <rational>

Init-keywords: None.

Description: The class of integers.

Implementations are required to support integers with at least 28 bits of precision. The overflow and underflow behavior is implementation-defined. (Some implementations may choose to have integers of unlimited size, but this is not required.)

The result of dividing two integers with / is implementation defined. Portable programs should use floor/, ceiling/, round/, or truncate/ to divide two integers.

Operations: The class <integer> provides the following operations:

Table 11-13   Functions on <integer>

Function	Description	Page
odd?	Tests for the property of being an odd number.	275
even?	Tests for the property of being an even number.	275
logior	Returns the bitwise inclusive or of its integer arguments.	284
logxor	Returns the bitwise exclusive or of its integer arguments.	284
logand	Returns the bitwise and of its integer arguments.	285
lognot	Returns the bitwise not of its integer argument.	285
logbit?	Tests the value of a particular bit in its integer argument.	285
ash	Performs an arithmetic shift on its first argument.	286

Table 11-14   Methods on <integer>

Function	Description	Page
lcm	Returns the least common multiple of its two arguments.	286
gcd	Returns the greatest common divisor of its two arguments.	287

Table 11-15   Methods on singleton(<integer>)

Function	Description	Page
`limited`	Returns a limited subtype of a class.	263

Collections

This section describes the built-in collections, Dylan's aggregate data structures.

Collections are used to hold groups of objects. Collections support iteration as well as random access through collection keys. An overview of collections is given in Chapter 8, "Collections."

Figure 11-4 shows the built-in collection classes and some of their characteristics.

Figure 11-4   The Collection Classes

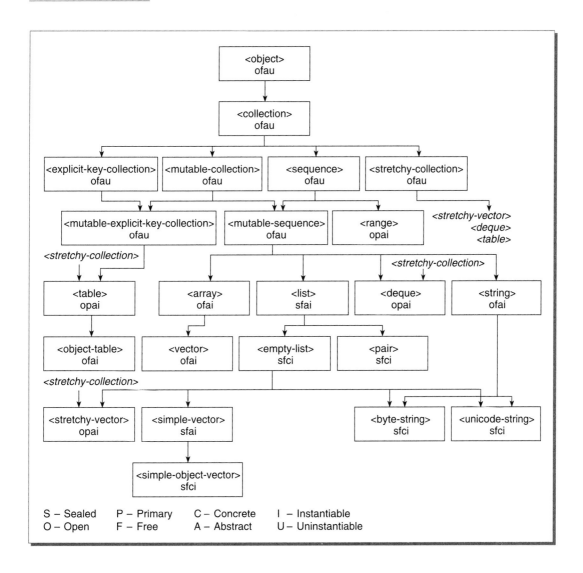

General Collections

<collection>   **[Open Abstract Class]**

The class of collections, aggregate data structures.

Superclasses: <object>

Init-keywords: None.

Description: The class of collections.

<collection> is the root class of the collection class hierarchy. It provides a set of basic operations on all collections.

The element type of <collection> is indefinite ⇐ <object>.

Operations: The class <collection> provides the following operations:

Table 11-16   Functions on <collection>

Function	Description	Page
do	Iterates over one or more collections for side effect.	327
map	Iterates over one or more collections and collects the results in a freshly allocated collection.	328
map-as	Iterates over one or more collections and collects the results in a freshly allocated collection of a specified type.	328

continued

Table 11-16   Functions on <collection> (continued)

Function	Description	Page
map-into	Iterates over one or more collections and collects the results in an existing mutable collection.	329
any?	Returns the first true value obtained by iterating over one or more collections.	330
every?	Returns true if a predicate returns true when applied to all corresponding elements of a set of collections.	331

Table 11-17   Generic Functions on <collection>

Function	Description	Page
element	Returns the collection element associated with a particular key.	300
key-sequence	Returns a sequence containing the keys of its collection argument.	299
reduce	Combines the elements of a collection and a seed value into a single value by repeatedly applying a binary function.	331
reduce1	Combines the elements of a collection into a single value by repeatedly applying a binary function, using the first element of the collection as the seed value.	332
member?	Returns true if a collection contains a particular value.	334
find-key	Returns the key in a collection such that the corresponding collection element satisfies a predicate.	335

continued

Table 11-17   Generic Functions on <collection> (continued)

Function	Description	Page
key-test	Returns the function used by its collection argument to compare keys.	298
forward- iteration- protocol	Returns a group of functions used to iterate over the elements of a collection.	337
backward- iteration- protocol	Returns a group of functions used to iterate over the elements of a collection in reverse order.	339

Table 11-18   Methods on <collection>

Function	Description	Page
=	Compares two objects for equality.	269
empty?	Returns true if its argument is empty.	294
size	Returns the size of its argument.	295
shallow-copy	Returns a copy of its argument.	292

Table 11-19   Methods on singleton(<collection>)

Function	Description	Page
limited	Returns a limited subtype of a class.	263

Explicit Key Collections

<explicit-key-collection>   **[Open Abstract Class]**

The class of all collections that are not sequences.

Superclasses: <collection>

Init-keywords: None.

Description: The class of all collections that are not sequences.

This class is disjoint from `<sequence>` because `key-test` is sealed over the domain `<sequence>`.

The element type of `<explicit-key-collection>` is indefinite ⇐ `<object>`.

Operations: The class `<explicit-key-collection>` provides the following operation:

Table 11-20   Methods on singleton(<explicit-key-collection>)

Function	Description	Page
limited	Returns a limited subtype of a class.	263

Sequences

<sequence>   **[Open Abstract Class]**

The class of collections whose keys are consecutive integers starting from zero.

Superclasses: `<collection>`

Init-keywords: None.

Description: The class of collections whose keys are consecutive integers starting from zero.

Sequences must be stable under iteration, and the iteration order must match the order of keys. Thus, the key associated with a sequence's iteration state can be determined by keeping a counter in parallel with the iteration state.

The default methods for `add`, `add-new`, `remove`, `choose`, `choose-by`, `intersection`, `union`, `remove-duplicates`, `copy-sequence`, `concatenate`, `reverse`, and `sort` all return new sequences that are instances of the `type-for-copy` of their primary sequence argument. However, more specialized methods are permitted to choose a more appropriate result class; for example, `copy-sequence` of a range returns another range, even though the `type-for-copy` value of a range is the `<list>` class.

`<sequence>` is disjoint from `<explicit-key-collection>` because of the sealed domain over the function `key-test` for `<sequence>`.

The element type of `<sequence>` is `indefinite` ⇐ `<object>`.

Operations: The class `<sequence>` provides the following operations:

Table 11-21   Functions on `<sequence>`

Function	Description	Page
concatenate	Returns the concatenation of one or more sequences in a sequence of a type determined by the `type-for-copy` of its first argument.	323
concatenate-as	Returns the concatenation of one or more sequences in a sequence of a specified type.	324
first	Returns the first element of a sequence.	303
second	Returns the second element of a sequence.	304
third	Returns the third element of a sequence.	304

Table 11-22   Generic Functions on `<sequence>`

Function	Description	Page
add	Adds an element to a sequence.	309
add!	Adds an element to a sequence.	310
add-new	Adds a new element to a sequence.	311
add-new!	Adds a new element to a sequence.	312
remove	Removes an element from a sequence.	312
remove!	Removes an element from a sequence.	313

continued

Table 11-22   Generic Functions on <sequence> (continued)

Function	Description	Page
choose	Returns those elements of a sequence that satisfy a predicate.	333
choose-by	Returns those elements of a sequence that correspond to those in another sequence that satisfy a predicate.	333
intersection	Returns the intersection of two sequences.	319
union	Returns the union of two sequences.	320
remove-duplicates	Returns a sequence without duplicates.	321
remove-duplicates!	Returns a sequence without duplicates.	322
copy-sequence	Returns a freshly allocated copy of some subsequence of a sequence.	323
replace-subsequence!	Replaces a portion of a sequence with the elements of another sequence.	325
reverse	Returns a sequence with elements in the reverse order of its argument sequence.	316
reverse!	Returns a sequence with elements in the reverse order of its argument sequence.	317
sort	Returns a sequence containing the elements of its argument sequence, sorted.	318
sort!	Returns a sequence containing the elements of its argument sequence, sorted.	318
last	Returns the last element of a sequence.	306
subsequence-position	Returns the position where a pattern appears in a sequence.	326

Table 11-23   Methods on <sequence>

Function	Description	Page
=	Compares two objects for equality.	269
key-test	Returns the function used by its collection argument to compare keys.	298

Table 11-24   Methods on singleton(<sequence>)

Function	Description	Page
limited	Returns a limited subtype of a class.	263

Mutable Collections

<mutable-collection>   **[Open Abstract Class]**

The class of collections that may be modified.

Superclasses: <collection>

Init-keywords: None.

Description: The class of collections that may be modified.

Every mutable collection is required to allow modification by implementing element-setter.

The element type of <mutable-collection> is indefinite ⇐ <object>.

Operations: The class `<mutable-collection>` provides the following operations:

Table 11-25   Functions on <mutable-collection>

Function	Description	Page
map-into	Iterates over one or more collections and collects the results in an existing mutable collection.	329

Table 11-26   Generic Functions on <mutable-collection>

Function	Description	Page
element-setter	Sets the collection element associated with a particular key.	301

Table 11-27   Methods on <mutable-collection>

Function	Description	Page
type-for-copy	Returns an appropriate type for creating mutable copies of its argument.	292

Table 11-28   Methods on singleton(<mutable-collection>)

Function	Description	Page
limited	Returns a limited subtype of a class.	263

<mutable-explicit-key-collection>   **[Open Abstract Class]**

The class of explicit-key-collections that can have elements replaced.

Superclasses: `<explicit-key-collection>` `<mutable-collection>`

Init-keywords: None.

Description: The class of explicit-key-collections that can have elements replaced.

The element type of `<mutable-explicit-key-collection>` is indefinite ⇐ `<object>`.

Operations: The class `<mutable-explicit-key-collection>` provides the following operations:

Table 11-29   Generic Functions on <mutable-explicit-key-collection>

Function	Description	Page
`remove-key!`	Modifies an explicit key collection so it no longer has a particular key.	335

Table 11-30   Methods on singleton(<mutable-explicit-key-collection>)

Function	Description	Page
`limited`	Returns a limited subtype of a class.	263

`<mutable-sequence>`   **[Open Abstract Class]**

The class of sequences that may be modified.

Superclasses: `<sequence>` `<mutable-collection>`

Init-keywords: None.

Description: The class of sequences that may be modified.

The element type of `<mutable-sequence>` is indefinite ⇐ `<object>`.

Operations: The class <mutable-sequence> provides the following operations:

Table 11-31   Functions on <mutable-sequence>

Function	Description	Page
first-setter	Sets the first element of a mutable sequence.	304
second-setter	Sets the second element of a mutable sequence.	305
third-setter	Sets the third element of a mutable sequence.	305

Table 11-32   Generic Functions on <mutable-sequence>

Function	Description	Page
last-setter	Sets the last element of a mutable sequence.	306

Table 11-33   Methods on singleton(<mutable-sequence>)

Function	Description	Page
limited	Returns a limited subtype of a class.	263

Stretchy Collections

<stretchy-collection>   **[Open Abstract Class]**

The class of collections that may grow or shrink to accommodate adding or removing elements.

Superclasses: <collection>

Init-keywords: None.

Description: The class of collections that may grow or shrink to accommodate adding or removing elements.

Stretchy collections allow `element-setter` to be called with a key that is not present in the collection, expanding the collection as necessary to add a new element in that case. Each concrete subclass of `<stretchy-collection>` must provide or inherit a method for `element-setter` that behaves as follows when there is not already an element present for the indicated key:

■ If the class is a subclass of `<explicit-key-collection>`, adds a new element to the collection with the indicated key.

■ If the class is a subclass of `<sequence>`, first calls `size-setter` on the key + 1 and the collection to expand the sequence. The key must be a non-negative integer.

The element type of `<stretchy-collection>` is indefinite $\Leftarrow$ `<object>`.

Operations: The class `<stretchy-collection>` provides the following operations:

Table 11-34   Methods on singleton(<stretchy-collection>)

Function	Description	Page
limited	Returns a limited subtype of a class.	263

Arrays

<array>   **[Open Abstract Instantiable Class]**

The class of sequences whose elements are arranged according to a Cartesian coordinate system.

Superclasses: `<mutable-sequence>`

Init-keywords: The make method on `singleton(<array>)` accepts the following keyword arguments. Note that these are not inherited by subclasses of `<array>`.

dimensions: An instance of <sequence> with elements that are instances of <integer>. This argument specifies the dimensions of the array. The size of the sequence specifies the rank (number of dimensions) of the array, and each integer in the sequence specifies the size of a dimension. This argument is required.

fill: An instance of <object> specifying an initial value for each element of the array. The default value is #f.

Description: The class of collections whose elements are arranged according to a Cartesian coordinate system.

An array element is referred to by a (possibly empty) series of indices. The length of the series must equal the rank of the array. Each index must be a non-negative integer less than the corresponding dimension. An array element may alternatively be referred to by an integer, which is interpreted as a row-major index.

Arrays typically use space efficient representations, and the average time required to access a randomly chosen element is typically sublinear to the number of elements.

Whe a multi-dimensional array is created, the concrete class that is actually instantiated cannot be any of the specified subclasses of <array>, which are all one-dimensional. Every implementation must have one or more concrete subclasses of <array> that are used for this purpose. These concrete subclasses have no specified names, and their names are not exported by the Dylan module.

When a single-dimensional array is created, the array created will be an instance of <vector>.

Each concrete subclass of <array> must either provide or inherit implementations of the functions element, element-setter, and dimensions.

The element type of <array> is indefinite ⇐ <object>.

Operations: The class <array> provides the following operations::

Table 11-35 Generic Functions on <array>

Function	Description	Page
rank	Returns the number of dimensions of an array.	296
row-major-index	Returns the row-major-index position of an array element.	297
aref	Returns the array element indicated by a set of indices.	302
aref-setter	Sets the array element indicated by a set of indices.	302
dimensions	Returns the dimensions of an array.	297
dimension	Returns the size of a specified dimension of an array.	298

Table 11-36 Methods on <array>

Function	Description	Page
size	Returns the size of its argument.	295
rank	Returns the number of dimensions of an array.	296
row-major-index	Returns the row-major-index position of an array element.	297
aref	Returns the array element indicated by a set of indices.	302
aref-setter	Sets the array element indicated by a set of indices.	302
dimension	Returns the size of a specified dimension of an array.	298

Table 11-37   Methods on singleton(<array>)

Function	Description	Page
make	Returns a general instance of its first argument.	258
limited	Returns a limited subtype of a class.	263

Vectors

<vector>   **[Open Abstract Instantiable Class]**

The class of arrays of rank one (i.e., exactly one dimension).

Superclasses: <array>

Init-keywords: The make method on singleton(<vector>) accepts the following keyword arguments. Note that these are not inherited by subclasses of <vector>.

size: An instance of <integer> specifying the size of the vector. The default value is 0.

fill: An instance of <object> specifying an initial value for each element of the vector. The default value is #f.

Description: The class of one-dimensional arrays.

<vector> has no direct instances; calling make on <vector> returns an instance of <simple-object-vector>.

Each concrete subclass of <vector> must either provide or inherit an implementation of size that shadows the method provided by <array>.

The element type of <vector> is indefinite $\Leftarrow$ <object>.

Operations: The class <vector> provides the following operations:

Table 11-38   Constructors for <vector>

Function	Description	Page
vector	Creates and returns a freshly allocated vector.	267

Table 11-39   Methods on <vector>

Function	Description	Page
dimensions	Returns the dimensions of an array.	297
element	Returns the collection element associated with a particular key.	300

Table 11-40   Methods on singleton(<vector>)

Function	Description	Page
make	Returns a general instance of its first argument.	258
limited	Returns a limited subtype of a class.	263

<simple-vector>   **[Sealed Abstract Instantiable Class]**

A predefined subclass of <vector> that provides an efficient implementation of fixed-length vectors.

Superclasses: <vector>

Init-keywords: The make method on singleton(<simple-vector>) accepts the following keyword arguments. Note that these are not inherited by subclasses of <simple-vector>.

size: An instance of <integer> specifying the size of the vector. The default value is 0.

fill: An instance of <object> specifying an initial value for each element of the vector. The default value is #f.

Description: The class of simple and efficient vectors.

The class <simple-vector> provides a constant time implementation for the element and element-setter functions. This property is shared by all subtypes of <simple-vector>.

Calling make on a <simple-vector> returns an instance of <simple-object-vector>. The size of a simple vector cannot be changed after the simple vector has been created.

Vector literals (created with the #[...] syntax) are general instances of <simple-vector>.

The element type of <simple-vector> is indefinite ⇐ <object>.

The class <simple-object-vector> and the type limited(<simple-vector>, of: <object>) have exactly the same instances, but neither is a subtype of the other. The relationship between them is simply that the make method for the type returns an instance of the class.

Operations: The class <simple-vector> provides the following operations:

Table 11-41 Methods on <simple-vector>

Function	Description	Page
element	Returns the collection element associated with a particular key.	300
element-setter	Sets the collection element associated with a particular key.	301

Table 11-42 Methods on singleton(<simple-vector>)

Function	Description	Page
make	Returns a general instance of its first argument.	258
limited	Returns a limited subtype of a class.	263

`<simple-object-vector>` **[Sealed Instantiable Class]**

The class of simple vectors that may have elements of any type.

Superclasses: `<simple-vector>`

Init-keywords: The class `<simple-object-vector>` supports the following init-keywords:

size: An instance of `<integer>` specifying the size of the vector. The default value is 0.

fill: An instance of `<object>` specifying the initial value for each element. The default value is #f.

Description: The class `<simple-object-vector>` represents vectors that may have elements of any type. It provides a constant time implementation for the element and element-setter functions.

The element type of `<simple-object-vector>` is `<object>`.

Operations: None.

`<stretchy-vector>` **[Open Abstract Instantiable Primary Class]**

The class of vectors that are stretchy.

Superclasses: `<vector>` `<stretchy-collection>`

Init-keywords: The class `<stretchy-vector>` supports the following init-keywords:

size: An instance of `<integer>` specifying the initial size of the stretchy vector. The default value is 0.

fill: An instance of `<object>` specifying the initial value for each element. The default value is #f.

Description: The class of vectors that are stretchy.

Because `<stretchy-vector>` is abstract and instantiable but has no specified subclasses, every implementation must provide one or more concrete subclass to instantiate. These concrete subclasses have no specified names, and their names are not exported by the Dylan module.

The element type of `<simple-vector>` is indefinite ⇐ `<object>`.

Operations: The class `<stretchy-vector>` provides the following operations:

Table 11-43 Methods on <stretchy-vector>

Function	Description	Page
add!	Adds an element to a sequence.	309
remove!	Removes an element from a sequence.	313

Table 11-44 Methods on singleton(<stretchy-vector>)

Function	Description	Page
limited	Returns a limited subtype of a class.	263

Deques

`<deque>`   **[Open Abstract Instantiable Primary Class]**

The class of double-ended queues.

Superclasses: `<mutable-sequence>` `<stretchy-collection>`

Init-keywords: The class `<deque>` supports the following init-keywords:

size: An instance of `<integer>` specifying the initial size of the deque. The default value is 0.

fill: An instance of `<object>` specifying the initial value for each element. The default value is #f.

Description: A subclass of sequence that supports efficient forward and backward iteration, and efficient addition and removal of elements from the beginning or end of the sequence.

Because `<deque>` is abstract and instantiable but has no specified subclasses, every implementation must provide one or more concrete subclasses to instantiate. These concrete subclasses have no specified names, and their names are not exported by the Dylan module.

The element type of <deque> is indefinite ⇐ <object>.

Operations: The class <deque> provides the following operations:

Table 11-45   Generic Functions on <deque>

Function	Description	Page
push	Adds an element to the front of a deque.	314
pop	Removes and returns the first element of a deque.	315
push-last	Adds an element to the end of a deque.	315
pop-last	Removes and returns an element from the end of a deque.	315

Table 11-46   Methods on <deque>

Function	Description	Page
add!	Adds an element to a sequence.	309
remove!	Removes an element from a sequence.	313

Table 11-47   Methods on singleton(<deque>)

Function	Description	Page
limited	Returns a limited subtype of a class.	263
make	Returns a general instance of its first argument.	258

Lists

Lists are constructed by linking together instances of <pair>. The head of a list contains an element, and the tail of the list contains a pointer to the next pair in the list. The list ends when the tail of a pair contains something besides another pair.

A **proper list** has a final pair with a tail containing the empty list.

An **improper list** does not have a final pair with a tail containing the empty list, either because the tail of its final pair is not the empty list, or because the list is circular and thus does not have a final pair. Except when their behavior on improper lists is documented explicitly, collection or sequence functions are not guaranteed to return an answer when an improper list is used as a collection or a sequence. At the implementation's option, these functions may return the correct result, signal a `<type-error>`, or (in the case of a circular list) fail to return.

When treated as a collection, the elements of a list are the heads of successive pairs in the list.

`<list>`   **[Sealed Instantiable Abstract Class]**

The class of linked lists.

Superclasses: `<mutable-sequence>`

Init-keywords: The make method on `singleton(<list>)` accepts the following keyword arguments. Note that these are not inherited by subclasses of `<list>`.

    `size:`   An instance of `<integer>` specifying the size of the list. The default value is `0`.

    `fill:`   An instance of `<object>` specifying the initial value for each element. The default value is `#f`.

Description: The class of linked lists.

    The `<list>` class is partitioned into two concrete subclasses, `<pair>` and `<empty-list>`. Calling make on `<list>` will return a linked list made from pairs and terminated with the empty list.

    The element type of `<list>` is `<object>`.

Operations: The class <list> provides the following operations:

Table 11-48 Constructors for <list>

Function	Description	Page
list	Creates and returns a freshly allocated list.	261
pair	Creates and returns a freshly allocated pair.	262

Table 11-49 Functions on <list>

Function	Description	Page
head	Returns the head of a list.	307
tail	Returns the tail of a list.	307

Table 11-50 Methods on <list>

Function	Description	Page
size	Returns the size of its argument.	295
=	Compares two objects for equality.	269
add!	Adds an element to a sequence.	309
remove!	Removes an element from a sequence.	313

Table 11-51 Methods on singleton(<list>)

Function	Description	Page
make	Returns a general instance of its first argument.	258

<pair> [Sealed Instantiable Class]

The class of lists that can have new values assigned to their heads and tails.

Superclasses: <list>

Init-keywords: None.

Description: The class of lists that can have new values assigned to their heads and tails.

The element type of <pair> is <object>.

Operations: The following operations are provided on <pair>:

Table 11-52   Functions on <pair>

Function	Description	Page
head-setter	Sets the head of a pair.	308
tail-setter	Sets the tail of a pair.	308

Table 11-53   Constructors for <pair>

Function	Description	Page
pair	Creates and returns a freshly allocated pair.	262

<empty-list> [Sealed Instantiable Class]

The class with only one instance, the empty list.

Superclasses: <list>

Init-keywords: None.

Description: The class <empty-list> has only one instance, the empty list. The empty list is a direct instance of <empty-list> and an indirect instance of <list>. Note that <empty-list> is not == to singleton (#()).

The element type of <empty-list> is <object>.

Operations: None.

Ranges

<range>   **[Open Abstract Instantiable Primary Class]**

The class of arithmetic sequences.

Superclasses: <sequence>

Init-keywords: The class <range> supports the following init-keywords:

from: An instance of <real> specifying the first value in the range. The default value is 0.

by: An instance of <real> specifying the step between consecutive elements of the range. The default value is 1.

to: An instance of <real> specifying an inclusive bound for the range. If by: is positive, the range will include numbers up to and including this value. If by: is negative, the range will include numbers down to to and including this value.
to: cannot be specified with above: or below:.

above: An instance of <real> specifying an exclusive lower bound for the range. The range will only include numbers above this value, regardless of the sign of by:.
above: cannot be specified with to: or below:.

below: An instance of <real> specifying an exclusive upper bound for the range. The range will only include numbers below this value, regardless of the sign of by:.
below: cannot be specified with to: or above:.

size: An instance of <integer> specifying the size of the range.

Description: The class <range> is used for creating sequences of numbers. Ranges may be infinite in size, and may run from higher numbers to lower numbers.

If size: is specified and none of to:, above: or below: is specified, then the size: argument determines the size of the range.

If size: is specified and one of to:, above: or below: is specified, than it is an error if the number of elements implied by the to:, above: or below: argument (and the by: argument, if present) does not agree with the number of elements specified by the size: argument.

Because <range> in abstract and instantiable but has no specified subclasses, every implementation must provide one or more concrete subclass to instantiate. These concrete subclasses have no specified names, and their names are not exported by the Dylan module.

The element type of <range> is indefinite $\Leftarrow$ <real>.

Operations: The class <range> provides the following operations:

Table 11-54   Methods on <range>

Function	Description	Page
member?	Returns true if a collection contains a particular value.	334
size	Returns the size of its argument.	295
copy-sequence	Returns a freshly allocated copy of some subsequence of a sequence.	323
=	Compares two objects for equality.	269
reverse	Returns a sequence with elements in the reverse order of its argument sequence.	316
reverse!	Returns a sequence with elements in the reverse order of its argument sequence.	317
intersection	Returns the intersection of two sequences.	319
type-for-copy	Returns an appropriate type for creating mutable copies of its argument.	292

Table 11-55   Methods on singleton(<range>)

Function	Description	Page
limited	Returns a limited subtype of a class.	263
make	Returns a general instance of its first argument.	258

Strings

<string>   **[Open Abstract Instantiable Class]**

The class of sequences with elements that are characters.

Superclasses: <mutable-sequence>

Init-keywords: The class <string> supports the following init-keywords:

size: An instance of <integer> specifying the size of the string. The default value is 0.

fill: An instance of <character> specifying the initial value for each element. The default value is ' ' (space).

Description: The class <string> is used for holding sequences of characters.

<string> has no direct instances; calling make on <string> will return an instance of a concrete subclass of <string>.

The element type of <string> is indefinite $\Leftarrow$ <character>.

Operations: The class <string> provides the following operations:

Table 11-56   Methods on <string>

Function	Description	Page
<	Returns true if its first operand is less than its second operand.	271
as-lowercase	Coerces an object to lowercase.	291
as-lowercase!	Coerces an object to lowercase in place.	291
as-uppercase	Coerces an object to uppercase.	290
as-uppercase!	Coerces an object to uppercase in place.	290

Table 11-57   Methods on singleton(<string>)

Function	Description	Page
limited	Returns a limited subtype of a class.	263

<byte-string>   **[Sealed Instantiable Class]**

The class of vectors with elements that are eight-bit characters.

Superclasses: <string> <vector>

Init-keywords: The class <byte-string> supports the following init-keywords:

size: An instance of <integer> specifying the size of the byte string. The default value is 0.

fill: An instance of <character> specifying the initial value for each element. The default value is ' ' (space).

Description: The class <byte-string> represents strings with elements that are eight bit characters. It provides constant time element and element-setter methods.

The element type of <byte-string> is indefinite $\Leftarrow K_2$ (where K_2 is a subtype of <character>).

Collections   **233**

Operations: The class <byte-string> provides the following operations:

Table 11-58   Methods on <byte-string>

Function	Description	Page
element	Returns the collection element associated with a particular key.	300
element-setter	Sets the collection element associated with a particular key.	301

<unicode-string>   **[Sealed Instantiable Class]**

The class of vectors with elements that are sixteen-bit Unicode characters.

Superclasses: <string> <vector>

Init-keywords: The class <unicode-string> supports the following init-keywords:

size: An instance of <integer> specifying the size of the unicode string. The default value is 0.

fill: An instance of <character> specifying the initial value for each element. The default value is ' ' (space).

Description: The class <unicode-string> represents strings with elements that are sixteen bit Unicode characters. It provides constant time element and element-setter methods.

The element type of <unicode-string> is indefinite $\Leftarrow K_1$ (where K_1 is a subtype of <character>).

Operations: The class `<unicode-string>` provides the following operations:

Table 11-59 Methods on <unicode-string>

Function	Description	Page
element	Returns the collection element associated with a particular key.	300
element-setter	Sets the collection element associated with a particular key.	301

Tables

Also called a hash table, a table is an unordered mapping between arbitrary keys and elements. Tables are the only predefined collections that are unstable under iteration.

Tables are stretchy in that they allow the addition and removal of keys. `<table>` and its subclasses are the only predefined classes that are stretchy but are not stretchy sequences.

For a complete description of tables, see "Tables" on page 122.

`<table>`   **[Open Abstract Instantiable Primary Class]**

The class of tables (also known as hash tables).

Superclasses: `<mutable-explicit-key-collection>` `<stretchy-collection>`

Init-keywords: The class <table> supports the following init-keyword:

size: An instance of <integer>. If specified, this value provides a hint to the implementation as to the expected number of elements to be stored in the table, which might be used to control how much space to initially allocate for the table. The default value is unspecified.

Description: The class <table> is the only predefined instantiable subclass of `<explicit-key-collection>`.

Every concrete subclass of <table> must provide or inherit a method for table-protocol. For details, see "Tables" on page 122.

<table> has no direct instances; calling make on <table> will return an instance of <object-table>.

The element type of <table> is indefinite $\Leftarrow$ <object>.

Operations: The class <table> provides the following operations:

Table 11-60   Generic Functions on <table>

Function	Description	Page
table-protocol	Returns functions used to implement the iteration protocol for tables.	340

Table 11-61   Methods on <table>

Function	Description	Page
forward-iteration -protocol	Returns a group of functions used to iterate over the elements of a collection.	337
table-protocol	Returns functions used to implement the iteration protocol for tables.	340
remove-key!	Modifies an explicit key collection so it no longer has a particular key.	335
element	Returns the collection element associated with a particular key.	300
element-setter	Sets the collection element associated with a particular key.	301
size	Returns the size of its argument.	295
key-test	Returns the function used by its collection argument to compare keys.	298

Table 11-62   Methods on singleton(<table>)

Function	Description	Page
limited	Returns a limited subtype of a class.	263
make	Returns a general instance of its first argument.	258

<object-table>   **[Open Abstract Instantiable Class]**

The class of tables that compare keys using == .

Superclasses: <table>

Init-keywords: None.

Description: Calling make on <table> will return a general instance of <object-table>. Because <object-table> is abstract and instantiable but has no specified subclasses, every implementation must provide one or more concrete subclasses to instantiate. These concrete subclasses have no specified names, and their names are not exported by the Dylan module.

The element type of <object-table> is indefinite $\Leftarrow$ <object>.

Operations: The class <object-table> provides the following operations:

Table 11-63   Methods on <object-table>

Function	Description	Page
table-protocol	Returns functions used to implement the iteration protocol for tables.	340

Table 11-64   Methods on singleton(<object-table>)

Function	Description	Page
limited	Returns a limited subtype of a class.	263

Functions

Functions are the objects that accept arguments, perform computations, and return values.

Figure 11-5 shows the built-in function classes and some of their characteristics.

Figure 11-5   The Function Classes

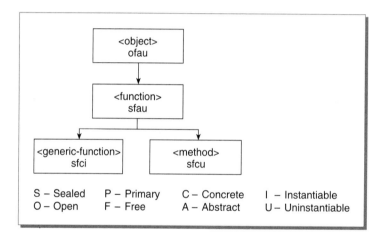

General Functions

`<function>`   **[Sealed Abstract Class]**

The class of objects that can be applied to arguments.

Superclasses: `<object>`

Init-keywords: None.

Description: All functions are instances of <function>. Functions are described in Chapter 6, "Functions."

Operations: The class <function> provides the following operations:

Table 11-65 Functions on <function>

Function	Description	Page
compose	Returns the composition of one or more functions.	346
complement	Returns a function that expresses the complement of a predicate.	346
disjoin	Returns a function that expresses the disjunction of one or more predicates.	347
conjoin	Returns a function that expresses the conjunction of one or more predicates.	347
curry	Returns a function based on an existing function and a number of default initial arguments.	348
rcurry	Returns a function based on an existing function and a number of default final arguments.	349
function-specializers	Returns the specializers of a function.	353
function-arguments	Returns information about the arguments accepted by a function.	354
function-return-values	Returns information about the values returned by a function.	354
applicable-method?	Tests if a function is applicable to sample arguments.	355
apply	Applies a function to arguments.	350
do	Iterates over one or more collections for side effect.	327

continued

Table 11-65   Functions on <function> (continued)

Function	Description	Page
map	Iterates over one or more collections and collects the results in a freshly allocated collection.	328
map-as	Iterates over one or more collections and collects the results in a freshly allocated collection of a specified type.	328
map-into	Iterates over one or more collections and collects the results in an existing mutable collection.	329
any?	Returns the first true value obtained by iterating over one or more collections.	330
every?	Returns true if a predicate returns true when applied to all corresponding elements of a set of collections.	331
reduce	Combines the elements of a collection and a seed value into a single value by repeatedly applying a binary function.	331
reduce1	Combines the elements of a collection into a single value by repeatedly applying a binary function, using the first element of the collection as the seed value.	332
find-key	Returns the key in a collection such that the corresponding collection element satisfies a predicate.	335
replace-elements!	Replaces those collection elements that satisfy a predicate.	336

continued

Table 11-65   Functions on <function> (continued)

Function	Description	Page
choose	Returns those elements of a sequence that satisfy a predicate.	333
choose-by	Returns those elements of a sequence that correspond to those in another sequence that satisfy a predicate.	333
do-handlers	Applies a function to all dynamically active handlers.	362

Generic Functions

<generic-function>   **[Sealed Instantiable Class]**

The class of functions that are made up of a number of individual methods.

Superclasses: <function>

Init-keywords: The class <generic-function> supports the following init-keywords:

required: An instance of <number> or <sequence>.

This argument represents the required arguments that the generic function accepts. If a sequence is supplied, the size of the sequence is the number of required arguments, and the elements of the sequence are the specializers. If a number is supplied, it is the number of required arguments, and the specializers default to <object>. If the argument is not supplied, or the supplied argument is neither a sequence nor a non-negative integer, an error is signaled.

rest?:   An instance of <boolean>.

A true value indicates that the generic function accepts a variable number of arguments. The default value is #f.

key: #f or an instance of <collection> whose elements are keywords.

If the value is a collection, then the generic function accepts keyword arguments, and the collection specifies the set of mandatory keywords for the generic function. A value of #f indicates that the generic function does not accept keyword arguments. The default value is #f.

all-keys?: An instance of <boolean>.

A true value indicates that the generic function accepts all keyword arguments. The default value is #f.

Description: The class of generic functions. Generic functions are described in Chapter 6, "Functions."

The arguments describe the shape of the generic function's parameter list, and thereby control which methods can be added to the generic function. See the section "Kinds of Parameter Lists" on page 86 and the section "Parameter List Congruency" on page 93 for the implications of these choices.

An error is signaled if the value of rest?: is true and the value of key: is a collection. While a method parameter list may specify both #rest and #key, a generic function parameter list cannot.

An error is signaled if the value of all-keys?: is true and the value of key: is #f.

A new generic function initially has no methods. An error will be signaled if a generic function is called before methods are added to it. Once a generic function is created, you can give it behavior by adding methods to it with add-method or define method.

Generic functions are not usually created by calling make directly. Most often they are created by define generic or implicitly by define method.

Operations: The class <generic-function> provides the following operations:

Table 11-66   Functions on <generic-function>

Function	Description	Page
generic-function-methods	Returns the methods of a generic function.	351
add-method	Adds a method to a generic function.	352
generic-function-mandatory-keywords	Returns the mandatory keywords of a generic function, if any.	353
sorted-applicable-methods	Returns all the methods in a generic function that are applicable to sample arguments, sorted in order of specificity.	356
find-method	Returns the method in a generic function that has particular specializers.	356
remove-method	Removes a method from a generic function.	357

Methods

<method>   **[Sealed Class]**

The class of functions that are applicable to arguments of a specified type.

Superclasses: <function>

Init-keywords: None.

Description: The class of methods. Methods are described in Chapter 6, "Functions."

Operations: The class <method> provides the following operations:

Table 11-67   Functions on <method>

Function	Description	Page
add-method	Adds a method to a generic function.	352
remove-method	Removes a method from a generic function.	357

Conditions

Conditions are used to describe and signal exceptional situations.

Figure 11-6 shows the built-in condition classes and some of their characteristics.

Figure 11-6   The Condition Classes

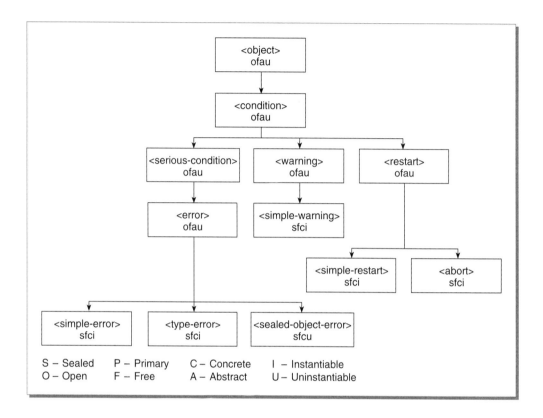

General Conditions

<condition>   **[Open Abstract Class]**

The class of objects used by the condition system to connect a signaler with an appropriate handler.

Superclasses: `<object>`

Init-keywords: None.

Description: The class of condition objects. A complete description of conditions is given in Chapter 7, "Conditions."

Operations: The class <condition> provides the following operations:

Table 11-68 Functions on <condition>

Function	Description	Page
signal	Signals a condition.	357
error	Signals a nonrecoverable error.	358
cerror	Signals a correctable error.	359
break	Invokes the debugger.	359

Table 11-69 Generic functions on <condition>

Function	Description	Page
default-handler	Called if no dynamic handler handles a condition.	361
return-query	Queries the user for values to return.	362
return-allowed?	Returns true if a condition's recovery protocol allows returning values.	363
return-description	Returns a description of a condition's returned values.	363

Table 11-70 Methods on <condition>

Function	Description	Page
default-handler	Called if no dynamic handler handles a condition.	361

Serious Conditions

<hr>

<serious-condition>   **[Open Abstract Class]**

<hr>

The class of conditions that cannot safely be ignored.

Superclasses: `<condition>`

Init-keywords: None.

Description: The class of conditions that cannot safely be ignored.

Operations: The following operation is defined on `<serious-condition>`:

Table 11-71   Methods on <serious-condition>

Function	Description	Page
`default-handler`	Called if no dynamic handler handles a condition.	361

Errors

<hr>

<error>   **[Open Abstract Class]**

<hr>

The class of conditions that represent something invalid about the program.

Superclasses: `<serious-condition>`

Init-keywords: None.

Description: The class of serious conditions that represent program errors.

               `<error>` is distinct from `<serious-condition>` so one can establish a handler for errors that does not also trap unpredictable environmental exceptions such as network problems.

Operations: None.

<simple-error>   **[Sealed Instantiable Class]**

The class of error conditions that consist of just an error message constructed from a format string and arguments.

Superclasses: <error>

Init-keywords: format-string:

An instance of <string>. A format string describing the error.

format-arguments:

An instance of <sequence>. Format arguments to splice into the format string to describe the error.

Description: The class of error conditions that consist of just an error message constructed from a format string and arguments.

The recovery protocol of <simple-error> is empty.

Operations: The class <simple-error> provides the following operations:

Table 11-72   Functions on <simple-error>

Function	Description	Page
condition-format-string	Returns the format string of a simple condition.	364
condition-format-arguments	Returns the format arguments of a simple condition.	364

<type-error>   **[Sealed Instantiable Class]**

The class of error conditions generated by type checks.

Superclasses: <error>

Init-keywords: value: An instance of <object>. The object whose type was checked.

type: An instance of <type>. The type that was expected. The error
             was signaled because the object was not of this type.

Description: The class of errors indicating that an object was not of the expected type.

The recovery protocol is empty.

Operations: The class <type-error> provides the following operations::

Table 11-73   Functions on <type-error>

Function	Description	Page
type-error-value	Returns the value that was not of the expected type.	365
type-error-expected-type	Returns the expected type of the type check that led to the type error.	365

<sealed-object-error>   [Sealed Class]

The class of errors that are generated by sealing violations.

Superclasses: <error>

Init-keywords: None.

Description: The class of errors that indicate the violation of a sealing restriction.

Operations: None.

Warnings

<warning>   [Open Abstract Class]

The class of conditions that are interesting to users but can safely be ignored.

Superclasses: <condition>

Init-keywords: None.

Operations: The following operation is defined on <warning>:

Table 11-74   Methods on <warning>

Function	Description	Page
default-handler	Called if no dynamic handler handles a condition.	361

Description: The class of conditions that can be safely ignored.

There is a default handler for <warning> that displays the warning in a user-interface dependent way and then returns #f. The recovery protocol is that any value can be returned and will be ignored.

<simple-warning>   **[Sealed Instantiable Class]**

A default class of warnings that are described by a warning string.

Superclasses: <warning>

Init-keywords: format-string:
> An instance of <string>. A format string describing the warning.

format-arguments:
> An instance of <sequence>. Format arguments to splice into the format string to describe the warning.

Description: The class of warnings described by a format string and arguments.

The recovery protocol is that any value can be returned and will be ignored.

Operations: The class <simple-warning> provides the following operations:

Table 11-75   Functions on <simple-warning>

Function	Description	Page
condition-format-string	Returns the format string of a simple condition.	364
condition-format-arguments	Returns the format arguments of a simple condition.	364

Restarts

<restart>	**[Open Abstract Class]**

The class of conditions used for restarting a computation.

Superclasses: <condition>

Init-keywords: condition: #f or an instance of <condition>. This argument is accepted and ignored by <restart>; some subclasses save the value of this initialization argument and use it to associate a restart with a particular condition from which the restart can recover. No such subclasses are defined as part of the language. Other restarts do not care; they can recover from any condition.

Description: The class of conditions used to correct an unusual situation.

There is a default handler for <restart> that signals an error reporting an attempt to use a restart for which no restart handler was established. The recovery protocol concept is not applicable to restarts.

Operations: The class <restart> provides the following operations:

Table 11-76   Generic functions on <restart>

Function	Description	Page
restart-query	Called to query the user and restart.	361

Table 11-77   Methods on <restart>

Function	Description	Page
default-handler	Called if no dynamic handler handles a condition.	361

<simple-restart>   **[Sealed Instantiable Class]**

A default class of restarts.

Superclasses: <restart>

Init-keywords: format-string:
                      An instance of <string>. A format string describing the restart.
                      format-arguments:
                      An instance of <sequence>. Format arguments to splice into
                      the format string to describe the restart.

Description: A default class of restarts.

                      Typical implementations will use the format string and format arguments to
                      produce a description of the restart.

Operations: The class <simple-restart> provides the following operations:

Table 11-78   Functions on <simple-restart>

Function	Description	Page
condition-format-string	Returns the format string of a simple condition.	364
condition-format-arguments	Returns the format arguments of a simple condition.	364

Aborts

<abort>   **[Sealed Instantiable Class]**

The class of conditions used to terminate a computation.

Superclasses: <restart>

Init-keywords: None.

Description: The class of conditions used to terminate a computation.

Handlers are expected to terminate execution of the current application command, or similar unit of execution, and return control to something like an application command loop. This is comparable to command-period on the Macintosh. The exact details of this feature depend on the particular environment, of course, but signaling an instance of <abort> is a uniform way to "get out."

Operations: None.

The Built-In Functions

Contents

Overview   257
Constructing and Initializing Instances   258
   General Constructor   258
   Initialization   260
   Specific Constructors   261
Equality and Comparison   267
   Logical Negation   268
   Equality Comparisons   268
   Magnitude Comparisons   271
Arithmetic Operations   274
   Properties   275
   Arithmetic Operations   277
Coercing and Copying Objects   287
   General Coercion Function   288
   Coercing Case   290
   Copying Objects   292
Collection Operations   294
   Collection Properties   294
   Selecting Elements   300
   Adding and Removing Elements   309
   Reordering Elements   316
   Set Operations   319
   Subsequence Operations   323
   Mapping and Reducing   327
   The Iteration Protocol   337
Reflective Operations on Types   343

Functional Operations   346
Function Application   350
Reflective Operations on Functions   351
Operations on Conditions   357
   Signaling Conditions   357
   Handling Conditions   361
   Introspection on Conditions   362

Overview

This chapter contains an entry for each function defined by Dylan.

The functions described below are annotated either as an "open generic function" or as a "function."

A function specified as an "open generic function" can be extended through the addition of programmer defined methods. The signature of the generic function constrains which methods can be added through the congruency rules described on page 93. The signature does not imply a set of predefined methods. For example, the signature of + is (`<object>`, `<object>`), but the predefined methods on + only cover subtypes of `<number>`. Particular behavior of the function is given in its description and in the description of its methods.

A function specified as a "function" cannot portably be extended through the addition of methods. Implementations are free to implement these functions as open generic functions, but programs that take advantage of such liberality will not be portable. The signature of such a function specifies the types of the arguments to which the function may be applicable, but does not necessarily imply that the function is applicable to all instances of the types. The exact behavior of the function is given in its description.

Implementations are allowed to define these generic functions and functions with signatures that are less restrictive than those given below. However, programs that take advantage of this liberality will not be portable.

When a method is specified, it describes the behavior of a generic function when applied to arguments of particular types. It does not imply that this behavior is implemented by a single method. A method described as "sealed" specifies a sealed domain covering the generic function and specializers of the method.

Where a sealed domain is specified, implementations are free to seal the domain or leave the domain unsealed. Portable programs should not rely on the domain being unsealed.

Constructing and Initializing Instances

Instance creation and initialization is performed by the open generic functions `make` and `initialize`. For an overview of the allocation and initialization process, see "Instance Creation and Initialization" beginning on page 64.

General Constructor

make	[Open Generic Function]

Returns a general instance of its first argument.

Signature: `make` *type* `#rest` *supplied-init-args* `#key #all-keys` ⇒ *instance*

Arguments: *type* An instance of `<type>`.

supplied-init-args Keyword/argument pairs.

Values: *instance* An `<object>`, which must be a general instance of *type*.

Description: Returns an instance of *type*, with characteristics specified by keyword arguments.

The *instance* returned is guaranteed to be a general instance of *type* but not necessarily a direct instance of *type*. This liberality allows `make` to be called on an abstract class or other type; it can instantiate and return a direct instance of one of the concrete subtypes of the abstract class or type.

The *instance* returned may or may not be newly allocated. If a new instance is allocated, `make` will call `initialize` on the instance before returning it.

Programmers may customize `make` for particular classes by defining methods specialized by singleton specializers. These methods may obtain the default `make` behavior, if desired, by calling next-method.

Note that the `<class>` method on `make` returns a newly allocated direct instance of its first argument.

make *class* `#rest` *supplied-init-args* `#key` ⇒ *object*   [G.F. Method]

The method on `<class>` creates an instance of *class*, calls `initialize` on the instance, and then returns the instance. An error is signaled if *class* is abstract.

A complete description of this method and its role in the initialization protocol is given in "Instance Creation and Initialization" on page 64.

make `(singleton (<array>))`
  `#key` *dimensions fill* ⇒ *array*   [Sealed G.F. Method]

The method on `singleton(<array>)` accepts *dimensions* and *fill* keyword arguments, and instantiates a concrete subclass of `<array>`. These arguments are described with the `<array>` class on page 218.

make `(singleton (<deque>))`
  `#key` *size fill* ⇒ *deque*   [Sealed G.F. Method]

The method on `singleton(<deque>)` accepts *size* and *fill* keyword arguments, and instantiates a concrete subclass of `<deque>`. These arguments are described with the `<deque>` class on page 225.

make `(singleton (<range>))`
  `#key` *from by to above below size* ⇒ *deque*   [Sealed G.F. Method]

The method on `singleton(<range>)` accepts a number of keyword arguments, and instantiates a concrete subclass of `<range>`. These arguments are described with the `<range>` class on page 230.

make `(singleton (<table>))`
  `#key` *size* ⇒ *object-table*   [Sealed G.F. Method]

The method on `singleton(<table>)` accepts *size* keyword argument, and instantiates `<object-table>`. The size argument is described with the `<table>` class on page 235.

make `(singleton (<vector>))`
  `#key` *size fill* ⇒ *simple-object-vector*   [Sealed G.F. Method]
make `(singleton (<simple-vector>))`
  `#key` *size fill* ⇒ *simple-object-vector*   [Sealed G.F. Method]

Methods on `singleton(<vector>)` and `singleton(<simple-vector>)` accept *size* and *fill* keyword arguments, and return an instance of

<simple-object-vector>. These arguments are described with the
<vector> class on page 221 and with the <simple-vector> class on
page 222.

make (singleton (<list>))
　　#key *size fill* ⇒ *list*   **[Sealed G.F. Method]**

A method on singleton(<list>) accepts *size* and *fill* keyword arguments.
These arguments are described with the <list> class on page 227.

Initialization

initialize   **[Open Generic Function]**

Performs instance initialization that cannot be specified declaratively by a class
definition.

Signature: initialize *instance* #key #all-keys ⇒ #rest *objects*

Arguments: *instance*   An instance of <object>.

Values: *objects*   Instances of <object>. The return values are ignored by
     make.

Description: Provides a way for users to handle initialization of instances which cannot be
expressed simply by init specifications. This is typically needed when a
computation requires inputs from multiple initialization arguments or slot
values, or a single computation needs to be used to initialize multiple slots.

By convention, all initialize methods should call next-method very early,
to make sure that any initializations from less specific classes are performed
first.

The initialize generic function permits all keywords and requires none. It
does this because the keyword argument checking is performed by the default
method on make.

initialize *object* **#key** ⇒ *object*   **[G.F. Method]**

This method does nothing. It is present so that it is always safe for
initialize methods to call next method, and so that it is safe for the default
make method to call initialize.

---

slot-initialized?   **[Open Generic Function]**

Tests whether a slot has been initialized

Signature: slot-initialized? *instance getter* ⇒ *boolean*

Arguments: *instance*   An instance of of <object>.

                 getter   An instance of <generic-function>.

Values: *boolean*   An instance of <boolean>.

Description: Returns true if the slot in *instance* that would be accessed by the *getter* generic
function is initialized. If the slot is not initialized, then false is returned.

slot-initialized? will signal an error if the *getter* does not access a slot in
the *instance*.

To support slot-initialized? for a virtual slot, programmers must define
a method for slot-initialized? that shares a protocol with the getter of
the slot.

Specific Constructors

---

list   **[Function]**

Creates and returns a freshly allocated list.

Signature: list #rest *arguments* ⇒ *list*

Arguments: *arguments*   The elements of the *list*. Instances of <object>.

Values: *list*   A freshly allocated instance of <list>.

Description: Returns a freshly allocated list containing the *arguments*, in order.

`pair`   **[Function]**

Creates and returns a freshly allocated pair.

Signature: `pair` *object1* , *object2* ⇒ *pair*

Arguments: *object1*   An instance of `<object>`.

               object2   An instance of `<object>`.

Values: *pair*   A freshly allocated instance of `<pair>`.

Description: Creates a freshly allocated pair whose head value is *object1* and tail value is *object2*.

```
pair (1, 2)
  ⇒ #(1 . 2)
pair (1, #(2, 3, 4, 5))
  ⇒ #(1, 2, 3, 4, 5)
```

Note that while the pair returned by `pair` is freshly allocated, it may be the beginning of a list, portions of which are not freshly allocated.

```
define variable *preexisting-list* = list(2, 3, 4)
define variable *new-list* = pair(1, *preexisting-list*)
*new-list*
  ⇒ #(1, 2, 3, 4)
tail(*new-list*) == *preexisting-list*
  ⇒ #t
third(*new-list*) := 'x'
*new-list*
  ⇒  #(1, 2, x, 4)
*preexisting-list*
  ⇒  #(2, x, 4)
```

range	[Function]

Creates and returns a range.

Signature: range #key *from to above below by size* ⇒ *range*

Arguments:

from	An instance of `<real>`. The default value is 0.
to	An instance of `<real>`.
above	An instance of `<real>`.
below	An instance of `<real>`.
by	An instance of `<real>`. The default value is 0.
size	An instance of `<real>`.

Values:

range	An instance of `<range>`.

Description: Creates an instance of `<range>`. The arguments correspond to the initialization arguments of `<range>`, described on page 230.

singleton	[Function]

Creates and returns a singleton.

Signature: singleton *object* ⇒ *singleton*

Arguments:

object	An instance of `<object>`.

Values:

singleton	An instance of `<singleton>`. The singleton for *object*.

Description: Returns a singleton for *object*. singleton(*object*) is equivalent to make(`<singleton>`, object: *object*). If a singleton for the specified object already exists, implementations are free to return it rather than allocate a new singleton.

limited	[Function]

Returns a limited subtype of a class.

Signature: limited *class* #key ⇒ *type*

| **Arguments:** | *class* | An instance of `<class>`. |
| **Values:** | *type* | An instance of `<type>`. |

Description: Returns a limited subtype of *class*. The available keyword arguments depend on the *class*. Not all classes support `limited`; those that do are documented in the method descriptions below.

Note that an implementation is not required to implement `limited` as a generic function, and so the behavior embodied in the following method descriptions need not actually be implemented by separate methods. The behavior is described as a set of methods for convenience of presentation only.

limited (singleton (`<integer>`)) **#key** *min max* ⇒ *type*[Sealed G.F. Method]

Returns a limited integer type, which is a subtype of `<integer>` whose instances are integers greater than or equal to *min* (if min: is specified) and less than or equal to *max* (if max: is specified). If no keyword arguments are specified, the result type is equivalent to `<integer>`. Limited integer types are not instantiable.

limited (singleton (`<collection>`))
    #key *of size* ⇒ *type*　　　　　　　　　　　　[Sealed G.F. Method]
limited (singleton (`<explicit-key-collection>`))
    #key *of size* ⇒ *type*　　　　　　　　　　　　[Sealed G.F. Method]
limited (singleton (`<mutable-collection>`))
    #key *of size* ⇒ *type*　　　　　　　　　　　　[Sealed G.F. Method]
limited (singleton (`<stretchy-collection>`))
    #key *of size* ⇒ *type*　　　　　　　　　　　　[Sealed G.F. Method]
limited (singleton (`<mutable-explicit-key-collection>`))
    #key *of size* ⇒ *type*　　　　　　　　　　　　[Sealed G.F. Method]
limited (singleton (`<sequence>`))
    #key *of size* ⇒ *type*　　　　　　　　　　　　[Sealed G.F. Method]
limited (singleton (`<mutable-sequence>`))
    #key *of size* ⇒ *type*　　　　　　　　　　　　[Sealed G.F. Method]

These methods return uninstantiable limited collection types.

limited (singleton (<table>))
> **#key** *of size* ⇒ *type*   [Sealed G.F. Method]

limited (singleton (<object-table>))
> **#key** *of size* ⇒ *type*   [Sealed G.F. Method]

These two methods return types that support a `size:` initialization keyword with the same behavior as `<table>`.

limited (singleton (<array>))
> **#key** *of size dimensions* ⇒ *type*   [Sealed G.F. Method]

This method returns a type that supports `dimensions:` and `fill:` initialization keywords with the same behavior as `<array>`. The default for fill is `#f` so if `instance?(#f, of)` is not true and the product of the *dimensions* is nonzero, the `fill:` initialization keyword is required because the default would cause a type error.

Instantiating *type* with a value of *dimensions* that has one element will return an instance of `limited(<simple-vector>, of: of)`.

limited (singleton (<vector>))
> **#key** *of size* ⇒ *type*   [Sealed G.F. Method]

This method returns the same types as the method on `singleton(<simple-vector>)`.

limited (singleton (<simple-vector>))
> **#key** *of size* ⇒ *type*   [Sealed G.F. Method]

limited (singleton (<stretchy-vector>))
> **#key** *of* ⇒ *type*   [Sealed G.F. Method]

limited (singleton (<deque>))
> **#key** *of* ⇒ *type*   [Sealed G.F. Method]

These three methods return types that support `size:` and `fill:` initialization keywords with the same behavior as the collection-class argument. The default for fill is `#f` so if `instance?(#f, of)` is not true and *size* is nonzero, the `fill:` initialization keyword is required because the default would cause a type error.

All general instances of `<simple-vector>` provide a constant time implementation of `element` and `element-setter`.

limited (singleton (<string>))
      #key *of size* ⇒ *type*   **[Sealed G.F. Method]**

The *of* argument must be a subtype of <character>. This method returns a type that supports size: and fill: initialization keywords with the same behavior as <string>. The default for fill: is ' ' so if instance?(' ', *of*) is not true and *size* is nonzero, the fill: initialization keyword is required because the default would cause a type error.

There are no specified subtypes of <character>, except for unions of singletons, which makes this method rather useless for portable programs. However, the method is provided because there might be useful subtypes of <character> in a particular implementation or in future versions of Dylan.

limited (singleton (<range>))
      #key *of* ⇒ *type*   **[Sealed G.F. Method]**

The *of* argument must be a subtype of <real>. This method returns a type that supports from:, to:, below:, above:, by:, and size: initialization keywords with the same behavior as <range>. Make of this type signals a <type-error> if any element of the range is not an instance of *of*.

---

type-union   **[Function]**

Returns the union of two or more types.

Signature: type-union *type1* #rest *more-types* ⇒ *type*

Arguments: *type1*   An instance of <type>.

                       more-types   Instances of <type>.

Values: *type*   An instance of <type>.

Description: Returns a type whose instances are the instances of *type1* and all the *more-types*. The type returned is not instantiable. A complete description of union types is given in "Union Types" on page 72.

```
define constant $my-enumerated-type =
                type-union(singleton(#"one"),
                           singleton(#"two"),
                           singleton(#"three"),
                           singleton(#"four"),
                           singleton(#"five"))
```

vector   **[Function]**

Creates and returns a freshly allocated vector.

Signature: vector #rest *arguments* ⇒ *vector*

Arguments: *arguments*   Instances of <object>.

Values: *vector*   A freshly allocated instance of <simple-object-vector>.
                                        Its elements are the *arguments*, in order.

Description: Returns a vector whose elements are the *arguments*, in order.

Equality and Comparison

Dylan provides an identity function, as well as a group of equality and
magnitude comparison functions that can be extended for user classes. The
functions ~=, ~==, >, <=, >=, min and max are defined in terms of == or = and
<. By extending the behavior of = and <, programs can extend the behavior of
the other functions.

For the protocol to work, user-defined methods on = and < must preserve the
following properties:

Identity: If (a = b), then (b = a).

Transitivity: If (a < b) and (b < c), then (a < c).

                    If (a = b) and (b = c), then (a = c).

Trichotomy: Exactly one of: (a < b), (a = b), (b < a) always holds
                    (on the assumption that these two operations are defined for
                    the objects in question).

In the general case, the behavior of comparison operators when applied to instances of <complex> is implementation defined. This is to allow implementations to support IEEE floating point when comparing NaNs. However, when instances of <rational> and instances of <float> are compared, it is defined that the instance of <float> is first converted to a rational and then an exact comparison is performed.

Logical Negation

~   **[Function]**

Returns true if its argument is false; otherwise returns false.

Signature: ~ *thing* ⇒ *boolean*

Arguments: *thing*   An instance of <object>.

Values: *boolean*   An instance of <boolean>.

Description: Returns #t if *thing* is false. Returns #f if *thing* is true.

Equality Comparisons

==   **[Function]**

Compares two objects for identity.

Signature: *object1* == *object2* ⇒ *boolean*

Arguments: *object1*   An instance of <object>.
                               object2   An instance of <object>.

Values: *boolean*   An instance of <boolean>.

Description: Returns true if *object1* and *object2* are identical. Otherwise, it returns false.

Objects are considered identical if they are computationally equivalent. That is, there is no way for any possible Dylan program to distinguish them.

At an implementation level, this will usually mean that the objects are pointers to the same storage or are the same immediate value. An extension is made for built-in number classes and characters. Because these objects are not mutable (i.e., cannot be changed), two of the same class with the same value will always be the same (and will thus be indistinguishable to programs).

~==   [Function]

Compares two objects for nonidentity.

Signature: *object1* ~== *object2* ⇒ *boolean*

Arguments: *object1*   An instance of `<object>`.
                  object2   An instance of `<object>`.

Values: *boolean*   An instance of `<boolean>`.

Description: Returns true if *object1* and *object2* are not identical. It returns false if they are identical.

If both arguments are instances of `<complex>` then the result is computed in an implementation-defined way. Otherwise, the result is computed by `~(object1 == object2)`.

=   [Open Generic Function]

Compares two objects for equality.

Signature: *object1* = *object2* ⇒ *boolean*

Arguments: *object1*   An instance of `<object>`.
                  object2   An instance of `<object>`.

Values: *boolean*   An instance of `<boolean>`.

Description: Returns true if *object1* and *object2* are equal. Otherwise, it returns false.

Programmers may define methods for = specialized on classes they define. A programmer may be required to provide an = method when defining subclasses of some predefined classes in order to fullfill the protocol of the class, as described below. For objects that do not have a more specific = method, = returns the same as ==.

= is not guaranteed to return. For example, it may not return when called on circular structures or otherwise unbounded structures.

In addition to the sealed domains specified by the methods below, = is sealed over the following domains:

```
<object>, <symbol>
<symbol>, <object>
<object>, <character>
<character>, <object>
<object>, <boolean>
<boolean>, <object>
```

object1 = object2 ⇒ boolean   [G.F. Method]

The default method on = calls == and returns the result returned by ==.

complex1 = complex2 ⇒ boolean   [Sealed G.F. Method]

Complex numbers are equal if they have the same mathematical value.

collection1 = collection2 ⇒ boolean   [G.F. Method]

Two collections are equal if they have identical key-test functions, they have the same keys (as determined by their key-test functions), the elements at corresponding keys are =, and neither collection is a dotted list.

sequence$_1$ = sequence$_2$ ⇒ boolean   [G.F. Method]

For sequences, = returns true if sequence$_1$ and sequence$_2$ have the same size and elements with = keys are =, and returns false otherwise.

list₁ = *list₂* ⇒ *boolean*   **[Sealed G.F. Method]**

For lists, = returns true if the two lists are the same size, corresponding elements of *list₁* and *list₂* are = and the final tails are =. It returns false otherwise.

list = *sequence* ⇒ *boolean*   **[G.F. Method]**
sequence = *list* ⇒ *boolean*   **[G.F. Method]**

For mixed lists and sequences, = returns true if the *list* is not a dotted list, both have the same size, and elements with = keys are =. It returns false otherwise.

range1 = *range2* ⇒ *boolean*   **[Sealed G.F. Method]**

When called with two ranges, = always terminates, even if one or both ranges are unbounded in size.

~=   **[Function]**

Compares two objects for inequality.

Signature: *object1* ~= *object2* ⇒ *boolean*

Arguments: *object1*   An instance of `<object>`.
                     object2   An instance of `<object>`.

Values: *boolean*   An instance of `<boolean>`.

Description: Returns true if *object1* and *object2* are not equal. It returns false if they are equal.

If both arguments are instances of `<complex>` then the result is computed in an implementation-defined way. Otherwise, the result is computed by the expression ~ (*object1* = *object2*).

Magnitude Comparisons

<   **[Open Generic Function]**

Returns true if its first operand is less than its second operand.

Signature: *object1* < *object2* ⇒ *boolean*

Arguments: *object1*   An instance of <object>.

                object2   An instance of <object>.

Values: *boolean*   An instance of <boolean>.

Description: Returns true if *object1* is less than *object2*.

The generic function < is sealed over the domain (<complex>, <complex>).

real1 < *real2* ⇒ *boolean*   [Sealed G.F. Method]

Built-in real numbers are compared by mathematical value.

character1 < *character2* ⇒ *boolean*   [Sealed G.F. Method]

Characters are compared by the ordinal value of the underlying character set. Character case is significant.

string1 < *string2* ⇒ *boolean*   [G.F. Method]

When both arguments are strings, < compares strings by comparing elements from left to right, using < and = on corresponding elements, and stopping when the elements are not =. If one string is a strict prefix of the other, the shorter string is considered the "smaller" one.

For variations on string comparison (such as comparisons that ignore case), different comparison operators must be used.

>   [Function]

Returns true if its first operand is greater than its second operand.

Signature: *object1* > *object2* ⇒ *boolean*

Arguments: *object1*   An instance of <object>.

                object2   An instance of <object>.

Values: *boolean*   An instance of <boolean>.

Description: Returns true if *object1* is greater than *object2*.

If both arguments are instances of `<complex>` then the result is computed in an implementation-defined way. Otherwise, the result is computed by the expression (*object2* < *object1*).

`<=`   **[Function]**

Returns true if its first operand is less than or equal to its second operand.

Signature: *object1* `<=` *object2* ⇒ *boolean*

Arguments: *object1*   An instance of `<object>`.

object2   An instance of `<object>`.

Values: *boolean*   An instance of `<boolean>`.

Description: Returns true if *object1* is less than or equal to *object2*.

If both arguments are instances of `<complex>` then the result is computed in an implementation-defined way. Otherwise, the result is computed by the expression ~ (*object2* < *object1*).

`>=`   **[Function]**

Returns true if its first operand is greater than or equal to its second operand.

Signature: *object1* `>=` *object2* ⇒ *boolean*

Arguments: *object1*   An instance of `<object>`.

object2   An instance of `<object>`.

Values: *boolean*   An instance of `<boolean>`.

Description: Returns true if *object1* is greater than or equal to *object2*.

If both arguments are instances of `<complex>` then the result is computed in an implementation-defined way. Otherwise, the result is computed by the expression ~ (*object1* < *object2*).

min	[Function]

Returns the least of its arguments.

Signature: min *object1* #rest *objects* ⇒ *object2*

Arguments: *object1*   An instance of <object>.

objects   Zero or more instances of <object>.

Values: *object2*   An instance of <object>.

Description: Returns the least of its arguments.

min operates by calling <, and therefore is applicable to any objects for which < is defined.

max	[Function]

Returns the greatest of its arguments.

Signature: max *object1* #rest *objects* ⇒ *object2*

Arguments: *object1*   An instance of <object>.

objects   Zero or more instances of <object>.

Values: *object2*   An instance of <object>.

Description: Returns the greatest of its arguments.

max operates by calling <, and therefore is applicable to any objects for which < is defined.

Arithmetic Operations

When instances of <rational> and instances of <float> are combined by a numerical function, the instance of <rational> is first converted to an instance of <float> of the same format as the original instance of <float>.

Properties

---

odd?   **[Function]**

Tests for the property of being an odd number.

Signature: odd? *integer* ⇒ *boolean*

Arguments: *integer*   An instance of `<integer>`.

Values: *boolean*   An instance of `<boolean>`.

Description: Returns true if its argument is an odd number.

---

even?   **[Function]**

Tests for the property of being an even number.

Signature: even? *integer* ⇒ *boolean*

Arguments: *integer*   An instance of `<integer>`.

Values: *boolean*   An instance of `<boolean>`.

Description: Returns true if its argument is an even number.

---

zero?   **[Open Generic Function]**

Tests for the property of being equal to zero.

Signature: zero? *object* ⇒ *boolean*

Arguments: *object*   An instance of `<object>`.

Values: *boolean*   An instance of `<boolean>`.

Description: Returns true if its argument is equal to zero.

zero? *complex* ⇒ *boolean*   **[Sealed G.F. Method]**

A method is defined for the class `<complex>`.

`positive?`   **[Open Generic Function]**

Tests for the property of being positive.

Signature: `positive?` *object* ⇒ *boolean*

Arguments: *object*   An instance of `<object>`.

Values: *boolean*   An instance of `<boolean>`.

Description: Returns true if its argument is positive.

positive? *real* ⇒ *boolean*   **[Sealed G.F. Method]**

A method is defined for the class `<real>`.

`negative?`   **[Open Generic Function]**

Tests for the property of being negative.

Signature: `negative?` *object* ⇒ *boolean*

Arguments: *object*   An instance of `<object>`.

Values: *boolean*   An instance of `<boolean>`.

Description: Returns true if its argument is negative.

negative? *real* ⇒ *boolean*   **[Sealed G.F. Method]**

A method is defined for the class `<real>`.

`integral?`   **[Open Generic Function]**

Tests for the property of being integral.

Signature: `integral?` *object* $\Rightarrow$ *boolean*

Arguments: *object*   An instance of `<object>`.

Values: *boolean*   An instance of `<boolean>`.

Description: Returns true if its argument is an integer.

> **`integral?` *object* $\Rightarrow$ *false***   **[G.F. Method]**
>
> A method is defined for the class `<object>` that returns `#f`.

> **`integral?` *real* $\Rightarrow$ *boolean***   **[Sealed G.F. Method]**
>
> A method is defined for real numbers that is equivalent to *real* `=` `round`(*real*).

Arithmetic Operations

`+`   **[Open Generic Function]**

Returns the sum of its arguments.

Signature: *object1* `+` *object2* $\Rightarrow$ `#rest` *objects*

Arguments: *object1*   An instance of `<object>`.
               object2   An instance of `<object>`.

Values: *objects*   Instances of `<object>`.

Description: Adds two objects and returns the sum.

> **_complex1_ `+` _complex2_ $\Rightarrow$ _complex_**   **[Sealed G.F. Method]**
>
> A predefined method returns the sum of two complex numbers.

`*`   **[Open Generic Function]**

Returns the product of its arguments.

Signature: *object1* * *object2* ⇒ #rest *objects*

Arguments: *object1* An instance of <object>.

object2 An instance of <object>.

Values: *objects* Instances of <object>.

Description: Multiplies two objects and returns the product.

complex1 * complex2 ⇒ **complex** [Sealed G.F. Method]

A predefined method returns the product of two complex numbers.

− _____ [Open Generic Function]

Returns the difference of its arguments.

Signature: *object1* − *object2* ⇒ #rest *objects*

Arguments: *object1* An instance of <object>.

object2 An instance of <object>.

Values: *objects* Instances of <object>.

Description: Subtracts *object2* from *object1* and returns the difference.

complex1 − complex2 ⇒ **complex** [Sealed G.F. Method]

A predefined method returns the difference of two complex numbers.

/ _____ [Open Generic Function]

Returns the quotient of its arguments.

Signature: *object1* / *object2* ⇒ #rest *objects*

Arguments: *object1* An instance of <object>.

object2 An instance of <object>.

Values: *objects*   Instances of <object>.

Description: Divides *object2* into *object1* and returns the quotient.

complex1 / complex2 ⇒ *complex*   **[Sealed G.F. Method]**

A predefined method returns the quotient of two complex numbers.

Division by zero signals an error.

The result of dividing two integers with / is implementation defined. Portable programs should use floor/, ceiling/, round/, or truncate/ to divide two integers.

negative   **[Open Generic Function]**

Returns the negation of an object.

Signature: negative *object1* ⇒ #rest *objects*

Arguments: *object1*   An instance of <object>.

Values: *objects*   Instances of <object>.

Description: Returns the negation of its argument. The unary minus operator is equivalent to a call to the negative in the current binding environment.

negative *real1* ⇒ *real2*   **[Sealed G.F. Method]**

A predefined method returns the additive inverse of a real number.

floor   **[Function]**

Truncates a real number toward negative infinity.

Signature: floor *real1* ⇒ *integer real2*

Arguments: *real1*   An instance of <real>.

The Built-In Functions

Values: *integer*   An instance of <integer>.

real2   An instance of <real>.

Description: Truncates *real1* toward negative infinity. The integer part is returned as *integer*, the remainder is returned as *real2*.

`ceiling`   **[Function]**

Truncates a real number toward positive infinity.

Signature: `ceiling` *real1* ⇒ *integer real2*

Arguments: *real1*   An instance of <real>.

Values: *integer*   An instance of <integer>.

real2   An instance of <real>.

Description: Truncates *real1* toward positive infinity. The integer part is returned as *integer*, the remainder is returned as *real2*.

`round`   **[Function]**

Rounds a real number toward the nearest mathematical integer.

Signature: `round` *real1* ⇒ *integer real2*

Arguments: *real1*   An instance of <real>.

Values: *integer*   An instance of <integer>.

real2   An instance of <real>.

Description: Rounds *real1* toward the nearest mathematical integer. The integer part is returned as *integer*, the remainder is returned as *real2*. If *real1* is exactly between two integers, then the result *integer* will be a multiple of two.

`truncate`   **[Function]**

Truncates a real number toward zero.

Signature: truncate *real1* ⇒ *integer real2*

Arguments: *real1*   An instance of <real>.

Values: *integer*   An instance of <integer>.
              real2   An instance of <real>.

Description: Truncates *real1* toward zero. The integer part is returned as *integer,* the remainder is returned as *real2.*

---

floor/   **[Function]**

Returns the floor of the quotient of two numbers.

Signature: floor/ *real1 real2* ⇒ *integer real3*

Arguments: *real1*   An instance of <real>.
              real2   An instance of <real>.

Values: *integer*   An instance of <integer>.
              real3   An instance of <real>.

Description: Divides *real2* into *real1* and truncates the result toward negative infinity. The integer part of the result is returned as *integer,* the remainder is returned as *real3.*

---

ceiling/   **[Function]**

Returns the ceiling of the quotient of two numbers.

Signature: ceiling/ *real1 real2* ⇒ *integer real3*

Arguments: *real1*   An instance of <real>.
              real2   An instance of <real>.

Values: *integer*   An instance of <integer>.
              real3   An instance of <real>.

Description: Divides *real2* into *real1* and truncates the result toward positive infinity. The integer part of the result is returned as *integer*, the remainder is returned as *real3*.

round/	[Function]

Rounds off the quotient of two numbers.

Signature: round/ *real1 real2* ⇒ *integer real3*

Arguments:

real1	An instance of `<real>`.
real2	An instance of `<real>`.

Values:

integer	An instance of `<integer>`.
real3	An instance of `<real>`.

Description: Divides *real2* into *real1* and rounds the result toward the nearest mathematical integer. The integer part of the result is returned as *integer*, the remainder is returned as *real3*. If the result of the division is exactly between two integers, then the result *integer* will be a multiple of two.

truncate/	[Function]

Returns the truncated quotient of two numbers.

Signature: truncate/ *real1 real2* ⇒ *integer real3*

Arguments:

real1	An instance of `<real>`.
real2	An instance of `<real>`.

Values:

integer	An instance of `<integer>`.
real3	An instance of `<real>`.

Description: Divides *real2* into *real1* and truncates the result toward zero. The integer part of the result is returned as *integer*, the remainder is returned as *real3*.

modulo	[Function]

Returns the second value of `floor/`.

Signature:	`modulo` *real1 real2* ⇒ *real3*	

Arguments:	*real1*	An instance of `<real>`.
	real2	An instance of `<real>`.

Values:	*real3*	An instance of `<real>`.

Description: Returns the second value of `floor/`(*real1*, *real2*).

`remainder`   **[Function]**

Returns the second value of `truncate/`.

Signature:	`remainder` *real1 real2* ⇒ *real3*	

Arguments:	*real1*	An instance of `<real>`.
	real2	An instance of `<real>`.

Values:	*real3*	An instance of `<real>`.

Description: Returns the second value of `truncate/`(*real1*, *real2*).

---

^   **[Open Generic Function]**

Raises an object to a specified power.

Signature:	*object1* ^ *object2* ⇒ `#rest` *objects*	

Arguments:	*object1*	An instance of `<object>`.
	object2	An instance of `<object>`.

Values:	*objects*	Instances of `<object>`.

Description: Returns *object1* raised to the power *object2*. An error is signaled if both arguments are zero.

The Built-In Functions

complex ^ integer ⇒ number   **[Sealed G.F. Method]**

A predefined method raises a complex number to an integral power and
returns the result.

---

abs   **[Open Generic Function]**

Returns the absolute value of its argument.

Signature: abs *object1* ⇒ #rest *objects*

Arguments: *object1*   An instance of <object>.

Values: *objects*   Instances of <object>.

Description: Returns the absolute value of *object1*.

abs complex ⇒ real   **[Sealed G.F. Method]**

A predefined method returns the absolute value of a complex number.

---

logior   **[Function]**

Returns the bitwise inclusive or of its integer arguments.

Signature: logior #rest *integers* ⇒ *integer*

Arguments: *integers*   Zero or more instances of <integer>.

Values: *integer*   An instance of <integer>.

Description: Returns the bitwise inclusive or of the *integers*.

---

logxor   **[Function]**

Returns the bitwise exclusive or of its integer arguments.

Signature: logxor #rest *integers* ⇒ *integer*

Arguments: *integers*   Zero or more instances of <integer>.

Values: *integer* An instance of <integer>.

Description: Returns the bitwise exclusive or of the *integers*.

---

logand [Function]

Returns the bitwise and of its integer arguments.

Signature: logand #rest *integers* ⇒ *integer*

Arguments: *integers* Zero or more instances of <integer>.

Values: *integer* An instance of <integer>.

Description: Returns the bitwise and of the *integers*.

---

lognot [Function]

Returns the bitwise not of its integer argument.

Signature: lognot *integer1* ⇒ *integer2*

Arguments: *integer1* An instance of <integer>.

Values: *integer2* An instance of <integer>.

Description: Returns the bitwise not of the *integer1*.

---

logbit? [Function]

Tests the value of a particular bit in its integer argument.

Signature: logbit? *index integer* ⇒ *boolean*

Arguments: *index* An instance of <integer>.
integer An instance of <integer>.

Values: *boolean* An instance of <boolean>.

Description: Returns true if the *index*th bit in *integer* is a one-bit; otherwise it returns false. Negative *integers* are treated as if they were in two's-complement notation.

---

ash   **[Function]**

Performs an arithmetic shift on its first argument.

Signature: ash *integer1 count* $\Rightarrow$ *integer2*

Arguments: *integer1*   An instance of <integer>.

count   An instance of <integer>.

Values: *integer2*   An instance of <integer>.

Description: Performs an arithmetic shift on the binary representation of *integer1*.

ash shifts *integer1* arithmetically left by *count* bit positions if *count* is positive, or right *count* bit positions if *count* is negative. The shifted value of the same sign as *integer1* is returned.

When ash moves bits to the left, it adds zero-bits at the right. When it moves them to the right, it discards bits.

ash is defined to behave as if *integer1* were represented in two's complement form, regardless of how integers are represented by the implementation.

```
ash(8, 1)
   ⇒ 16
ash(32, -1)
   ⇒ 16
```

---

lcm   **[Open Generic Function]**

Returns the least common multiple of its two arguments.

Signature: lcm *object1 object2* $\Rightarrow$ *object3*

Arguments: *object1*   An instance of <object>.

object2   An instance of <object>.

Values: *object3*   An instance of <object>.

Description: Returns the least common multiple of *object1* and *object2*.

lcm *integer1 integer2* ⇒ *integer3*   **[Sealed G.F. Method]**

A predefined method returns the least common multiple of two integers.

gcd   **[Open Generic Function]**

Returns the greatest common divisor of its two arguments.

Signature: gcd *object1 object2* ⇒ *object3*

Arguments: *object1*   An instance of <object>.
                     object2   An instance of <object>.

Values: *object3*   An instance of <object>.

Description: Returns the greatest common divisor of *object1* and *object2*.

gcd *integer1 integer2* ⇒ *integer3*   **[Sealed G.F. Method]**

A predefined method returns the greatest common divisor of two integers.

Coercing and Copying Objects

The following functions are used to coerce, copy, or simply return objects.

identity   **[Function]**

Returns its argument.

Signature: identity *object* ⇒ *object*

Arguments: *object*   An instance of <object>.

Values: *object*   An instance of `<object>`; the same object that was passed in as an argument.

Description: Returns *object* unaltered.

---

values   **[Function]**

Returns its arguments as multiple values.

Signature: values #rest *the-values* ⟹   #rest *the-values*

Arguments: *the-values*   Zero or more instances of `<object>`.

Values: *the-values*   Zero or more instances of `<object>`; the objects that were passed as arguments.

Description: Returns *the-values* as multiple values.

```
values(1, 2, 3);
⟹ 1    // first value returned
   2    // second value returned
   3    // third value returned
```

General Coercion Function

---

as   **[Open Generic Function]**

Coerces an object to a type.

Signature: as *type object* ⟹ *instance*

Arguments: *type*   An instance of `<type>`.
                  object   An instance of `<object>`.

Values: *instance*   An instance of `<object>`. It must be an instance of *type*.

Description: Coerces *object* to *type*. That is, it returns an instance of *type* that has the same contents as *object*. If *object* is already an instance of *type*, it is returned unchanged. In general, the value returned may or may not be freshly allocated.

Predefined methods allow coercion between integers and characters, between strings and symbols, and between collection types. No methods are predefined for other classes. Programs may define additional methods.

as *collection-type collection* ⇒ *instance-of-collection-type*   [G.F. Method]

When converting between collection types, the return value will have the same number of elements as *collection*. If the *collection* is an instance of <sequence> and the *collection-type* is a subtype of <sequence>, the elements will be in the same order. The individual elements may also undergo some conversion. The specific collection types for which as is defined is implementation defined.

as (singleton (<integer>)) *character* ⇒ *integer*   [Sealed G.F. Method]

This method on as returns a numeric equivalent for *character*. The integer returned is implementation dependent.

as (singleton (<character>)) *integer* ⇒ *character*   [Sealed G.F. Method]

This method on as returns the character equivalent to *integer*. The meaning of *integer* is implementation dependent.

as (singleton (<symbol>)) *string* ⇒ *symbol*   [Sealed G.F. Method]

This method on as returns the symbol that has the name *string*. If the symbol does not yet exist, it is created. This method on as will always return the same symbol for strings of the same characters, without regard to alphabetic case.

```
as (<symbol>, "foo")
  ⇒  #"foo"
#"FOO" == as (<symbol>, "foo")
  ⇒  #t
#"Foo"
  ⇒  #"foo"
```

as (singleton (<string>)) **symbol** ⇒ **string**   [Sealed G.F. Method]

This method on as returns the name of the symbol, which will be a string.

```
as (<string>, #"Foo")
  ⇒ "Foo"
```

Coercing Case

as-uppercase   [Open Generic Function]

Coerces an object to uppercase.

Signature: as-uppercase *object1* ⇒ *object2*

Arguments: *object1*   An instance of <object>.

Values: *object2*   An instance of <object>.

Description: Coerces an object to uppercase and returns the resulting new object.

object1 is not modified by this operation.

as-uppercase *character* ⇒ **uppercase-character**   [Sealed G.F. Method]

This method returns the uppercase equivalent for *character*. If *character* already is uppercase or does not exist in two cases, it is returned unchanged.

as-uppercase *string* ⇒ **new-string**   [G.F. Method]

This method is equivalent to map (as-uppercase, *string*).

as-uppercase!   [Open Generic Function]

Coerces an object to uppercase in place.

Signature: as-uppercase! *object* ⇒ *object*

Arguments: *object*   An instance of <object>.

Values: *object*   An instance of <object>; the same object that was passed in as an argument.

Description: Coerces an object to uppercase in place and returns the modified object.

object may be modified by this operation, and the result will be == to the *object*.

as-uppercase! *string* ⇒ *string*   **[G.F. Method]**

This method is equivalent to map-into(*string* , as-uppercase , *string*).

---

as-lowercase   **[Open Generic Function]**

Coerces an object to lowercase.

Signature: as-lowercase *object1* ⇒ *object2*

Arguments: *object1*   An instance of <object>.

Values: *object2*   An instance of <object>.

Description: Coerces an object to lowercase and returns the resulting new object.

object1 will not be modified by this operation.

as-lowercase *character* ⇒ *lowercase-character*   **[Sealed G.F. Method]**

The <character> method on as-lowercase returns the lowercase equivalent for *character*. If *character* already is lowercase or does not exist in two cases, it is returned unchanged.

as-lowercase *string* ⇒ *new-string*   **[G.F. Method]**

This method is equivalent to map(as-lowercase, *string*).

---

as-lowercase!   **[Open Generic Function]**

Coerces an object to lowercase in place.

Signature: as-lowercase! *object* ⇒ *object*

Arguments:	*object*	An instance of `<object>`.
Values:	*object*	An instance of `<object>`; the same object that was passed in as an argument.

Description: Coerces an object to lowercase in place and returns the modified object.

object may be modified by this operation, and the result will be `==` to the *object*.

---

as-lowercase! *string* ⇒ *string* [G.F. Method]

This method is equivalent to `map-into`(*string* , `as-lowercase`, *string*).

Copying Objects

`shallow-copy` **[Open Generic Function]**

Returns a copy of its argument.

Signature:	`shallow-copy` *object1* ⇒ `#rest` *objects*	
Arguments:	*object1*	An instance of `<object>`.
Values:	*objects*	Instances of `<object>`.

Description: Returns a new object that has the same contents as *object1*. The contents are not copied but are the same objects contained in *object1*.

There is a predefined method for instances of `<collection>`. For other classes, the programmer must provide a method.

---

shallow-copy *collection* ⇒ *new-collection* **[G.F. Method]**

The method for `<collection>` creates a new object by calling `make` on the `type-for-copy` of *collection* and filling it with the same elements as *collection*.

`type-for-copy` **[Open Generic Function]**

Returns an appropriate type for creating mutable copies of its argument.

Signature:	`type-for-copy` *object* $\Rightarrow$ *type*	
Arguments:	*object*	An instance of `<object>`.
Values:	*type*	An instance of `<type>`.
Description:		Returns an appropriate type for creating mutable copies of *object*.

Returns an appropriate type for creating mutable copies of *object*.

The `type-for-copy` value of a collection must be an instantiable subtype of `<mutable-collection>`. For collections that are themselves mutable, the collection's actual class is generally the most appropriate (assuming it is instantiable). The `type-for-copy` value for a sequence should be a subtype of `<sequence>`, and the `type-for-copy` value of an explicit-key-collection should be a subtype of `<explicit-key-collection>`.

type-for-copy *object* $\Rightarrow$ *type*   [G.F. Method]

The method on `<object>` returns the result of calling `object-class` on the *object*.

type-for-copy *mutable-collection* $\Rightarrow$ *type*   [G.F. Method]

The method on `<mutable-collection>` returns the result of calling `object-class` on the *mutable-collection*.

type-for-copy *limited-collection* $\Rightarrow$ *type*   [Sealed G.F. Method]

For a type L_1 created by `limited(C, of: T, size: S)` where C is not `<range>`, `type-for-copy` of an object made by instantiating L_1 returns a type L_2 that satisfies each of the following:

- L_2 is either a class or a limited collection type.

- L_2 is a subtype of C.

- L_2's element type is equivalent to T.

- If L_2 is a limited collection type, its size attribute is `#f`.

type-for-copy *range* $\Rightarrow$ `<list>`   [Sealed G.F. Method]

The method on `<range>` returns `<list>`.

type-for-copy *limited-range* ⇒ **<list>**　　　　　　**[Sealed G.F. Method]**

The method on instances of limited(singleton(<range>)...) returns
<list>, the same as for any instance of <range>.

Collection Operations

The generic functions described in this section have predefined methods for the
built-in collection classes (and sequence classes, where appropriate). The
details of these predefined methods have not yet been specified.

Note to implementors: Functions such as map, map-as that return a new
collection cannot rely on the type they instantiate having a valid default for
fill:. Therefore, when the size of the result is nonzero, these functions should
compute the first element of the result before making the collection and specify
that element as the fill: value. Otherwise a spurious type error could occur
when making the collection.

Collection Properties

empty?　　　　　　　　　　　　　　　　　　　**[Open Generic Function]**

Returns true if its argument is empty.

Signature:　　empty? *object* ⇒ *boolean*

Arguments:　　*object*　　　　　An instance of <object>.

Values:　　　　*boolean*　　　　An instance of <boolean>.

Description:　　Returns true if *object* is empty. Otherwise returns #f.

empty? *collection* ⇒ *boolean*　　　　　　　　**[G.F. Method]**

A set of methods defined for the class <collection> returns true if the
collection has zero elements.

size   **[Open Generic Function]**

Returns the size of its argument.

Signature: size *object* ⇒ #rest *objects*

Arguments: *object*   An instance of <object>.

Values: *objects*   Instances of <object>.

Description: Returns the size of *object*.

size *collection* ⇒ *integer-or-false*   **[G.F. Method]**

When called on a collection, size returns the numbers of keys in the collection. This default method simply counts while iterating through the collection. size may return #f for collections of unbounded size.

size *array* ⇒ *size*   **[G.F. Method]**

The method for <array> is equivalent to

```
reduce(\*, 1, dimensions (array))
```

size *list* ⇒ *integer-or-false*   **[Sealed G.F. Method]**

For circular lists, size is guaranteed to terminate and return #f. For noncircular lists, size returns an integer size value.

size *range* ⇒ *size*   **[Sealed G.F. Method]**

For unbounded ranges, size always terminates and returns #f. For finite ranges, size returns an integer.

size *table* ⇒ *size*   **[Sealed G.F. Method]**

The class <table> provides an implementation of size for use by its subclasses. The method returns an instance of <integer>.

size-setter   **[Open Generic Function]**

Sets the size of an object.

Signature: size-setter *new-size object* $\Rightarrow$ *new-size*

Arguments: *new-size*   An instance of <object>.
                 object   An instance of <object>.

Values: *new-size*   An instance of <object>.

Description: Sets the size of *object* to *new-size*.

object is modified by this operation.

Methods are provided for stretchy sequences; that is, for collections that are instances both of <stretchy-collection> and of <sequence>.

size-setter sets the size of a stretchy sequence to be *new-size*. The stretchy sequence is modified by this operation. If *new-size* is less than or equal to the original size of the stretchy sequence, then the first *new-size* elements of the stretchy sequence are retained at the same positions. If *new-size* is greater than the original size of the stretchy sequence, then the previous elements of the stretchy sequence are retained at the same positions, and enough new elements are added to reach the new size. The value of each new element is the same as would have been used if the stretchy sequence had been created with make, specifying size: *new-size* but not fill:.

It is not specified how size-setter adds new elements to the stretchy sequence. In particular, it is not required to call add! or any other predefined function.

rank   **[Open Generic Function]**

Returns the number of dimensions of an array.

Signature: rank *array* $\Rightarrow$ *rank*

Arguments: *array*   An instance of <array>.

Values: *rank*   An instance of <integer>.

Description: Returns the number of dimensions (the rank) of *array*.

rank *array* ⇒ *rank*   [G.F. Method]

The method for `<array>` computes `rank` by calling `size` on the `dimensions` of `array`.

---

row-major-index   **[Open Generic Function]**

Returns the row-major-index position of an array element.

Signature: row-major-index *array* #rest *subscripts* ⇒ *index*

Arguments: *array*   An instance of `<array>`.

              subscripts   Instances of `<integer>`.

Values: *index*   An instance of `<integer>`.

Description: Computes the position according to the row-major ordering of `array` for the element that is specified by `subscripts`, and returns the position of that element.

An error is signaled if the number of subscripts is not equal to the rank of the array. An error is signaled if any of the subscripts are out of bounds for array.

row-major-index *array* #rest *subscripts* ⇒ *index*   [G.F. Method]

The method for `<array>` computes the *index* using the *subscripts* and the result of calling `dimensions` on the *array*.

---

dimensions   **[Open Generic Function]**

Returns the dimensions of an array.

Signature: dimensions *array* ⇒ *sequence*

Arguments: *array*   An instance of `<array>`.

Values: *sequence*   An instance of `<sequence>`. The elements of this sequences will be instances of `<integer>`.

Description: Returns the dimensions of *array*, as a sequence of integers. The consequences are undefined if the resulting sequence is modified. This function forms the basis for all the other array operations. Each concrete subclass of `<array>` must either provide or inherit an implementation of this function.

dimensions *vector* ⇒ *sequence*   **[G.F. Method]**

Returns a sequence whose single element is the size of the vector.

`dimension`   **[Open Generic Function]**

Returns the size of a specified dimension of an array.

Signature: `dimension` *array axis* ⇒ *dimension*

Arguments: *array*   An instance of `<array>`.

                axis   An instance of `<integer>`.

Values: *dimension*   An instance of `<integer>`.

Description: Returns the *axis* dimension of `array`.

axis must be a non-negative integer less than the rank of `array`. An error is signaled if *axis* is out of bounds for `array`.

dimension *array axis* ⇒ *dimension*   **[G.F. Method]**

The method for `<array>` calls `element` on the result of calling `dimensions` on the `array`, using the `axis` number as the key.

`key-test`   **[Open Generic Function]**

Returns the function used by its collection argument to compare keys.

Signature: `key-test` *collection* ⇒ *test-function*

Arguments: *collection*   An instance of `<collection>`.

Values: *test-function* An instance of `<function>`. The function used by the collection to compare keys.

Description: Returns the function used by *collection* to compare keys.

All collection classes must provide or inherit a method that returns a result consistent with their iteration protocol and `element` methods. A given method for `key-test` must return the same value (compared with `==`) each time it is called.

key-test *sequence* ⇒ *test-function*   **[Sealed G.F. Method]**

The method of `key-test` for sequences returns the function `==`.

key-test *table* ⇒ *test-function*   **[Sealed G.F. Method]**

The method of `key-test` for instances of `<table>` returns the first value of `table-protocol`(*table*).

key-sequence   **[Open Generic Function]**

Returns a sequence containing the keys of its collection argument.

Signature: key-sequence *collection* ⇒ *keys*

Arguments: *collection*   An instance of `<collection>`.

Values: *keys*   An instance of `<sequence>` containing the keys of *collection*.

Description: Returns a sequence containing the keys of *collection*.

Although elements may be duplicated in a collection, keys, by their nature, must be unique; two different elements in a collection may not share a common key, even though distinct keys may yield identical elements.

The order in which the keys from *collection* appear in the key sequence is unspecified if *collection* is unstable under iteration. In particular, different calls to `key-sequence` with the same argument may yield differently ordered key sequences. If *collection* is stable under iteration, however, the resulting sequence of keys will be in the natural order for *collection*.

Selecting Elements

element   **[Open Generic Function]**

Returns the collection element associated with a particular key.

Signature: element *collection key* #key *default* ⇒ *element*

Arguments: *collection*   An instance of <collection>.

                   key   An instance of <object>.

                   default   An instance of <object>.

Values: *element*   An instance of <object>.

Description: Returns the element associated with *key* in *collection*. If no element is associated
                   with *key*, then the behavior of element depends on whether it was called with
                   a *default* argument: if a *default* argument was passed, its value is returned;
                   otherwise, an error is signaled.

                   All collections are required to implement element.

element *simple-vector* *index* #key *default* ⇒ *element*   **[Sealed G.F. Method]**

There is a constant time implementation of element for all general instances
of <simple-vector>.

element *unicode-string index* #key *default* ⇒ *character*   **[Sealed G.F. Method]**

The class <unicode-string> provides a constant time implementation for
the element function.

element *byte-string index* #key *default* ⇒ *character*   **[Sealed G.F. Method]**

The class <byte-string> provides a constant time implementation for the
element function.

element *table key* #key *default* ⇒ *element*   **[Sealed G.F. Method]**

The class <table> provides a default implementation for the element function.

element-setter   **[Open Generic Function]**

Sets the collection element associated with a particular key.

Signature: element-setter *new-value mutable-collection key* ⇒ *new-value*

Arguments: *new-value*   An instance of <object>.

mutable-collection An instance of <mutable-collection>.

key   An instance of <object>.

Values: *new-value*   Zero or more instances of <object>.

Description: Alters *mutable-collection* so that the value associated with *key* will subsequently be *new-value*. If *mutable-collection* is stretchy, element-setter may also change its size (for example, by adding new keys with values).

An error is signaled if a program calls element-setter with a key that is not already a key to *collection*, unless the collection is stretchy.

Stretchy collections allow element-setter to be called with a key that is not present in the collection, expanding the collection as necessary to add a new element in that case. Each concrete subclass of <stretchy-collection> must provide or inherit a method for element-setter that behaves as follows when there is not already an element present for the indicated key:

■ If the class is a subclass of <explicit-key-collection>, adds a new element to the collection with the indicated key.

■ If the class is a subclass of <sequence>, first calls size-setter on the key + 1 and the collection to expand the sequence. The key must be a non-negative integer.

element-setter *new-element simple-vector index*   **[Sealed G.F. Method]**
⇒ *new-element*

There is a constant time implementation of element-setter for all general instances of <simple-vector>.

element-setter *new-value table key*   [Sealed G.F. Method]

The class <table> provides an implementation of element-setter for use by its subclasses. If no element with the given *key* exists, element-setter will add the *key* and *new-value* to the table.

element-setter *character unicode-string index*   [Sealed G.F. Method]
⇒ *character*

The class <unicode-string> provides a constant time implementation for the element-setter function.

element-setter *character byte-string index* ⇒ *character* [Sealed G.F. Method]

The class <byte-string> provides a constant time implementation for the element-setter function.

---

aref   **[Open Generic Function]**

Returns the array element indicated by a set of indices.

Signature: aref *array* #rest *indices* ⇒ *element*

Arguments: *array*   An instance of <array>.
                     indices   Instances of <integer>.

Values: *element*   An instance of <object>.

Description: Returns the element of *array* indicated by *indices*.

                     An error is signaled if the number of *indices* is not equal to the rank of the *array*.
                     An error is signaled if any of the *indices* are out of bounds for the *array*.

aref *array* **#rest** *indices* ⇒ *element*   **[G.F. Method]**

The method for <array> calls element on the *array*, using as the key the result of applying row-major-index to the *array* and *indices*.

---

aref-setter   **[Open Generic Function]**

Sets the array element indicated by a set of indices.

Signature: `aref-setter` *new-value array* `#rest` *indices* ⇒ *new-value*

Arguments:

new-value	An instance of `<object>`.
array	An instance of `<array>`.
indices	Instances of `<integer>`.

Values:

new-value	An instance of `<object>`.

Description: Sets the element of *array* indicated by *indices* to the *new-value* and returns the *new-value*.

array is modified by this operation.

An error is signaled if the number of *indices* is not equal to the rank of the *array*. An error is signaled if any of the *indices* are out of bounds for *array*. An error is signaled if the *array* is limited to hold objects of a particular type and the new value is not an instance of that type.

`aref-setter` *new-value* *array* `#rest` *indices* ⇒ *new-value*   [G.F. Method]

The method for `<array>` calls `element-setter` on the array and new value, using as the key the result of applying `row-major-index` to the `array` and *indices*.

`first`   [Function]

Returns the first element of a sequence.

Signature: `first` *sequence* `#key` *default* ⇒ *value*

Arguments:

sequence	An instance of `<sequence>`.
default	An instance of `<object>`.

Values:

value	An instance of `<object>`.

Description: Returns the first element of the *sequence* by calling `element` with the supplied arguments and the corresponding index.

Note that because `element` is zero-based, `first(seq)` is equivalent to `element(seq, 0)` and `seq[0]`.

second   **[Function]**

Returns the second element of a sequence.

Signature: second *sequence* #key *default* ⇒ *value*

Arguments: *sequence*   An instance of <sequence>.

                  default   An instance of <object>.

Values: *value*   An instance of <object>.

Description: Returns the second element of the *sequence* by calling element with the
                  supplied arguments and the corresponding index.

third   **[Function]**

Returns the third element of a sequence.

Signature: third *sequence* #key *default* ⇒ *value*

Arguments: *sequence*   An instance of <sequence>.

                  default   An instance of <object>.

Values: *value*   An instance of <object>.

Description: Returns the third element of the *sequence* by calling element with the supplied
                  arguments and the corresponding index.

first-setter   **[Function]**

Sets the first element of a mutable sequence.

Signature: first-setter *new-value mutable-sequence* ⇒ *new-value*

Arguments: *new-value*   An instance of <object>.

                  mutable-sequence An instance of <mutable-sequence>.

Values: *new-value*   An instance of <object>.

Description: Sets the first element of the *mutable-sequence* and returns the *new-value*, by calling `element-setter` with the supplied arguments and the corresponding index.

Note that because `element-setter` is zero-based, `first-setter(val, seq)` is equivalent to `element-setter(val, seq, 0)` and `seq[0] := val`.

---

second-setter   **[Function]**

Sets the second element of a mutable sequence.

Signature: second-setter *new-value mutable-sequence* ⇒ *new-value*

Arguments: *new-value*   An instance of <object>.

mutable-sequence An instance of <mutable-sequence>.

Values: *new-value*   An instance of <object>.

Description: Sets the second element of the *mutable-sequence* and returns the *new-value*, by calling `element-setter` with the supplied arguments and the corresponding index.

---

third-setter   **[Function]**

Sets the third element of a mutable sequence.

Signature: third-setter *new-value mutable-sequence* ⇒ *new-value*

Arguments: *new-value*   An instance of <object>.

mutable-sequence An instance of <mutable-sequence>.

Values: *new-value*   An instance of <object>.

Description: Sets the third element of the *mutable-sequence* and returns the *new-value*, by calling `element-setter` with the supplied arguments and the corresponding index.

last   **[Open Generic Function]**

Returns the last element of a sequence.

Signature: last *sequence* #key *default* ⇒ *value*

Arguments: *sequence*   An instance of <sequence>.

                 default   An instance of <object>.

Values: *value*   Zero or more instances of <object>.

Description: Returns the last element of *sequence*.

                 If the sequence is empty, then the behavior of last depends on whether it was
                 called with a *default* argument. If the *default* argument was supplied, its value
                 is returned; otherwise, an error is signaled.

```
last (#("emperor", "of", "china"))
  ⇒  "china"
```

last-setter   **[Open Generic Function]**

Sets the last element of a mutable sequence.

Signature: last-setter *new-value mutable-sequence* ⇒ *new-value*

Arguments: *new-value*   An instance of <object>.

                 mutable-sequence An instance of <mutable-sequence>.

Values: *new-value*   An instance of <object>.

Description: Replaces the last element of *mutable-sequence* with *new-value*.

                 mutable-sequence is modified by this operation.

                 new-value must obey any type restrictions for elements of *mutable-sequence* . An
                 error is signaled if *mutable-sequence* is empty or unbounded.

```
define variable my-list = list (1, 2, 3)
my-list
  ⇒  #(1, 2, 3)
```

```
last (my-list) := 4
  ⇒  4
my-list
  ⇒  #(1, 2, 4)

define variable my-empty-vector = vector()
my-empty-vector
  ⇒  #[]
last (my-empty-vector) := 4
{error}
```

---

head   **[Function]**

Returns the head of a list.

Signature: head *list* ⇒ *object*

Arguments: *list*   An instance of <list>.

Values: *object*   An instance of <object>.

Description: Returns the head of *list*.

If *list* is a pair, head returns the value of the head slot. If *list* is the empty list, head returns the empty list.

```
head (#(4, 5, 6))
  ⇒  4
head (#())
  ⇒  #()
```

---

tail   **[Function]**

Returns the tail of a list.

Signature: tail *list* ⇒ *object*

Arguments: *list*   An instance of <list>.

The Built-In Functions

Values: *object*   An instance of `<object>`.

Description: Returns the tail of *list*.

If *list* is a pair, `tail` returns the value of the tail slot. If *list* is the empty list, `tail` returns the empty list.

```
tail (#(4, 5, 6))
 ⇒  #(5, 6)
tail (#())
 ⇒  #()
```

`head-setter`   **[Function]**

Sets the head of a pair.

Signature: `head-setter` *object pair* ⇒ *object*

Arguments: *object*   An instance of `<object>`.
pair   ·   An instance of `<pair>`.

Values: *object*   An instance of `<object>`.

Description: Sets the head of *pair* to contain *object* and returns *object*.

pair is modified by this operation.

```
define variable x = list (4, 5, 6)
head (x) := 9
 ⇒  9
x
 ⇒  #(9, 5, 6)
```

`tail-setter`   **[Function]**

Sets the tail of a pair.

Signature: `tail-setter` *object pair* ⇒ *object*

Arguments:	*object*	An instance of `<object>`.
	pair	An instance of `<pair>`.
Values:	*object*	An instance of `<object>`.

Description: Sets the tail of *pair* to contain *object* and returns *object*.

pair is modified by this operation.

```
define variable x = list (4, 5, 6)
tail (x) := #(9, 8, 7)
  ⇒  #(9, 8, 7)
x
  ⇒  #(4, 9, 8, 7)
tail (x) := "dot"
  ⇒  "dot"
x
  ⇒  #(4, 9, 8 . "dot")
```

Adding and Removing Elements

---

add   **[Open Generic Function]**

Adds an element to a sequence.

Signature: add *source-sequence new-element* ⇒ *result-sequence*

Arguments:	*source-sequence*	An instance of `<sequence>`.
	new-element	An instance of `<object>`.
Values:	*result-sequence*	An instance of `<sequence>`.

Description: Returns a sequence that contains *new-element* and all the elements of *source-sequence*. The *result-sequence* may or may not be freshly allocated. It may share structure with a preexisting sequence.

source-sequence is not modified by this operation.

The *result-sequence*'s size is one greater than the size of *source-sequence*. The generic function add doesn't specify where the new element will be added, although individual methods may do so.

```
define variable *numbers* = #(3, 4, 5)
add (*numbers*, 1)
  ⇒  #(1, 3, 4, 5)
*numbers*
  ⇒  #(3, 4, 5)
```

---

add!   **[Open Generic Function]**

Adds an element to a sequence.

Signature: add! *source-sequence new-element* ⇒ *result-sequence*

Arguments: *source-sequence*   An instance of <sequence>.

            new-element   An instance of <object>.

Values: *result-sequence*   An instance of <sequence>.

Description: Returns a sequence that contains *new-element* and all the elements of *source-sequence*. The *result-sequence* may or may not be freshly allocated. It may share structure with a preexisting sequence. *source-sequence* and *result-sequence* may or may not be ==.

source-sequence may be modified by this operation.

result-sequence's size is one greater than the size of *source-sequence*. The generic function add! doesn't specify where the new element will be added, although individual methods may do so.

```
define variable *numbers* = list (3, 4, 5)
add! (*numbers*, 1)
  ⇒  #(1, 3, 4, 5)
*numbers*
  ⇒  {undefined}
```

add! *deque new-value* ⇒ *deque*   **[Sealed G.F. Method]**

The result of add! on a deque is == to the *deque* argument, which is modified
by this operation. add! adds *new-element* at the beginning of the *deque*.

add! *stretchy-vector new-element* ⇒ *stretchy-vector*   **[Sealed G.F. Method]**

The result of add! on a stretchy vector is == to the *stretchy-vector* argument,
which is modified by this operation. add! adds *new-element* at the end of the
stretchy-vector.

add! *list element* ⇒ *pair*   **[Sealed G.F. Method]**

The result of add! on a list is equivalent to (pair *element list*). The result
will share structure with the *list* argument, but it will not be == to the
argument, and the argument will not be modified.

---

add-new   **[Open Generic Function]**

Adds a new element to a sequence.

Signature: add-new *source-sequence new-element* #key *test* ⇒ *result-sequence*

Arguments: *source-sequence*   An instance of <sequence>.

                  new-element   An instance of <object>.

                  test   An instance of <function>. The default is ==.

Values: *result-sequence*   An instance of <sequence>.

Description: Adds *new-element* to source-sequence if it is not already an element of
source-sequence, as determined by the *test* function. If *new-element* is already a
member of *source-sequence*, then *source-sequence* is returned unmodified.

If an element is added, add-new operates just as add would.

The *test* function may be noncommutative: it is always called with an element
from *source-sequence* as its first argument and *new-element* as its second
argument.

```
add-new (#(3, 4, 5), 1)
  ⇒  #(1, 3, 4, 5)
add-new (#(3, 4, 5), 4)
  ⇒  #(3, 4, 5)
```

---

add-new!   **[Open Generic Function]**

Adds a new element to a sequence.

Signature: add-new! *source-sequence new-element* #key *test* ⇒ *result-sequence*

Arguments: *source-sequence*   An instance of <sequence>.

new-element   An instance of <object>.

test   An instance of <function>. The default is ==.

Values: *result-sequence*   An instance of <sequence>.

Description: Adds *new-element* to source-sequence if it is not already an element of *source-sequence*, as determined by the *test* function. If *new-element* is already a member of *source-sequence*, then *source-sequence* is returned unmodified.

If an element is added, add-new! operates just as add! would.

The *test* function may be noncommutative: it is always called with an element from *sequence* as its first argument and *new-element* as its second argument.

```
add-new! (list (3, 4, 5), 1)
  ⇒  #(1, 3, 4, 5)
add-new! (list (3, 4, 5), 4)
  ⇒  #(3, 4, 5)
```

---

remove   **[Open Generic Function]**

Removes an element from a sequence.

Signature: remove *source-sequence value* #key *test count* ⇒ *result-sequence*

Arguments: *source-sequence*   An instance of <sequence>.

value   An instance of <object>.

test	An instance of <function>. The default is ==.	
count	An instance of <integer> or #f. The default is #f.	

Values: *result-sequence*   An instance of <sequence>.

Description: Returns a sequence consisting of the elements of *source-sequence* not equal to *value*. The *result-sequence* may or may not be freshly allocated. However, the *source-sequence* is never modified by remove.

test is a function that determines whether an element is equal to *value*. The *test* function may be noncommutative: it is always called with an element from *source-sequence* as its first argument and *value* as its second argument.

If *count* is #f, then all copies of *value* are removed. Otherwise, no more than *count* copies of *value* are removed (so additional elements equal to *value* might remain in *result-sequence*).

```
define variable *old-list* = list(1, 2, 3)
define variable *new-list* = remove(*old-list*, 1)
*new-list*
 ⇒  #(2, 3)
*new-list* == tail(*old-list*)
 ⇒  {undefined}
```

---

remove!   **[Open Generic Function]**

Removes an element from a sequence.

Signature: remove! *source-sequence value* #key *test count* ⇒ *result-sequence*

Arguments:
source-sequence	An instance of <sequence>.
value	An instance of <object>.
test	An instance of <function>. The default is ==.
count	An instance of <integer> or #f. The default is #f.

Values: *result-sequence*   An instance of <sequence>.

Description: Returns a sequence consisting of the elements of *source-sequence* not equal to *value*. The *result-sequence* may or may not be freshly allocated, may or may not be == to the *source-sequence,* and may or may not share structure with the *source-sequence.* The *source-sequence* may be modified by `remove!`.

test is a function that determines whether an element is equal to *value.* The *test* function may be noncommutative: it is always called with an element from *source-sequence* as its first argument and *value* as its second argument.

If *count* is #f, then all copies of *value* are removed. Otherwise, no more than *count* copies of *value* are removed (so additional elements equal to *value* might remain in *result-sequence*).

remove! *deque value* **#key** *test count* ⇒ *deque*   [Sealed G.F. Method]

The result of `remove!` on a deque is == to the *deque* argument. The argument is modified by this operation.

remove! *stretchy-vector element* **#key** *test count*   [Sealed G.F. Method]
⇒ *stretchy-vector*

The result of `remove!` on a stretchy vector is == to the *stretchy-vector* argument. The argument is modified by this operation.

remove! *list element* **#key** *test count* ⇒ *list*   [Sealed G.F. Method]

The result of `remove!` on a list may or may not be == to the *list* argument. The argument may be modified by this operation.

---

push   **[Open Generic Function]**

Adds an element to the front of a deque.

Signature: push *deque new-value* ⇒ *new-value*

Arguments: *deque*   An instance of <deque>.

   new-value   An instance of <object>.

Values: *new-value*   An instance of <object>. The same object that was passed in as an argument.

Description: Augments *deque* by adding *new-value* to its front.

deque is modified by this operation.

---

pop   **[Open Generic Function]**

Removes and returns the first element of a deque.

Signature: pop *deque* ⇒ *first-element*

Arguments: *deque*   An instance of <deque>.

Values: *first-element*   An instance of <object>.

Description: Removes the first element from *deque* and returns it.

deque is modified by this operation.

---

push-last   **[Open Generic Function]**

Adds an element to the end of a deque.

Signature: push-last *deque new-value* ⇒ *new-value*

Arguments: *deque*   An instance of <deque>.
                  new-value   An instance of <object>.

Values: *new-value*   An instance of <object>. The same object that was passed in as an argument.

Description: Augments *deque* by adding *new-value* to its end.

deque is modified by this operation.

---

pop-last   **[Open Generic Function]**

Removes and returns an element from the end of a deque.

Signature: pop-last *deque* ⇒ *last-element*

Arguments:	*deque*	An instance of <deque>.
Values:	*last-element*	An instance of <object>.

Description: Removes the last element from *deque* and returns it.

deque is modified by this operation.

Reordering Elements

---

reverse   **[Open Generic Function]**

Returns a sequence with elements in the reverse order of its argument sequence.

Signature: reverse *source-sequence* ⟹ *result-sequence*

Arguments: *source-sequence*   An instance of <sequence>.

Values: *result-sequence*   An instance of <sequence>.

Description: Returns a sequence containing the same elements as *source-sequence,* but in reverse order. The *result-sequence* is generally of the same class as the *source-sequence.*

The *result-sequence* may or may not be freshly allocated. The *source-sequence* is not modified by this operation.

The consequences are undefined if the *source-sequence* is unbounded (circular or infinite).

```
define variable *x* = list("bim", "bam", "boom")
*x*
  ⇒  #("bim", "bam", "boom")
reverse(*x*)
  ⇒  #("boom", "bam", "bim")
*x*
  ⇒  #("bim", "bam", "boom")
```

reverse *range* ⇒ *new-range*   **[Sealed G.F. Method]**

Reversing a range produces another range. An unbounded range cannot be reversed.

`reverse!`   **[Open Generic Function]**

Returns a sequence with elements in the reverse order of its argument sequence.

Signature: `reverse!` *source-sequence* ⇒ *result-sequence*

Arguments: *source-sequence*   An instance of `<sequence>`.

Values: *result-sequence*   An instance of `<sequence>`.

Description: Returns a sequence containing the same elements as *source-sequence*, but in reverse order. The *result-sequence* is generally of the same class as the *source-sequence*.

The *source-sequence* may be modified by this operation. The *result-sequence* may or may not be freshly allocated. The *source-sequence* and the *result-sequence* may or may not be ==. Programs should never rely on this operation performing a side-effect on an existing sequence, but should instead use the value returned by the function.

The consequences are undefined if the *source-sequence* is unbounded (circular or infinite).

```
define variable *x* = list("bim", "bam", "boom")
*x*
  ⇒  #("bim", "bam", "boom")
reverse!(*x*)
  ⇒  #("boom", "bam", "bim")
*x*
  ⇒  {undefined}
```

reverse! *range* ⇒ *range*   **[Sealed G.F. Method]**

The result of `reverse!` on a range is == to the *range* argument. An unbounded range cannot be reversed.

sort   **[Open Generic Function]**

Returns a sequence containing the elements of its argument sequence, sorted.

Signature: sort *source-sequence* #key *test stable* ⇒ *result-sequence*

Arguments: *source-sequence*   An instance of `<sequence>`.

                      test   An instance of `<function>`. The default is `<`.

                      stable   An instance of `<object>`, treated as a boolean.

Values: *result-sequence*   An instance of `<sequence>`.

Description: Returns a sequence containing the elements of *source-sequence* sorted into
                      ascending order. The *result-sequence* may or may not be freshly allocated. The
                      source-sequence is not modified by this operation.

                      sort determines the relationship between two elements by giving elements to
                      the *test*. The first argument to the *test* function is one element of *source-sequence*;
                      the second argument is another element of *source-sequence*. *test* should return
                      true if and only if the first argument is strictly less than the second (in some
                      appropriate sense). If the first argument is greater than or equal to the second
                      (in the appropriate sense), then the *test* should return `#f`.

                      If *stable* is supplied and not `#f`, a possibly slower algorithm will be used that
                      will leave in their original order any two elements, x and y, such that *test(x, y)*
                      and *test(y, x)* are both false.

```
define variable *numbers* = vector(3, 1, 4, 1, 5, 9)
*numbers*
  ⇒ #[3, 1, 4, 1, 5, 9]
sort (*numbers*)
  ⇒  #[1, 1, 3, 4, 5, 9]
*numbers*
  ⇒  #[3, 1, 4, 1, 5, 9]
```

sort!   **[Open Generic Function]**

Returns a sequence containing the elements of its argument sequence, sorted.

Signature: sort! *source-sequence* #key *test stable* ⇒ *result-sequence*

Arguments: *source-sequence*   An instance of `<sequence>`.

test   An instance of `<function>`. The default is `<`.

stable   An instance of `<object>`, treated as a boolean.

Values: *result-sequence*   An instance of `<sequence>`.

Description: Returns a sequence containing the elements of *source-sequence* sorted into ascending order. The *result-sequence* may or may not be freshly allocated. The *source-sequence* may be modified by this operation. The *result-sequence* may or may not be `==` to *source-sequence*. After this operation, the contents of *source-sequence* are undefined.

Programs should never rely on this operation performing a side-effect on an existing sequence, but should instead use the value returned by the function.

`sort!` determines the relationship between two elements by giving elements to the *test*. The first argument to the *test* function is one element of *source-sequence*; the second argument is another element of *source-sequence*. *test* should return true if and only if the first argument is strictly less than the second (in some appropriate sense). If the first argument is greater than or equal to the second (in the appropriate sense), then the *test* should return `#f`.

If *stable* is supplied and not `#f`, a possibly slower algorithm will be used that will leave in their original order any two elements, x and y, such that *test(x, y)* and *test(y, x)* are both false.

```
define variable *numbers* = vector(3, 1, 4, 1, 5, 9)
*numbers*
  ⇒ #[3, 1, 4, 1, 5, 9]
sort! (*numbers*)
  ⇒  #[1, 1, 3, 4, 5, 9]
*numbers*
  ⇒  {undefined}
```

Set Operations

`intersection`   **[Open Generic Function]**

Returns the intersection of two sequences.

The Built-In Functions

Signature: `intersection` *sequence1 sequence2* #key *test* ⇒ *new-sequence*

Arguments:

sequence1	An instance of `<sequence>`.
sequence2	An instance of `<sequence>`.
test	An instance of `<function>`. The default is `==`.

Values:

new-sequence	An instance of `<sequence>`.

Description: Returns a new sequence containing only those elements of *sequence1* that also appear in *sequence2*.

test is used to determine whether an element appears in *sequence2*. It is always called with an element of *sequence1* as its first argument and an element from *sequence2* as its second argument. The order of elements in the result sequence is not specified.

new-sequence may or may not share structure with the *sequence1* and *sequence2*.

```
? intersection (#("john", "paul", "george", "ringo"),
                #("richard", "george", "edward", "charles"),
                test: \=)
#("george")
```

intersection *range1 range2* **#key** *test* ⇒ *range*   **[Sealed G.F. Method]**

`intersection` applied to two ranges and a test of `==` (the default) will produce another range as its result, even though the `type-for-copy` of a range is not `<range>`. If either *range1* or *range2* is unbounded, this method is guaranteed to terminate only if the *test* is `==`.

`union`   **[Open Generic Function]**

Returns the union of two sequences.

Signature: `union` *sequence1 sequence2* #key *test* ⇒ *new-sequence*

Arguments:

sequence1	An instance of `<sequence>`.
sequence2	An instance of `<sequence>`.
test	An instance of `<function>`. The default is `==`.

Values: *new-sequence*   An instance of `<sequence>`.

Description: Returns a sequence containing every element of *sequence1* and *sequence2*.

If the same element appears in both argument sequences, this will not cause it to appear twice in the result sequence. However, if the same element appears more than once in a single argument sequence, it may appear more than once in the result sequence.

test is used for all comparisons. It is always called with an element from *sequence1* as its first argument and an element from *sequence2* as its second argument. The order of elements in the *new-sequence* is not specified.

new-sequence may or may not share structure with *sequence1* or *sequence2*.

```
union (#("butter", "flour", "sugar", "salt", "eggs"),
       #("eggs", "butter", "mushrooms", "onions", "salt"),
       test: \=)
  ⇒  #("salt", "butter", "flour", "sugar", "eggs",
       "mushrooms", "onions")
```

`remove-duplicates`   **[Open Generic Function]**

Returns a sequence without duplicates.

Signature: `remove-duplicates` *source-sequence* #key *test* ⇒ *result-sequence*

Arguments: *source-sequence*   An instance of `<sequence>`.

                   test   An instance of `<function>`. The default is ==.

Values: *result-sequence*   An instance of `<sequence>`.

Description: Returns a sequence that contains all the unique elements from *source-sequence* but no duplicate elements.

test is the function used to determine whether one element is a duplicate of another. The *test* argument may be noncommutative; it will always be called with its arguments in the same order as they appear in *source-sequence*.

The *result-sequence* may or may not be freshly allocated. However, the *source-sequence* will not be modified by this operation.

```
remove-duplicates (#("spam", "eggs", "spam",
                      "sausage", "spam", "spam"),
                   test: \=)
  ⇒  #("spam", "eggs", "sausage")
or
  ⇒  #("eggs", "spam", "sausage")
or
  ⇒  #("eggs", "sausage", "spam")
```

remove-duplicates!   **[Open Generic Function]**

Returns a sequence without duplicates.

Signature: remove-duplicates! *source-sequence* #key *test* ⇒ *result-sequence*

Arguments: *source-sequence*   An instance of `<sequence>`.

               test   An instance of `<function>`. The default is `==`.

Values: *result-sequence*   An instance of `<sequence>`.

Description: Returns a sequence that contains all the unique elements from *source-sequence* but no duplicate elements.

test is the function used to determine whether one element is a duplicate of another. The *test* argument may be noncommutative; it will always be called with its arguments in the same order as they appear in *source-sequence*.

The *result-sequence* may or may not be freshly allocated, may or may not share structure with the *source-sequence,* and may or may not be `==` to the *source-sequence.* The *source-sequence* may or may not be modified by the operation.

```
define variable *menu* = #("spam", "eggs", "spam",
                           "sausage", "spam", "spam")
remove-duplicates! (*menu*, test: \=)
  ⇒  #("spam", "eggs", "sausage")
or
  ⇒  #("eggs", "spam", "sausage")
or
```

```
  ⇒  #("eggs", "sausage", "spam")
*menu*
  ⇒  {undefined}
```

Subsequence Operations

copy-sequence   **[Open Generic Function]**

Returns a freshly allocated copy of some subsequence of a sequence.

Signature: copy-sequence   *source* #key *start end* ⇒ *new-sequence*

Arguments: *source*   An instance of `<sequence>`.

start   An instance of `<integer>`. The default is 0.

end   An instance of `<integer>`. The default is the size of *source*.

Values: *new-sequence*   A freshly allocated instance of `<sequence>`.

Description: Creates a freshly allocated sequence containing the elements of *source* between *start* and *end*.

```
define constant hamlet = #("to", "be", "or", "not", "to", "be")
hamlet == copy-sequence (hamlet)
  ⇒  #f
copy-sequence (hamlet, start: 2, end: 4)
  ⇒  #("or", "not")
```

copy-sequence *range* #key *start end* ⇒ *new-range*   **[Sealed G.F. Method]**

When applied to a range, `copy-sequence` returns another range, even though the `type-for-copy` of a range is the `<list>` class.

concatenate   **[Function]**

Returns the concatenation of one or more sequences in a sequence of a type determined by the `type-for-copy` of its first argument.

Signature: `concatenate` *first-sequence* #rest *more-sequences* ⇒ *result-sequence*

Arguments: *first-sequence*   An instance of `<sequence>`.

　　　　　　　more-sequences   Instances of `<sequence>`.

Values: *result-sequence*   An instance of `<sequence>`.

Description: Returns a sequence containing all the elements of all the sequences, in order.

The *result-sequence* will be an instance of the `type-for-copy` value for *first-sequence*. It may or may not be freshly allocated. The *result-sequence* may be created by calling `make` on the indicated type, with a `size:` initialization argument whose value is the sum of the sizes of the argument sequences. (For this reason, the `type-for-copy` value of *first-sequence* must support the `size:` init-keyword.)

new-sequence may share structure with any of the argument sequences, but it is not guaranteed to do so. The argument sequences will not be modified by this operation.

```
concatenate ("low-", "calorie")
 ⇒  "low-calorie"
```

`concatenate-as`   **[Function]**

Returns the concatenation of one or more sequences in a sequence of a specified type.

Signature: `concatenate-as` *type first-sequence* #rest *more-sequences* ⇒ *result-sequence*

Arguments: *type*   An instance of `<type>`, which must be a subtype of `<mutable-sequence>`

　　　　　　　first-sequence   An instance of `<sequence>`.

　　　　　　　more-sequences   Instances of `<sequence>`.

Values: *result-sequence*   An instance of *type*, and therefore also an instance of `<sequence>`.

Description: Returns a sequence containing all the elements of all the sequences, in order.

The *result-sequence* will be an instance of *type*. It may or may not be freshly allocated.

type must be a subtype of `<mutable-sequence>` and acceptable as the first argument to `make`. `size:` with a non-negative integer value must be an acceptable initarg for `make` of *type*. The *result-sequence* may be created by calling `make` on *type*, with a `size:` initialization argument whose value is the sum of the sizes of the arguments.

```
concatenate-as (<string>, #('n', 'o', 'n'), #('f', 'a', 't'))
  ⇒  "nonfat"
```

`replace-subsequence!`	**[Open Generic Function]**

Replaces a portion of a sequence with the elements of another sequence.

Signature: `replace-subsequence!` *target-sequence insert-sequence* `#key` *start end*
⇒ *result-sequence*

Arguments:

target-sequence	An instance of `<sequence>`.
insert-sequence	An instance of `<sequence>`.
start	An instance of `<integer>`. The default is 0.
end	An instance of `<integer>`. The default is the size of *target-sequence*.

Values: *result-sequence*   An instance of `<sequence>`.

Description: `replace-subsequence!` returns a sequence with the same elements as *target-sequence*, except that elements of the indicated subsequence of *target-sequence* are replaced by all the elements of *insert-sequence*. The subsequence to be overridden begins at index *start* and ends at index *end*.

result-sequence may or may not share structure with *source-sequence* or *insert-sequence*, and it may or may not be `==` to *source-sequence* or *insert-sequence*. *source-sequence* may or may not be modified by the operation. *insert-sequence* will not be modified by this operation.

```
define variable *original* = list ("a", "b", "c", "d", "e")
```

```
*new* := replace-subsequence! (*original*, #("x", "y", "z"), end: 1))
   #("x", "y", "z", "b", "c", "d", "e")

*new* := replace-subsequence! (*new*, #("x", "y", "z"), start: 4))
   #("x", "y", "z", "b", "x", "y", "z")

*new* := replace-subsequence! (*new*, #("a", "b", "c"),
                                           start: 2, end: 4))
   #("x", "y", "a", "b", "c", "x", "y", "z")
```

---

subsequence-position   **[Open Generic Function]**

Returns the position where a pattern appears in a sequence.

Signature: subsequence-position   *big pattern* #key *test count* ⇒ *index*

Arguments: *big*   An instance of `<sequence>`.

                  pattern   An instance of `<sequence>`.

                  test   An instance of `<function>`. The default is `==`.

                  count   An instance of `<integer>`. The default is `1`.

Values: *index*   `#f` or an instance of `<integer>`.

Description: Searches *big* for a subsequence that is element-for-element equal to *pattern*, as determined by the *test* argument.

test is applied to elements of successive subsequences of *big* and corresponding elements of the *pattern* to determine whether a match has occurred. If a subsequence is found, `subsequence-position` returns the index at which the subsequence starts; otherwise, it returns `#f`. If there is more than one match, *count* determines which subsequence is selected. A *count* of 1 (the default) indicates that the first match should be returned.

```
subsequence-position ("Ralph Waldo Emerson", "Waldo")
   ⇒  6
```

Mapping and Reducing

Simple Mapping

The following mapping functions (do, map, map-as, map-into, any?, every?) iterate over a number of source collections. Each time through the iteration, a function is applied to one element from each of the source collections. The number of arguments to the function is equal to the number of source collections.

The functions vary in how they handle the results of each function application.

do	[Function]

Iterates over one or more collections for side effect.

Signature: do *function collection* #rest *more-collections* ⇒ *false*

Arguments: *function*   An instance of <function>.

collection   An instance of <collection>.

more-collections   Instances of <collection>.

Values: *false*   #f.

Description: Applies *function* to corresponding elements of all the *collections* and returns #f. If all the *collections* are sequences, do guarantees that they will be processed in their natural order.

```
do (method (a b) print (a + b) end,
    #(100, 100, 200, 200),
    #(1, 2, 3, 4))
101
102
203
204
   ⇒   #f
```

map	[Function]

Iterates over one or more collections and collects the results in a freshly allocated collection.

Signature: map   *function collection* #rest *more-collections* ⇒ *new-collection*

Arguments: *function*   An instance of `<function>`.

collection   An instance of `<collection>`.

more-collections   Instances of `<collection>`.

Values: *new-collection*   A freshly allocated instance of `<collection>`.

Description: Creates a freshly allocated collection whose elements are obtained by calling *function* on corresponding elements of all the *collections*. If all the *collections* are sequences, processing is performed in the natural order.

`map` returns a collection whose value is an instance of the `type-for-copy` value of *collection*. The new collection is created by calling `make` on that type, with a `size:` initialization argument whose value is the number of corresponding elements in the *collections*.

```
map (\+,
     #(100, 100, 200, 200),
     #(1, 2, 3, 4))
  ⇒  #(101, 102, 203, 204)
```

map-as	[Function]

Iterates over one or more collections and collects the results in a freshly allocated collection of a specified type.

Signature: map-as *type function collection* #rest *more-collections* ⇒ *new-collection*

Arguments: *type*   An instance of `<type>`. It must be an instantiable subtype of `<mutable-collection>`.

function   An instance of `<function>`.

collection   An instance of `<collection>`.

more-collections   Instances of `<collection>`.

Values: *new-collection*   A freshly allocated instance of `<mutable-collection>`.

Description: Creates a freshly allocated collection of type *type* whose elements are obtained by applying *function* to corresponding elements of the *collection* arguments. *type* must be acceptable as the first argument to `make`. `size:` with a non-negative integer value must be an acceptable initarg for `make` of *type*. *new-collection* is created by calling `make` on *type*, with a `size:` initialization argument whose value is the number of corresponding elements in the *collections*. If all the *collections* are sequences (including *new-collection*), processing is done in the natural order.

```
map-as (<vector>, \+,
        #(100, 100, 200, 200),
        #(1, 2, 3, 4))
  ⇒  #(101, 102, 203, 204)
```

`map-into`   **[Function]**

Iterates over one or more collections and collects the results in an existing mutable collection.

Signature: `map-into` *mutable-collection function collection* `#rest` *more-collections* ⇒ *mutable-collection*

Arguments: *mutable-collection* An instance of `<mutable-collection>`.

function   An instance of `<function>`.

collection   An instance of `<collection>`.

more-collections   Instances of `<collection>`.

Values: *mutable-collection* An instance of `<mutable-collection>`.

Description: Returns the *mutable-collection* argument after modifying it by replacing its elements with the results of applying *function* to corresponding elements of *collection* and *more-collections*.

If *mutable-collection* and all the other *collections* are sequences, processing is done in the natural order.

When *mutable-collection* is an instance of `<stretchy-collection>`, the usual alignment requirement (described in "Collection Alignment" on page 120) is relaxed. In this case, the key sequence of *mutable-collection* is not considered during alignment. Rather, only the key sequences for the source *collections* are aligned, with *function* called on the corresponding elements. The result of each call to *function* is then stored into *mutable-collection* with the corresponding key (possibly stretching *mutable-collection* in the process), using `element-setter`. Other keys in *mutable-collection* remain undisturbed.

mutable-collection may be the same object as *collection* or any of the *more-collections*.

An error is signaled if *mutable-collection* does not have the same `key-test` function as the rest of the *collections*. This is true even if it is a `<stretchy-collection>` and therefore does not get aligned.

```
define variable x = list (10, 9, 8, 7)
map-into (x, \+, #(1, 2, 3, 4), #(100, 100, 200, 200))
  ⇒  #(101, 102, 203, 204)
x
  ⇒  #(101, 102, 203, 204)
```

---

any?   **[Function]**

Returns the first true value obtained by iterating over one or more collections.

Signature: any? *function collection* `#rest` *more-collections* ⇒ *value*

Arguments: *function*   An instance of `<function>`.

collection   An instance of `<collection>`.

more-collections   Instances of `<collection>`.

Values: *value*   An instance of `<object>`.

Description: Applies *function* to groups of corresponding elements of *collection* and *more-collections*. If an application of *function* returns true, then any? returns that true value. Otherwise *function* returns #f when applied to every such group, and any? returns #f.

If all the *collections* are sequences, any? operates in natural order. In all cases, any? stops on the first true value returned by *function*.

```
any? (\>, #(1, 2, 3 ,4), #(5, 4, 3, 2))
  ⇒  #t
any? (even?, #(1, 3, 5, 7))
  ⇒  #f
```

---

every?   **[Function]**

Returns true if a predicate returns true when applied to all corresponding
elements of a set of collections.

Signature: every? *function collection* #rest *more-collections* ⇒ *value*

Arguments: *function*   An instance of <function>.

collection   An instance of <collection>.

more-collections   Instances of <collection>.

Values: *value*   An instance of <boolean>.

Description: Applies *function* to groups of corresponding elements of *collection* and
more-collections. If an application of *function* returns false, then every? returns
#f. Otherwise *function* returns a true value when applied to every such group,
and every? returns #t.

If all the *collections* are sequences, every? operates in natural order. In all
cases, every? stops on the first false value returned by *function*.

```
every? (\>, #(1, 2, 3, 4), #(5, 4, 3, 2))
  ⇒  #f
every? (odd?, #(1, 3, 5, 7))
  ⇒  #t
```

Extensible Mapping Functions

---

reduce   **[Open Generic Function]**

Combines the elements of a collection and a seed value into a single value by
repeatedly applying a binary function.

Signature:	`reduce` *function initial-value collection* $\Rightarrow$ *value*	

Arguments:	*function*	An instance of `<function>`.
	initial-value	An instance of `<object>`.
	collection	An instance of `<collection>`.

Values:	*value*	An instance of `<object>`.

Description: Returns the result of combining the elements of *collection* and *initial-value* according to *function*.

If *collection* is empty, `reduce` returns *initial-value*; otherwise, *function* is applied to *initial-value* and the first element of *collection* to produce a new value. If more elements remain in the *collection*, then *function* is called again, this time with the value from the previous application and the next element from *collection*. This process continues until all elements of *collection* have been processed.

function is a binary function used to combine all the elements of *collection* into a single value. Processing is always done in the natural order for *collection*.

```
define variable high-score = 10
reduce (max, high-score, #(3, 1, 4, 1, 5, 9))
  ⇒  10
reduce (max, high-score, #(3, 12, 9, 8, 8, 6))
  ⇒  12
```

`reduce1`   **[Open Generic Function]**

Combines the elements of a collection into a single value by repeatedly applying a binary function, using the first element of the collection as the seed value.

Signature:	`reduce1` *function collection* $\Rightarrow$ *value*	

Arguments:	*function*	An instance of `<function>`.
	collection	An instance of `<collection>`.

Values:	*value*	An instance of `<object>`.

Description: Returns the combination of the elements of *collection* according to *function*.

An error is signaled if *collection* is empty.

`reduce1` is similar to `reduce`, except that the first element of *collection* is taken as the initial value, and all the remaining elements of *collection* are processed as if by `reduce`. (In other words, the first value isn't used twice.)

For unstable collections, "first" element effectively means "an element chosen at random." Processing is done in the natural order for *collection*.

```
reduce1 (\+, #(1, 2, 3, 4, 5))
  ⇒  15
```

`choose`   **[Open Generic Function]**

Returns those elements of a sequence that satisfy a predicate.

Signature: `choose` *predicate source-sequence* ⇒ *result-sequence*

Arguments: *predicate*   An instance of `<function>`.

source-sequence   An instance of `<sequence>`.

Values: *result-sequence*   An instance of `<sequence>`.

Description: Returns a sequence containing those elements of *source-sequence* that satisfy *predicate*. The *result-sequence* may or may not be freshly allocated.

```
choose (even?, #(3, 1, 4, 1, 5, 8, 9))
  ⇒  #(4, 8)
```

`choose-by`   **[Open Generic Function]**

Returns those elements of a sequence that correspond to those in another sequence that satisfy a predicate.

Signature: `choose-by` *predicate test-sequence value-sequence* ⇒ *result-sequence*

Arguments: *predicate*   An instance of `<function>`.

test-sequence   An instance of `<sequence>`.

value-sequence   An instance of <sequence>.

Values: *result-sequence*   An instance of <sequence>.

Description: Returns a sequence containing the elements from *value-sequence* that correspond to elements in *test-sequence* that satisfy *predicate*. The *result-sequence* may or may not be freshly allocated.

```
choose-by (even?, range (from: 1),
           #("a", "b", "c", "d", "e", "f", "g", "h", "i"))
   ⇒  #("b", "d", "f", "h")
```

Other Mapping Functions

member?	**[Open Generic Function]**

Returns true if a collection contains a particular value.

Signature: member? *value collection* #key *test* ⇒ *boolean*

Arguments: *value*   An instance of <object>.

collection   An instance of <collection>.

test   An instance of <function>. The default is ==.

Values: *boolean*   An instance of <boolean>.

Description: Returns true if *collection* contains *value* as determined by *test*. Otherwise returns false.

The *test* function may be noncommutative: it is always called with *value* as its first argument and an element from *collection* as its second argument.

```
define constant flavors = #(#"vanilla", #"pistachio", #"ginger")
member? (#"vanilla", flavors)
   ⇒  #t
member? (#"banana", flavors)
   ⇒  #f
```

member? *val range* #key *test* ⇒ *boolean*   **[Sealed G.F. Method]**

If *range* is unbounded, this method is guaranteed to terminate if *test* is ==.

find-key   **[Open Generic Function]**

Returns the key in a collection such that the corresponding collection element satisfies a predicate.

Signature: find-key *collection function* #key *skip failure* ⇒ *key*

Arguments: *collection*   An instance of <collection>.

                  predicate   An instance of <function>.

                  skip   An instance of <integer>. The default is 0.

                  failure   An instance of <object>. The default is #f.

Values: *key*   An instance of <object>.

Description: Returns a key value such that (*predicate* (element *collection key*)) is true. If no element in *collection* satisfies *predicate*, find-key returns *failure*.

The *skip* argument indicates that the first *skip* matching elements should be ignored. If *skip* or fewer elements of *collection* satisfy *predicate*, then *failure* is returned. If collection is not stable under iteration, then skip is only useful for finding out whether collection contains at least *skip* elements which satisfy *predicate*; it is not useful for finding a particular element.

```
flavors
 ⇒  #(#"vanilla", #"pistachio", #"ginger")
find-key (flavors, has-nuts?)
 ⇒  1
flavors[1]
 ⇒  #"pistachio"
```

remove-key!   **[Open Generic Function]**

Modifies an explicit key collection so it no longer has a particular key.

Signature: remove-key! *collection key* ⇒ *boolean*

Arguments: *collection*   An instance of `<mutable-explicit-key-collection>`.

            key   An instance of `<object>`.

Values: *boolean*   An instance of `<boolean>`.

Description: Modifies *collection* so that it no longer has a key equal to *key*. Equality is determined by *collection*'s key-test function.

The *boolean* return value will be #t if the *key* was present and removed, or #f if the key was not present and hence not removed.

remove-key! *table key* ⇒ *table*   **[Sealed G.F. Method]**

There is a predefined method on `<table>`.

---

replace-elements!   **[Open Generic Function]**

Replaces those collection elements that satisfy a predicate.

Signature: replace-elements! *mutable-collection predicate new-value-fn* #key *count* ⇒ *mutable-collection*

Arguments: *mutable-collection* An instance of `<mutable-collection>`.

            predicate   An instance of `<function>`.

            new-value-fn   An instance of `<function>`.

            count   An instance of `<integer>` or #f. The default is #f.

Values: *mutable-collection* An instance of `<mutable-collection>`.

Description: Replaces those elements of *mutable-collection* for which *predicate* returns true. The elements are replaced with the value of calling *new-value-fn* on the existing element. If *count* is #f, all of the matching elements are replaced. Otherwise, no more than *count* elements are replaced.

mutable-collection may be modified by this operation.

```
define variable numbers = list (10, 13, 16, 19)
replace-elements! (numbers, odd?, double)
   ⇒  #(10, 26, 16, 38)
```

<u>fill!</u>   **[Open Generic Function]**

Fills a collection with a specified value.

Signature: fill! *mutable-collection value* #key *start end* ⇒ *mutable-collection*

Arguments: *mutable-collection* An instance of `<mutable-collection>`.

 value   An instance of `<object>`.

 start   An instance of `<integer>`.

 end   An instance of `<integer>`.

Values: *mutable-collection* An instance of `<mutable-collection>`.

Description: Modifies *mutable-collection* so that `element` (*mutable-collection*, *key*) returns *value* for every *key*.

 If *mutable-collection* is a sequence, then *start* and *end* keywords may be specified to indicate that only a part of the sequence should be filled. *start* is considered an inclusive bound and defaults to 0; *end* is an exclusive bound and defaults to the length of the sequence.

```
define variable numbers = list (10, 13, 16, 19)
fill! (numbers, 3, start: 2)
 ⇒  #(10, 13, 3, 3)
```

The Iteration Protocol

<u>forward-iteration-protocol</u>   **[Open Generic Function]**

Returns a group of functions used to iterate over the elements of a collection.

Signature: forward-iteration-protocol *collection*
 ⇒ *initial-state limit next-state finished-state? current-key current-element current-element-setter copy-state*

Arguments: *collection*   An instance of `<collection>`.

Values: *initial-state*   An instance of `<object>`. The initial iteration state object.

limit   An instance of `<object>` that is used by the *finished-state?* function to determine whether the iteration has been completed.

next-state   An instance of `<function>`. Its signature is

                 `next-state` *collection state* ⇒ *new-state*

                 This function steps the iteration by producing a new state from the associated *collection* and *state*. The *next-state* function may or may not modify the *state* argument; it is an error to use a state value after it has been passed to the associated *next-state* function. The *copy-state* function provides a mechanism for saving a particular state in an iteration for later resumption.

finished-state? An instance of `<function>`. Its signature is

                 `finished-state?` *collection state limit* ⇒ *boolean*

                 This function returns `#t` if the iteration of the collection has been completed, i.e., there are no other elements of the collection to consider. It returns `#f` otherwise. It is an error to use a finished state in a call to the associated *next-state, current-element, current-key* or *current-element-setter* functions.

current-key   An instance of `<function>`. Its signature is

                 `current-key` *collection state* ⇒ *key*

                 This function returns the unique key associated with *state* in the *collection*. If the *current-key* function were called once with each *state* value produced during an iteration over a collection, the resulting sequence of values would contain every key from the collection exactly once; it would be the key-sequence of the collection.

current-element An instance of `<function>`. Its signature is

                 `current-element` *collection state* ⇒ *element*

                 This function returns the element of *collection* currently indicated by *state*.

current-element-setter An instance of `<function>`. Its signature is

                 `current-element-setter` *value collection state* ⇒ *value*

This function sets the element of *collection* indicated by *state* to *value* and returns *value*. If *collection* is not an instance of <mutable-collection>, or if the *value* is not of a type acceptable to the collection, an error is signaled.

copy-state An instance of <function>. Its signature is

copy-state *collection state* ⇒ *new-state*

This function returns a state that represents the same point in the iteration over *collection* as is represented by *state*.

Description: Returns eight values used to implement iteration over the *collection* argument.

Only the *collection* argument this function was called with may be used as the *collection* argument to functions returned by this function. Only the *initial-state* object and state objects returned by the *next-state* and *copy-state* functions may be used as the *state* argument to functions returned by this function. Only the *limit* object may be used as the *limit* argument to the *finished-state?* function. An example of the use of the iteration protocol is the following definition of a single-argument version of the do function:

```
define method do1 (f :: <function>, c :: <collection>)
  let (init, limit, next, end?, key, elt) =
                 forward-iteration-protocol(c);
  for (state = init then next(c, state),
    until: end?(c, state, limit))
    f(elt(c, state));
  end for;
end method do1;
```

forward-iteration-protocol *table*
⇒ *initial-state limit next-state finished-state? current-key current-element*
current-element-setter copy-state   **[Sealed G.F. Method]**

The method for <table> implements the iteration protocol in terms of the function table-protocol.

backward-iteration-protocol   **[Open Generic Function]**

Returns a group of functions used to iterate over the elements of a collection in reverse order.

Signature: `backward-iteration-protocol` *collection*
⇒ *initial-state limit next-state finished-state? current-key current-element current-element-setter copy-state*

Arguments: *collection*   An instance of `<collection>`.

Values: *initial-state*   An instance of `<object>`.

limit   An instance of `<object>`.

next-state   An instance of `<function>`.

finished-state?   An instance of `<function>`.

current-key   An instance of `<function>`.

current-element   An instance of `<function>`.

current-element-setter   An instance of `<function>`.

copy-state   An instance of `<function>`.

Description: Returns eight values used to implement reverse iteration over the *collection* argument.

Some collection classes that are stable under iteration support the ability to iterate in the reverse of the natural order, by providing a method on the generic function `backward-iteration-protocol`. The eight values returned by this function are analogous to the corresponding values returned by `forward-iteration-protocol`.

The Table Protocol

The class `<table>` provides an implementation of the iteration protocol, using the function `table-protocol`. Every concrete subclass of `<table>` must provide or inherit a method for `table-protocol`. A complete description of the table protocol is given in "Tables" on page 122.

`table-protocol`	**[Open Generic Function]**

Returns functions used to implement the iteration protocol for tables.

Signature: `table-protocol` *table* ⇒ *test-function hash-function*

Arguments: *table*   An instance of `<table>`.

Values: *test-function*   An instance of `<function>`. Its signature is

test-function *key1 key2* ⇒ *boolean*

test-function is used to compare keys. It returns true if the keys are members of the same equivalence class according to the table's equivalence predicate.

hash-function   An instance of `<function>`. Its signature is

hash-function *key* ⇒ *id state*

hash-function computes the hash code of the *key*, using the hash function associated with the table's equivalence predicate. The hash code is returned as two values, *id* (an integer) and *state* (a hash state).

Description: Returns the test-function and hash-function for the `<table>`. These functions are in turn used to implement the other collection operations on `<table>`.

`table-protocol` *object-table* ⇒ *test-function hash-function*[Sealed G.F. Method]

The method for `<object-table>` returns `==` as the *test-function* and `object-hash` as the *hash-function*.

The method for `<object-table>` could be written as

```
define method table-protocol (table :: <object-table>)
    => test-function :: <function>,
        hash-function :: <function>;
  values(\==, object-hash);
end method table-protocol;
```

---

merge-hash-codes   **[Function]**
_____

Returns a hash-code created from the merging of two argument hash codes.

Signature: merge-hash-codes *id1 state1 id2 state2* `#key` *ordered*
                  ⇒ *merged-id merged-state*

Arguments: *id1*   An instance of `<integer>`.

	state1	An instance of `<object>`.
	id2	An instance of `<integer>`.
	state2	An instance of `<object>`.
	ordered	An instance of `<boolean>`.
Values:	*merged-id*	An instance of `<integer>`.
	merged-state	An instance of `<object>`.

Description: Computes a new hash code by merging the argument hash codes in some implementation dependent way. This can be used, for example, to generate a hash-code for an object by combining hash codes of some of its parts.

id1, *id2*, and *merged-id* are all integers. *state1*, *state2*, and *merged-state* are all hash states. *ordered* is a boolean and determines whether the algorithm used to perform the merge is permitted to be order dependent. If false, which is the default, then the merged result must be independent of the order in which the argument pairs are provided. If true, then the order of the argument pairs matters because the algorithm used need not be either commutative or associative. It is best to provide a true value for *ordered* when possible, as this may result in a better distribution of hash ids. However, *ordered* must only be true if this will not cause the hash function to violate the second constraint on hash functions, described on page 123.

state1 and *state2* should be the value of `$permanant-hash-state` or hash-states returned from previous calls to `merge-hash-codes` or `object-hash`.

`object-hash`   **[Function]**

The hash function for the equivalence predicate `==`.

Signature: `object-hash` *object* ⇒ *hash-id hash-state*

Arguments: *object*   An instance of `<object>`.

Values: *hash-id*   An instance of `<integer>`.
           hash-state   An instance of `<object>`.

Description: Returns a hash-code for *object* that corresponds to the equivalence predicate ==. It is made available as a tool for writing hash functions in which the object identity of some component of a key is to be used in computing the hash code. It returns a hash id (an integer) and associated hash state for the object, computed in some implementation dependent manner. The values returned by `object-hash` when called repeatedly on the same object might not be the same for each call. If the *hash-id* value changes then the *hash-state* value will also change.

Reflective Operations on Types

The following functions return information on types and test type membership. They provide part of the implementation of the type protocol, as described in "The Type Protocol" beginning on page 49.

`instance?`	**[Function]**

Tests whether an object is an instance of a type.

Signature: `instance?` *object type* $\Rightarrow$ *boolean*

Arguments:
object	An instance of `<object>`.
type	An instance of `<type>`.

Values:
boolean	An instance of `<boolean>`.

Description: Returns true if *object* is a general instance of *type*.

`subtype?`	**[Function]**

Tests whether a type is a subtype of another type.

Signature: `subtype?` *type1 type2* $\Rightarrow$ *boolean*

Arguments:
type1	An instance of `<type>`.
type2	An instance of `<type>`.

Values: *boolean*   An instance of `<boolean>`.

Description: Returns true if *type₁* is a subtype of *type₂*. Subtype rules are given in "The Type Protocol" on page 49.

`object-class`   **[Function]**

Returns the class of an object.

Signature: `object-class` *object* ⇒ *class*

Arguments: *object*   An instance of `<object>`.

Values: *class*   An instance of `<class>`.

Description: Returns the class of which *object* is a direct instance.

`all-superclasses`   **[Function]**

Returns the class precedence list a class.

Signature: `all-superclasses` *class* ⇒ *sequence*

Arguments: *class*   An instance of `<class>`.

Values: *sequence*   An instance of `<sequence>`. Each element in the sequence is
                                      an instance of `<class>`.

Description: Returns the class precedence list of *class*. This is an ordered sequence of *class* and all its superclasses, as described in "Computing the Class Precedence List" on page 54.

The result *sequence* should never be destructively modified. Doing so may cause unpredictable behavior. If *class* is sealed, an implementation may choose to signal an error of type `<sealed-object-error>` rather than returning the sequence of all superclasses.

direct-superclasses   **[Function]**

Returns the direct superclasses of a class.

Signature: direct-superclasses *class* $\Rightarrow$ *sequence*

Arguments: *class*   An instance of <class>.

Values: *sequence*   An instance of <sequence>. Each element in the sequence is
                                 an instance of <class>.

Description: Returns the direct superclasses of *class* in a sequence. These are the classes that
                  were passed as arguments to make or define class when the *class* was
                  created. The order of the classes in the sequence is the same as the order in
                  which they were passed to define class or make when *class* was created.

                  The result *sequence* should never be destructively modified. Doing so may
                  cause unpredictable behavior. If *class* is sealed, an implementation may choose
                  to signal an error of type <sealed-object-error> rather than returning the
                  direct superclasses.

direct-subclasses   **[Function]**

Returns the direct subclasses of a class.

Signature: direct-subclasses *class* $\Rightarrow$ *sequence*

Arguments: *class*   An instance of <class>.

Values: *sequence*   An instance of <sequence>. Each element in the sequence is
                                 an instance of <class>.

Description: Returns the direct subclasses of *class* in a sequence. These are the classes that
                  have *class* as a direct superclass. The order of the classes in the sequence is not
                  significant.

                  The result *sequence* should never be destructively modified. Doing so may
                  cause unpredictable behavior. If *class* is sealed, an implementation may choose
                  to signal an error of type <sealed-object-error> rather than returning the
                  direct subclasses.

Functional Operations

The following operations are used to create new functions from other functions or objects. Often the Dylan compiler will have special knowledge of these operations to allow for efficient in-line compilation.

---

compose   **[Function]**

Returns the composition of one or more functions.

Signature: compose *function1* #rest *more-functions* ⇒ *function*

Arguments: *function1*   An instance of <function>.

more-functions   Instances of <function>.

Values: *function*   An instance of <function>.

Description: When called with just a single argument, compose returns that argument.

When called with two arguments, compose returns a function that applies the second function to its arguments and then applies the first function to the (single) result value.

With three or more arguments, compose composes pairs of argument functions, until a single composite function is obtained. (It doesn't matter if the pairings are done from the left or from the right, as long as the order of application is preserved.)

```
define constant number-of-methods =
   compose(size, generic-function-methods)

define constant root-position = compose(position, root-view)
```

---

complement   **[Function]**

Returns a function that expresses the complement of a predicate.

Signature:	`complement` *predicate* $\Rightarrow$ *function*	
Arguments:	*predicate*	An instance of `<function>`.
Values:	*function*	An instance of `<function>`.

Description: Returns a function that applies *predicate* to its arguments. If the *predicate* returns `#f`, the complement returns `#t`; otherwise, the complement returns `#f`. For example, `odd?` could be defined as `complement(even?)`.

```
choose(complement(zero?), #(1, 3, 0, 4, 0, 0, 3))
  ⇒  #(1, 3, 4, 3)
```

`disjoin`   **[Function]**

Returns a function that expresses the disjunction of one or more predicates.

Signature:	`disjoin` *predicate1* `#rest` *more-predicates* $\Rightarrow$ *function*	
Arguments:	*predicate1*	An instance of `<function>`.
	more-predicates	Functions.
Values:	*function*	An instance of `<function>`.

Description: Returns a single function, termed the disjunction of its argument functions. The disjunction accepts any number of arguments and operates by applying the predicates, in order, to the arguments. If any of the predicates returns true, the remaining predicates (if any) are not applied, and the true result is returned. Otherwise, all the predicates will be applied, and `#f` returned.

A disjunction is similar to an | expression of calls to the predicates.

```
define constant nonzero? = disjoin(positive?, negative?);
nonzero?(4)
  ⇒  #t
```

`conjoin`   **[Function]**

Returns a function that expresses the conjunction of one or more predicates.

Signature: `conjoin` *predicate1* #rest *more-predicates* ⇒ *function*

Arguments: *predicate1*   An instance of `<function>`.

more-predicates   Instances of `<function>`.

Values: *function*   An instance of `<function>`.

Description: Returns a single function, termed the conjunction of its argument functions. The conjunction accepts any number of arguments and operates by applying the predicates, in order, to the arguments. If any of the predicates returns `#f`, the remaining predicates (if any) are not applied and `#f` is immediately returned. Otherwise, all the predicates will be applied, and the result of the last application is returned.

A conjunction is similar to an `&` expression of calls to the predicates.

```
choose(conjoin(positive?, integral?), #(-1, -3, 5, -3.7, 3.5, 7))
   ⇒ #(5, 7)
```

---

curry   **[Function]**

Returns a function based on an existing function and a number of default initial arguments.

Signature: `curry` *function* #rest *curried-args* ⇒ *new-function*

Arguments: *function*   An instance of `<function>`.

curried-args   Instances of `<object>`.

Values: *new-function*   An instance of `<function>`.

Description: Returns a function that applies *function* to *curried-args* plus its own arguments, in that order. For example `curry (\>, 6)` is a predicate that returns true for values less than 6; `curry (\=, "x")` is a predicate that tests for equality with the string `"x"`; `curry (\+, 1)` is an incrementing function; `curry (concatenate, "set-")` is a function that concatenates the string `"set-"` to any additional sequences it is passed.

```
define constant all-odd? = curry(every?, odd?)
all-odd?(list(1, 3, 5))
  ⇒ #t

define constant less-than-10? = curry(\>, 10)
less-than-10?(4)
  ⇒ #t
```

`rcurry`	[Function]

Returns a function based on an existing function and a number of default final arguments.

Signature: rcurry *function* #rest *curried-args* ⇒ *new-function*

Arguments: *function*   An instance of `<function>`.

                curried-args   Instances of `<object>`.

Values: *new-function*   An instance of `<function>`.

Description: Returns a function that applies *function* to *curried-args* plus its own arguments, with the *curried-args* occurring last.

rcurry ("right" curry) operates just like curry, except it allows the rightmost arguments of *function* to be specified in advance, rather than the leftmost arguments. For example, rcurry (\>, 6) is a predicate that returns true for values greater than 6.

```
define constant number? = rcurry(instance?, <number>)
number?(4)
  ⇒ #t
number?("string")
  ⇒ #f

define constant greater-than-10? = rcurry(\>, 10)
greater-than-10?(4)
  ⇒ #f
```

always	[Function]

Returns a function that always returns a particular object.

Signature: always *object* $\Rightarrow$ *function*

Arguments: *object*   An instance of <object>.

Values: *function*   An instance of <function>.

Description: Returns a function that can be called with any number of arguments. The function ignores its arguments and always returns *object*.

```
define constant menu = always("spam!")
menu("today")
  ⇒ "spam!"
menu("tomorrow")
  ⇒ "spam!"
menu(4, 5, 6)
  ⇒ "spam!"
```

Function Application

apply	[Function]

Applies a function to arguments.

Signature: apply *function argument* #rest *more-arguments* $\Rightarrow$ #rest *values*

Arguments: *function*   An instance of <function>.

argument   An instance of <object> or, if there are no *more-arguments*, an instance of <sequence>.

more-arguments Instances of <object>. The last *more-arguments* must be an instance of <sequence>.

Values: *values*   Instances of <object>.

Description: Calls *function* and returns the values that *function* returns. The *argument* and *more-arguments* supply the arguments to *function*. All but the last of *argument* and *more-arguments* are passed to *function* individually. The last of *argument* and *more-arguments* must be a sequence. This sequence is not passed as a single argument to *function*. Instead, its elements are taken individually as arguments to *function*.

```
apply(max, list(3, 1, 4, 1, 5, 9))
  ⇒  9
apply(min 5, 7 list(3, 1, 4))
  ⇒  1

define constant make-string =
      method (#rest init-args) => string :: <string>;
        apply(make, <string>, init-args)
      end;
make-string(fill: 'a', size: 10)
  ⇒  "aaaaaaaaaa"
```

Reflective Operations on Functions

The following functions provide information on and manipulate other functions.

`generic-function-methods`	**[Function]**

Returns the methods of a generic function.

Signature: `generic-function-methods` *generic-function* ⇒ *sequence*

Arguments: *generic-function* An instance of `<generic-function>`.

Values: *sequence* An instance of `<sequence>`. Each element in the sequence is an instance of `<method>`.

Description: Returns a sequence of all of the methods in *generic-function*. The order of the methods in the sequence is not significant. The sequence returned should never be destructively modified. Doing so may cause unpredictable behavior.

If *generic-function* is sealed, an implementation may choose not to return a sequence of methods, but instead signal an error of type `<sealed-object-error>`.

`add-method`   **[Function]**

Adds a method to a generic function.

Signature: `add-method` *generic-function method* $\Rightarrow$ *new-method old-method*

Arguments: *generic-function*   An instance of `<generic-function>`.
                  method   An instance of `<method>`.

Values: *new-method*   An instance of `<method>`.
                  old-method   `#f` or an instance of `<method>`.

Description: Adds *method* to *generic-function*, thereby modifying the *generic-function*.

Programs do not commonly call `add-method` directly. It is called by `define method`.

If you add a method to a generic function, and the generic function already has a method with the exact same specializers, then the old method is replaced with the new one.

A single method may be added to any number of generic functions.

`add-method` returns two values. The first is the new *method*. The second will be either the method in *generic-function* that is being replaced by *method*, or it will be `#f` if no method is being replaced.

`add-method` may signal an error of type `<sealed-object-error>` if adding the method or replacing an existing method would cause a sealing violation.

If *generic-function* is sealed, or if *method* is in a sealed domain of *generic-function*, then an error of type `<sealed-object-error>` is signaled.

generic-function-mandatory-keywords   **[Function]**

Returns the mandatory keywords of a generic function, if any.

Signature: generic-function-mandatory-keywords *generic-function* ⇒ *keywords*

Arguments: *generic-function*   An instance of <generic-function>.

Values: *keywords*   The object #f or an instance of <collection>.

Description: If *generic-function* accepts keyword arguments, generic-function-mandatory-keywords returns a collection of the mandatory keywords for *generic-function*. This collection will be empty if the generic function accepts keywords but does not have any mandatory keywords. generic-function-mandatory-keywords returns #f if *generic-function* does not accept keyword arguments.

The collection returned should never be destructively modified. Doing so may cause unpredictable behavior.

function-specializers   **[Function]**

Returns the specializers of a function.

Signature: function-specializers *function* ⇒ *sequence*

Arguments: *function*   An instance of <function>.

Values: *sequence*   An instance of <sequence>. The elements of the sequence are instances of <type>.

Description: Returns a sequence of the specializers for *function*. The length of the sequence will equal the number of required arguments of *function*. The first element of the sequence will be the specializer of the first argument of *function*, the second will be the specializer of the second argument, and so on.

The sequence returned should never be destructively modified. Doing so may cause unpredictable behavior.

function-arguments   [Function]

Returns information about the arguments accepted by a function.

Signature: function-arguments *function* ⇒ *required-number rest-boolean kwd-sequence*

Arguments: *function*   An instance of <function>.

Values: *required-number*   An instance of <integer>.

                  rest-boolean   An instance of <boolean>.

                  kwd-sequence   Either #f or the symbol #"all" or an instance of
                                      <collection> whose elements are instances of <keyword>.

Description: Returns three values:

■ *required-number* is the number of required arguments accepted by the function.

■ *rest-boolean* indicates whether the function accepts a variable number of arguments.

■ *kwd-sequence* indicates whether the function accepts keyword arguments. If the value is #f then the function does not accept keyword arguments. Otherwise, the function does accept keyword arguments, and the value is either a collection of the keywords that are permissible for any call to the function, or the symbol #"all" if all keywords are permitted by the function.

Note that particular calls to a generic function may accept additional keywords not included in the third value returned by function-arguments, by virtue of their being recognized by applicable methods.

function-return-values   [Function]

Returns information about the values returned by a function.

Signature: function-return-values *function* ⇒ *return-value-types rest-return-value*

Arguments: *function*   An instance of <function>.

Values: *return-value-types* An instance of `<sequence>`. The elements of the sequence are instances of `<type>`.

rest-return-value An instance of `<type>` or `#f`.

Description: Returns two values:

■ *return-value-types* is a sequence of the types of values returned by the function. The length of the sequence equals the number of required return values of the function. The first element of the sequence is the type of the first return value, the second is the type of the second return value, etc. This sequence returned should never be destructively modified. Doing so may cause unpredictable behavior.

■ *rest-return-value* indicates whether the function returns a variable number of values and, if so, the type of values that may be returned after the required return values. If the function does not return a variable number of values, `#f` is returned; otherwise a type is returned.

`applicable-method?`   **[Function]**

Tests if a function is applicable to sample arguments.

Signature: `applicable-method?` *function* `#rest` *sample-args* ⇒ *boolean*

Arguments: *function*   An instance of `<function>`.

sample-args   Instances of `<object>`.

Values: *boolean*   An instance of `<boolean>`.

Description: Returns true if *function* is a method that would be applicable to *sample-args* or if it is a generic function that contains a method that would be applicable to *sample-args*.

Note that if *function* is a generic function, then calling it with the *sample-args* may still signal an error, even if `applicable-method?` returns true. This is because the generic function may contain methods that are ambiguous relative to the *sample-args*. See "Method Specificity" on page 96 for a complete description of ambiguous methods.

If *function* is a sealed generic function, `applicable-method?` may signal an error of type `<sealed-object-error>`.

`sorted-applicable-methods`   **[Function]**

Returns all the methods in a generic function that are applicable to sample
arguments, sorted in order of specificity.

Signature: `sorted-applicable-methods` *generic-function* `#rest` *sample-args*
                   ⇒ *sorted-methods unsorted-methods*

Arguments: *generic-function*   An instance of `<generic-function>`.

                   sample-args   Instances of `<object>`.

Values: *sorted-methods*   An instance of `<sequence>`. Elements of the sequence are
                                          instances of `<method>`.

                   unsorted-methods   An instance of `<sequence>`. Elements of the collection are
                                          instances of `<method>`.

Description: Returns two sequences that, taken together, contain the methods in
                   generic-function that are applicable to the *sample-args. sorted-methods* contains
                   methods that are more specific than every method that follows them.
                   unsorted-methods begins at the first point of ambiguity; it contains the methods
                   that cannot be sorted.

                   The sequences returned should never be destructively modified. Doing so may
                   cause unpredictable behavior.

                   If *generic-function* is sealed, an implementation may choose not to return two
                   sequences of methods, but instead signal an error of type
                   `<sealed-object-error>`.

`find-method`   **[Function]**

Returns the method in a generic function that has particular specializers.

Signature: `find-method` *generic-function specializers* ⇒ *found-method*

Arguments: *generic-function*   An instance of `<generic-function>`.

                   specializers   An instance of `<sequence>`. Elements of the sequence are
                                          instances of `<type>`.

Values: *found-method*   `#f` or an instance of `<method>`.

Description: Returns the method in *generic-function* that has the specializers in *specializers* as its specializers. The specializers must match exactly for a method to be returned.

If *generic-function* is sealed, an implementation may choose to signal an error of type `<sealed-object-error>` rather than return a value.

`remove-method`	**[Function]**

Removes a method from a generic function.

Signature: `remove-method` *generic-function method* ⇒ *method*

Arguments: *generic-function*   An instance of `<generic-function>`.

               method   An instance of `<method>`.

Values: *method*   An instance of `<method>`.

Description: Removes *method* from *generic-function* and returns *method*.

This operation modifies the *generic-function*.

If *generic-function* is sealed, or if *method* is in a sealed domain of *generic-function*, then an error of type `<sealed-object-error>` is signaled.

Operations on Conditions

The following functions are used to create, signal, handle, and examine conditions.

Signaling Conditions

`signal`	**[Function]**

Signals a condition.

Signatures: signal *condition* ⇒ #rest *values*
signal *string* #rest *arguments* ⇒ #rest *values*

Arguments (1): *condition*   An instance of <condition>.

Arguments (2): *string*   An instance of <string>.

arguments   Instances of <object>.

Values: *values*   Instances of <object>.

Description: Signals the *condition*, trying each active dynamic handler, the most recent first.
If all dynamic handlers decline, signal calls default-handler (*condition*).
If a handler returns, all the values that it returned are returned from signal. If
signal returns when *condition*'s recovery protocol does not allow returning,
some handler has violated protocol; signal does not check for this error. If
condition is a restart, the caller of signal should always assume that it might
return.

The second form signals a condition of type <simple-warning>.

---

error   **[Function]**

Signals a nonrecoverable error.

Signatures: error *condition* ⇒ {*will never return*}
error *string* #rest *arguments* ⇒ {*will never return*}

Arguments (1): *condition*   An instance of <condition>.

Arguments (2): *string*   An instance of <string>.

arguments   Instances of <object>.

Values: None. error will never return.

Description: error is similar to signal but never returns; if a handler returns, error
invokes the debugger immediately. error is used to make it clear that a
program does not expect to receive control again after signaling a condition
and might enable the compiler to generate slightly more compact code.

The second form signals a condition of type <simple-error>.

`cerror`	[Function]

Signals a correctable error.

Signatures: `cerror` *restart-description condition* ⇒ *false*
                  `cerror` *restart-description string* #rest *arguments* ⇒ *false*

Arguments (1):   *restart-description* An instance of `<string>`, interpreted as a format string.

                     condition   An instance of `<condition>`.

Arguments (2):   *restart-description* An instance of `<string>`, interpreted as a format string.

                     string   An instance of `<string>`.

                     arguments   Instances of `<object>`.

Values: *false*   #f.

Description: `cerror` is the same as `error` but first establishes a handler for
                   `<simple-restart>`, with a format string of *restart-description* and format
                   arguments of a sequence containing the *arguments*.

                   If the restart handler is invoked, `cerror` returns #f; otherwise, `cerror` never
                   returns. If `cerror` returns, the program should take the corrective actions
                   promised in the *restart-description*. `cerror` is the standard way to signal
                   correctable errors when no special class of restart condition is required.

`break`	[Function]

Invokes the debugger.

Signatures: `break` *condition* ⇒ *false*
                  `break` *string* #rest *arguments* ⇒ *false*
                  `break` ⇒ *false*

Arguments (1):   *condition*   An instance of `<condition>`.

Arguments (2):   *string*   An instance of `<string>`, interpreted as a format string.

                     arguments   Instances of `<object>`, interpreted as format arguments.

Arguments (3):   None.

Values: *false*   #f.

Description: Obtains a condition in the same way as signal but then invokes the debugger
immediately without signaling first. break establishes a <simple-restart>
so the debugger can continue execution. This is useful for breakpoints. break
always returns #f. With no arguments, a default message string is used.

The behavior of the debugger is implementation-defined.

---

check-type   **[Function]**

Checks an object to ensure that it is an instance of a specified type.

Signature: check-type *value type* ⇒ *value*

Arguments: *value*   An instance of <object>.

                  type   An instance of <type>.

Values: *value*   An instance of <object>.

Description: Checks *value* to ensure that it is an instance of *type*, and signal an error of type
<type-error> if it is not.

---

abort   **[Function]**

Aborts and never returns.

Signature: abort

Arguments: None.

Values: None. abort will never return.

Description: Performs error(make (<abort>)).

This function is provided as a convenient shortcut. The call is to error, rather
than to signal, to guarantee that abort will never return.

Handling Conditions

`default-handler`	**[Open Generic Function]**

Called if no dynamic handler handles a condition.

Signature: default-handler *condition* ⇒ #rest *values*

Arguments: *condition* An instance of <condition>.

Values: *values* Instances of <object>.

Description: Called if no dynamic handler handles a condition.

> **default-handler** *condition* ⇒ **false** **[G.F. Method]**
>
> A predefined method on <condition> simply returns #f.

> **default-handler** *serious-condition* ⇒ **{does not return}** **[G.F. Method]**
>
> A predefined method on <serious-condition> invokes an implementation-defined debugger.

> **default-handler** *warning* ⇒ **false** **[G.F. Method]**
>
> A predefined method on <warning> prints the warning's message in an implementation-defined way and then returns #f.

> **default-handler** *restart* ⇒ **{does not return}** **[Sealed G.F. Method]**
>
> A predefined method on <restart> signals an error.

`restart-query`	**[Open Generic Function]**

Called to query the user and restart.

Signature: restart-query *restart* ⇒ #rest *values*

Arguments: *restart* An instance of <restart>.

Values: *values*   Instances of <object>.

Description: Engages the interactive user in a dialog and stores the results in slots of *restart*.

This function is designed to be called from a handler, after making a restart and before signaling it. The debugger uses restart-query, for example.

restart-query *restart* ⇒ *object*   [G.F. Method]

There is a default method for <restart> that does nothing.

---

return-query   **[Open Generic Function]**

Queries the user for values to return.

Signature: return-query *condition* ⇒ #rest *values*

Arguments: *condition*   An instance of <condition>.

Values: *values*   Instances of <object>.

Description: If the recovery protocol of *condition* allows returning values, this engages the program user in a dialog and returns the results as any number of values, which the handler should return.

return-query should not be called if return-allowed? returns #f. Programs that define condition classes whose recovery protocol allows returning values should ensure that there is an appropriate method for this function defined on or inherited by the condition class.

Introspection on Conditions

---

do-handlers   **[Function]**

Applies a function to all dynamically active handlers.

Signature: do-handlers *function* ⇒ *false*

Arguments: *function*   An instance of <function>.

Values: *false*   #f.

Description: Applies *function* to all dynamically active handlers, the most recently established first. *function* receives four arguments: *type*, *test*, *function*, and *init-arguments*. The arguments describe a dynamically active handler. All arguments have dynamic extent and must not be modified. *test* defaults to a function that always returns #t. *init-arguments* will be an empty sequence if it was not supplied by the handler.

---

return-allowed?   **[Open Generic Function]**

Returns true if a condition's recovery protocol allows returning values.

Signature: return-allowed? *condition* ⇒ *boolean*

Arguments: *condition*   An instance of <condition>.

Values: *boolean*   An instance of <boolean>.

Description: Returns #t if the recovery protocol of *condition* allows returning values, or #f if it does not.

There is a default method for <condition> that returns #f. Programs which define condition classes whose recovery protocol allows returning values should ensure that there is an appropriate method for this function defined on or inherited by the condition class.

return-allowed? *condition* ⇒ *false*   **[G.F. Method]**

There is a default method for <condition> that returns #f.

---

return-description   **[Open Generic Function]**

Returns a description of a condition's returned values.

Signature: return-description *condition* ⇒ *description*

Arguments: *condition*   An instance of <condition>.

Values: *description*   #f or an instance of <string> or an instance of <restart>.

Description: If the recovery protocol of this condition allows returning values, `return-description` returns a description of the meaning of returning values.

This *description* can be a restart, a string, or `#f`. `return-description` should not be called if `return-allowed?` returns `#f`. If you define your own condition class whose recovery protocol allows returning values, you need to define a method for `return-description` unless the inherited method is suitable.

`condition-format-string`   **[Function]**

Returns the format string of a simple condition.

Signature: `condition-format-string` *simple-condition* ⇒ *format-string*

Arguments: *simple-condition*   An instance of `<simple-error>`, `<simple-warning>`, or `<simple-restart>`.

Values: *format-string*   An instance of `<string>`.

Description: Returns the format string that was supplied as an initialization argument when the *simple-condition* was created.

`condition-format-arguments`   **[Function]**

Returns the format arguments of a simple condition.

Signature: `condition-format-arguments` *simple-condition* ⇒ *format-args*

Arguments: *simple-condition*   An instance of `<simple-error>`, `<simple-warning>`, or `<simple-restart>`.

Values: *format-args*   An instance of `<sequence>`.

Description: Returns the sequence of format arguments that was supplied as an initialization argument when the *simple-condition* was created.

`type-error-value`	**[Function]**

Returns the value that was not of the expected type.

Signature: `type-error-value` *type-error* ⇒ *object*

Arguments: *type-error*   An instance of `<type-error>`.

Values: *object*   An instance of `<object>`.

Description: Returns the value that was not of the expected type, and thereby led to the type error.

`type-error-expected-type`	**[Function]**

Returns the expected type of the type check that led to the type error.

Signature: `type-error-expected-type` *type-error* ⇒ *type*

Arguments: *type-error*   An instance of `<type-error>`.

Values: *type*   An instance of `<type>`.

Description: Returns the expected type of the type check that led to the type error.

Other Built-In Objects

Contents

Other Built-In Objects   369

Other Built-In Objects

Dylan contains a small number of predefined unique program constants, described below.

#t   [**\<boolean\>**]

The canonical true value.

#f   [**\<boolean\>**]

The false value.

$permanent-hash-state   [**\<object\>**]

A hash state that is always valid.

This is an implementation-dependent hash state that indicates that the associated hash id is always valid, and does not depend on any mutable property of the object that can be changed without a visible modification to the object.

#()   [**\<empty-list\>**]

The empty list.

The Built-In Macros and Special Definitions

Contents

Overview   373
Definitions   373
Local Declarations   389
Statements   393
  Conditionals   394
  Iteration Constructs   399
  Other Statement Macros   404
Function Macros   409
  Assignment   409
  Conditional Execution   412

Overview

This chapter contains descriptions of the built-in macros and special definitions defined by Dylan.

The syntax used in this chapter is described in "Manual Notation" on page 6.

Definitions

Definitions are used to declare the overall structure of a program. They often define one or more module bindings, but do not always do so. Definitions can only appear at top level in a program. Definitions do not return values.

Table 14-1   Definitions

Macro	Description	Page
define variable	Defines and initializes a variable binding in the current module.	374
define constant	Defines and initializes a constant binding in the current module.	375
define generic	Defines a constant binding in the current module and initializes it to a new generic function.	376
define method	Adds a method to a generic function, and potentially defines a constant binding in the current module containing a new generic function.	377
define class	Defines a constant binding in the current module and initializes it to a new class.	378
define module	Defines and names a module, describing the imports and exports of the module.	380

continued

Table 14-1 Definitions (continued)

Macro	Description	Page
define library	Defines and names a library, describing the imports and exports of the library.	386
define domain	Restricts the ways in which a generic function and set of types can be extended, thereby enabling additional error checking and compiler optimization.	388
define macro	Defines a constant module binding containing a macro.	389

define variable [Definition]

Defines and initializes a variable binding in the current module.

Macro Call: define { *adjective* }* variable *variables* = *init*

Arguments:

adjective unreserved-name$_{bnf}$. The adjectives allowed are implementation dependent.

variables variable$_{bnf}$ | (variable-list$_{bnf}$)

init expression$_{bnf}$

Description: define variable defines variable bindings in the current module.

The values returned by *init* are used to initialize the bindings. The first value returned is bound to the first *variable*, the second value to the second *variable*, etc. The last *variable* may be preceded by #rest, in which case it is bound to a sequence containing all the remaining values.

If more than one binding is defined, the *variables* are enclosed in parentheses and separated by commas.

```
define variable *elapsed-time* = 0;

define variable (*whole-part*, *remainder*) = truncate(*amount*);

define variable (*first-value*, #rest *rest-values*)
            = get-initial-orders();
```

Module bindings may be specialized. This ensures that their value will always be of a given type. An attempt to initialize or assign the binding to a value not of that type will signal an error of type <type-error>.

```
define variable *elapsed-time* :: <integer> = 0;

define variable *front-window* :: type-union (<window>, singleton(#f))
                = initial-front-window();

define variable (*whole-part* :: <integer>, *remainder* :: <real>)
                = truncate(*amount*);
```

---

define constant   **[Definition]**

Defines and initializes a constant binding in the current module.

Macro Call: define { *adjective* }* constant *constants* = *init*

Arguments: *adjective*   unreserved-name*bnf*. The adjectives allowed are implementation dependent.

  constants   variable*bnf* | (variable-list*bnf*)

  init   expression*bnf*

Description: define constant defines constant bindings in the current module.

The values returned by *init* are used to initialize the constant bindings. The first value returned is bound to the first *constant*, the second value to the second *constant*, etc. The last *constant* may be preceded by #rest, in which case it is bound to a sequence containing all the remaining values.

If more than one *constant* is defined, the *constants* are enclosed in parentheses and separated by commas.

```
define constant $start-time = get-current-time();

define constant $pi = 3.14159;

define constant ($whole-pie, $piece-pie) = truncate($pi);
```

Module constants may be specialized. This ensures that their value is of a given type. An attempt to initialize the constant to a value not of that type will signal an error of type `<type-error>`.

```
define constant $start-time :: <integer> = get-current-time();
```

A constant binding cannot be assigned a new value. However, the object that is the value of the constant binding is not necessarily itself immutable. For example, if a constant binding contains a sequence, the elements of the sequence may be settable.

---

define generic   [Definition]

Defines a constant binding in the current module and initializes it to a new generic function.

Macro Call: define { *adjective* }* generic *name parameter-list* [*options*]

Arguments: *adjective*   unreserved-name*bnf*. The allowed adjectives are `sealed` and `open`. These adjectives are mutually exclusive. The default is `sealed`. Additional implementation-defined adjectives may be supported.

    name   variable-name*bnf*

    parameter-list   ([parameters*bnf*]) [=> *values*]

    options   comma-property-list*bnf*

    values   variable*bnf* | ([values-list*bnf*])

Description: `define generic` is used to define generic functions.

It defines a constant module binding with the name *name*, and initializes it to a new generic function described by the *adjectives*, *parameter-list* and *options*.

The *adjectives* specify whether the generic function is sealed. A complete description of generic function sealing is given in "Declaring Characteristics of Generic Functions" on page 135.

The *parameter-list* specifies the parameters and return values of the generic function and thereby constrains which methods may be added to it. For a complete description of these constraints, see "Parameter List Congruency" on page 93. A generic function parameter list may not include a next-method parameter, and its keyword parameters may include neither type specializers nor default initial values.

The *options* are alternating keywords and values. No options are defined by the language. They may be supplied by individual implementations.

The following example defines a generic function of two required arguments and one return value. All methods added to the generic function must also take two arguments and return one value. The first argument will always be specialized to a subtype of <animal>, the second argument will always be specialized to a subtype of <number>, and the return value will always be specialized to a subtype of <number>.

```
define generic cut-hair (subject :: <animal>, new-length :: <number>)
                     => (new-length :: <number>)
```

The use of the same name for a parameter and return value indicates that the parameter is returned as the value. This is only a convention; it is not enforced by the language.

The following example defines a generic function with one required parameter and one mandatory keyword parameter, `strength:`. Methods added to the generic function must have one required parameter, they must accept keyword arguments, and they must permit the keyword argument `strength:`.

```
define generic brew (brand :: <coffee-brand>, #key strength)
                   => (coffee :: <coffee>)
```

---

define method   **[Definition]**

Adds a method to a generic function, and potentially defines a constant binding in the current module containing a new generic function.

Macro Call: define { *adjective* }* method *name parameter-list*
  [*body*]
end [method] [*name*]

Arguments: *adjective*   unreserved-name*bnf*. The allowed adjective is `sealed`.
          Additional implementation-defined *adjectives* may be supported.

        name   variable-name*bnf*

parameter-list	parameter-list$_{bnf}$
body	body$_{bnf}$.

Description: `define method` creates a method and adds it to the generic function in *name*. If the module binding *name* is not already defined, it is defined as with `define generic`. Thus, `define method` will create a new generic function or extend an old one, as needed.

The *adjective* allows a sealing declaration to be made about the generic function to which the method is added. The effect of this adjective is described in "Abbreviations for Define Sealed Domain" on page 138.

The *parameter-list* describes the parameters and return values of the method, including their number and type. The method can be called only with arguments that match the types of the parameters, and the method will always return values in the quantity and typed declared. Methods added to a generic function must have parameter lists that are congruent with the generic function's parameter list. A complete description of parameter lists is given in "Parameter Lists" on page 84.

When the method is called, new local bindings are created for the parameters, initialized to the arguments of the call. The *body* is then executed in the environment containing these bindings.

```
define method tune (device :: <radio>) => (station :: <station>)
  // method body goes here
end method tune
```

---

define class   **[Definition]**

Defines a constant binding in the current module and initializes it to a new class.

Macro Call:
```
define { class-adjective }* class name ( { superclass } , + )
  { slot-spec | init-arg-spec | inherited-slot-spec } ; *
end [ class ] [ name ]
```

Arguments: *class-adjective*   unreserved-name$_{bnf}$. The allowed adjectives are `abstract`, `concrete`, `primary`, `free`, `sealed`, and `open`. Additional implementation-dependent class-adjectives may be supported.

The Built-In Macros and Special Definitions

name	variable-name$_{bnf}$
superclass	expression$_{bnf}$
slot-spec	{ *slot-adjective* }* [*allocation*] `slot` *getter-name* [`::` *type*] [*init-expression*] { , *slot-option* }*
init-arg-spec	[`required`] `keyword` symbol$_{bnf}$ [*init-expression*] { , *init-arg-option* }*
inherited-slot-spec	`inherited slot` *getter-name* [*init-expression*] { , *inherited-option* }*
slot-adjective	unreserved-name$_{bnf}$. Supported slot-adjectives are `constant` and `sealed`. Additional implementation-dependent slot-adjectives may be supported.
allocation	unreserved-name$_{bnf}$. Supported allocations are `instance`, `class`, `each-subclass`, and `virtual`. Additional implementation-defined allocations may be supported.
getter-name	variable-name$_{bnf}$
type	operand$_{bnf}$
init-expression	= expression$_{bnf}$
slot-option	*setter-option* | *init-keyword-option* | *required-init-keyword-option* | *init-value-option* | *init-function-option* | *type-option*
init-arg-option	*type-option* | *init-value-option* | *init-function-option*
inherited-option	*init-value-option* | *init-function-option*
setter-option	`setter:` { variable-name$_{bnf}$ | `#f` }
init-keyword-option	`init-keyword:` symbol$_{bnf}$
required-init-keyword-option	`required-init-keyword:` symbol$_{bnf}$

init-value- *option*	`init-value:` expression$_{bnf}$
init-function- *option*	`init-function:` expression$_{bnf}$
type-option	`type:` expression$_{bnf}$

Description:

`define class` is used to define classes.

It defines a constant module binding with the name *name*, and initializes it to a new class.

The *class-adjectives* provide sealing information about the class. Among the adjectives, `abstract` and `concrete` are mutually exclusive, `primary` and `free` are mutually exclusive, and `sealed` and `open` are mutually exclusive. Additional implementation-defined adjectives may be supported. See "Declaring Characteristics of Classes" on page 134 for a complete description of these adjectives.

The *superclasses* are the classes from which the new class directly inherits. The rules of inheritance are described in "Class Inheritance" on page 53 and "Computing the Class Precedence List" on page 54.

The *init-expression, required-init-keyword-option, init-value-option,* and *init-function-option* are all mutually exclusive in a single *slot-spec, init-arg-spec,* or *inherited-slot-spec.*

Each *slot-spec* describes a slot specification in the class. Slot specifications are described in "Slot Specifications" on page 58

Each *init-arg-spec* describes the handling of an initialization argument specification of the class. Initialization argument specifications are described in "Initialization Argument Specifications" on page 68.

Each *inherited-slot-spec* describes an inherited slot specification of the class. Inherited slot specifications are described in "Inherited Slot Specifications" on page 67.

define module   **[Definition]**

Defines and names a module, describing the imports and exports of the module.

The Built-In Macros and Special Definitions

Macro Call:

```
define module module-name
  { export-clause | create-clause | use-clause } ; *
end [ module ] [ module-name ]
```

Arguments:

module-name	name$_{bnf}$
export-clause	export { ordinary-name$_{bnf}$ } , *
create-clause	create { ordinary-name$_{bnf}$ } , *
use-clause	use *used-module* { , *option* }*
used-module	ordinary-name$_{bnf}$
option	*import-option* |
	exclude-option |
	prefix-option |
	rename-option |
	export-option
import-option	import: all | { { *variable-spec* } , * }
variable-spec	name$_{bnf}$ [=> name$_{bnf}$]
exclude-option	exclude: { { name$_{bnf}$ } , * }
prefix-option	prefix: string-literal$_{bnf}$
rename-option	rename: { { name$_{bnf}$ => name$_{bnf}$ } , * }
export-option	export: all | { { name$_{bnf}$ } , * }

Description:

define module defines a module with the given name. It describes which modules are used by the module being defined, which bindings are imported from the used modules, and which bindings are exported by the module being defined.

Circular use relationships among modules are not allowed. The graph of the module-uses-module relation must be directed and acyclic.

Like other definitions, module definitions are only allowed at top level. Like all constituents, module definitions are contained in a module. The names of bindings being imported and exported in a module definition refer to bindings in the module being defined and the modules being used. These are not affected by the module that contains the module definition.

There is no prohibition against macros that expand into module definitions.

- *module-name* is the name of the module being defined. Note that no binding is created for this name. The namespaces of modules, libraries, and bindings are distinct. The module name is scoped within the library containing the module.

- An *export-clause* specifies bindings that are to be exported from the module being defined. Each name is the name of one such binding. These bindings must be defined by a definition in the module being defined. It is an error if any of the bindings were imported from other modules. It is allowed for the same name to appear more than once, since this is sometimes useful for documentation purposes.

- A *create-clause* specifies that the named bindings are to be declared owned by and exported from the module being defined. Each name is the name of a binding to declare and export. These bindings must not be defined by a definition in the module being defined, and they must not be imported from another module. They must be defined by a definition in a module that uses the module being defined. It is allowed for the same name to appear more than once, since this is sometimes useful for documentation purposes.

- Each *use-clause* describes a set of bindings to be imported from another module. There may be multiple use clauses and there may even be multiple use clauses importing from the same module. If there are multiple use clauses importing from the same module, the bindings imported are the sum of the binding imported by each use clause. Because of renaming, it is possible for the same binding to imported multiple times under different names. This is not an error.

  Within a use clause, the *used-module* is the name of the module being used, and the options control which bindings are to be imported from that module, whether and how they should be renamed, and whether they should be reexported from the module being defined. Each of these options applies within the scope of the particular use clause, and does not affect the behavior of other use clauses (even if the other use clauses indicate the same module). The various options may each appear no more than once in a single use clause. They may appear in any order.

  - An *import-option* describes which bindings should be imported. It can be the name `all`, or a series of comma-delimited *variable-specs* enclosed in curly braces. The default is `all`, indicating that all bindings should be imported. If a series of *variable-specs* is specified, only the indicated variables are imported.

☐ A *variable-spec* is a name, or two names separated by an arrow. In the first form, the binding has the same name in the module being used and the module being defined. In the second form the binding is renamed as it is imported. The name preceding the arrow is the name of the binding in the module being used, and the name following the arrow is the name of the binding in the module being defined.

☐ An *exclude-option* indicates bindings that should not be imported from the module being used. The default is the empty set. This option may only specify a nonempty set if the import option is `all`.

☐ A *prefix-option* indicates a prefix to be given to all binding names as they are imported. This option can be overriden for individual bindings by supplying a renaming in a rename option or import option. The default prefix option is the empty string.

☐ A *rename-option* indicates how individual bindings should be renamed as they are imported. It is a comma-delimited series of entries surrounded by curly braces. Each entry is a pair of names separated by an arrow. The name preceding the arrow is the name of the binding in the module being used, and the name following the arrow is the name of the binding in the module being defined. The default for this option is the empty set.

☐ An *export-option* indicates which imported bindings should be reexported from the module being defined. It can be the name `all`, or a series of comma-delimited names enclosed in curly braces. Each name is the name of the binding in the module being defined as well as the name under which it will be exported. (There is no option to rename on export) Each binding indicated must have been imported by this use clause. It is allowed for the same name to appear more than once, as this is sometimes useful for documentation purposes. `all` indicates that all the bindings imported by this use clause should be exported. The default value for this option is the empty set.

```
define module graphics
   use dylan;
   create draw-line,
          erase-line,
          invert-line,
          skew-line,
          frame-rect,
          fill-rect,
          erase-rect,
```

```
            invert-rect;
    end module graphics;

    define module lines
      use dylan;
      use graphics,
        import: {draw-line,
                   erase-line,
                   invert-line,
                   skew-line};
    end module lines;

    define module rectangles
      use dylan;
      use graphics,
        prefix: "graphics$",
        exclude: {skew-line};
    end module rectangles;

    define module dylan-gx
      use dylan, export: all;
      use graphics,
        rename: {skew-line => warp-line},
          export: all;
    end module dylan-gx;
```

The modules created by these module declarations would have access to bindings with the following names:

```
graphics
        draw-line
        erase-line
        invert-line
        skew-line
        frame-rect
        fill-rect
```

```
        erase-rect
        invert-rect
        plus all the bindings in the Dylan module
```

lines

```
        draw-line
        erase-line
        invert-line
        skew-line
        plus all the bindings in the Dylan module
```

rectangles

```
        graphics$draw-line
        graphics$erase-line
        graphics$invert-line
        graphics$frame-rect
        graphics$fill-rect
        graphics$erase-rect
        graphics$invert-rect
        plus all the bindings in the Dylan module
```

dylan-gx

```
        draw-line
        erase-line
        invert-line
        warp-line
        frame-rect
        fill-rect
        erase-rect
        invert-rect
        plus all the bindings in the Dylan module
```

The lines and rectangles modules do not export any variables. They are presumably used to provide definitions for the variables created and exported by the graphics modules. The difference between the graphics module and the dylan-gx module is that one variable is renamed, and the dylan-gx module exports the variables that it imports from the dylan module, while the graphics module does not.

`define library` [Definition]

Defines and names a library, describing the imports and exports of the library.

Macro Call:
```
define library library-name
  { export-clause | use-clause } ; *
end [ library ] [ library-name ]
```

Arguments:

library-name	name*bnf*
use-clause	use *used-library* { , *option* }*
export-clause	export { ordinary-name*bnf* } , *
used-library	ordinary-name*bnf*
option	*import-option*	
	exclude-option	
	prefix-option	
	rename-option	
	export-option
import-option	import: all	{ { *module-spec* } , * }
module-spec	name*bnf* [=> name*bnf*]
exclude-option	exclude: { { name*bnf* } , * }
prefix-option	prefix: string-literal*bnf*
rename-option	rename: { { name*bnf* => name*bnf* } , * }
export-option	export: all	{ { name*bnf* } , * }

Description:
`define library` defines a library with the given name. It describes which libraries are used by the library being defined, which modules are imported from the used libraries, and which modules are exported by the library being defined.

Circular use relationships among libraries are not allowed. The graph of the library-uses-library relation must be directed and acyclic.

Like other definitions, library definitions are only allowed at top level. Like all constituents, library definitions are contained in a module. The names of modules being imported and exported by a library definition do not refer to bindings, and are not affected by the environment in which the library definition occurs.

There is no prohibition against macros that expand into library definitions.

- *library-name* is the name of the library being defined. Note that no binding is created for this name. The namespaces of libraries, modules, and bindings are distinct. The library name is scoped along with the other library names in the program.

- An *export-clause* specifies modules that are to be exported from the library being defined. Each name is the name of one such module. It is an error if any of the modules were imported from other libraries. It is allowed for the same name to appear more than once, since this is sometimes useful for documentation purposes.

- Each *use-clause* describes a set of modules to be imported from another library. There may be multiple use clauses and there may even be multiple use clauses importing from the same library. If there are multiple use clauses importing from the same library, the modules imported are the sum of the modules imported by each use clause. Because of renaming, it is possible for the same module to imported multiple times under different names. This is not an error.

Within a use clause, the *used-library* is the name of the library being used. The mechanism by which this name is associated with another library is implementation defined.

The *options* control which modules are to be imported from that library, whether and how they should be renamed, and whether they should be reexported from the library being defined. Each of these options applies within the scope of the particular use clause, and does not affect the behavior of other use clauses (even if the other use clauses indicate the same library). The various options may each appear no more than once in a single use clause. They may appear in any order.

  - An *import-option* describes which modules should be imported. It can be the name `all`, or a series of comma-delimited *module-specs* enclosed in curly braces. The default is `all`, indicating that all modules should be imported. If a series of *module-specs* is specified, only the indicated modules are imported.

  - A *module-spec* is a name, or two names separated by an arrow. In the first form, the module has the same name in the library being used and the library being defined. In the second form the module is renamed as it is imported. The name preceding the arrow is the name of the module in the library being used, and the name following the arrow is the name of the module in the library being defined.

☐ An *exclude-option* indicates modules that should not be imported from the library being used. The default is the empty set. This option may only specify a nonempty set if the import option is `all`.

☐ A *prefix-option* indicates a prefix to be given to all module names as they are imported. This option can be overriden for individual modules by supplying a renaming in the rename option or import option. The default prefix option is the empty string.

☐ A *rename-option* indicates how individual modules should be renamed as they are imported. It is a comma-delimited series of entries surrounded by curly braces. Each entry is a pair of names separated by an arrow. The name preceding the arrow is the name of the module in the library being used, and the name following the arrow is the name of the module in the library being defined. The default for this option is the empty set.

☐ An *export-option* indicates which imported modules should be reexported from the library being defined. It can be the name `all`, or a series of comma-delimited names enclosed in curly braces. Each name is the name of the module in the library being defined as well as the name under which it will be exported. (There is no option to rename on export) Each module indicated must have been imported by this use clause. It is allowed for the same name to appear more than once, as this is sometimes useful for documentation purposes. `all` indicates that all the modules imported by this use clause should be exported. The default value for this option is the empty set.

`define sealed domain`   **[Definition]**

Restricts the ways in which a generic function and set of types can be extended, thereby enabling additional error checking and compiler optimization.

Macro Call: `define sealed domain` *generic-function* ({ *type* } ,*)

Arguments: *generic-function* variable-name$_{bnf}$

type   expression$_{bnf}$

Description: define sealed domain seals the specified *generic-function* over the domain indicated by the *types*. For a complete description of the rules governing define sealed domain and the implications of a define sealed domain definition, see "Define Sealed Domain" on page 135.

- *generic-function* is the name of a module binding containing an explicitly defined generic function.

- Each *type* is an expression, the value of which must be a type. The number of *types* must be the same as the number of required arguments accepted by *generic-function*.

---

define macro   **[Special Definition]**

Defines a constant module binding containing a macro.

Macro Call: define macro *macro-definition*

Arguments: *macro-definition*   macro-definition*bnf*

Description: See Chapter 10, "Macros," for a complete description of the macro system.

Note that define macro is not a defining macro but a special definition. It is not named by a binding, and so it cannot being excluded or renamed using module operations.

Local Declarations

Local declarations are used to create bindings or install handlers that are active for the remainder of the innermost body containing the declaration. Bindings created by local declarations can be referenced only in the remaining program text of the body. Handlers installed are active while the execution of the remainder of the body is active, which includes the time during which any functions called from the remainder of the body are active.

Table 14-2   Local Declarations

Macro	Description	Page
let	Creates and initializes new local bindings within the smallest enclosing implicit body.	390
local	Creates new local bindings within the smallest enclosing implicit body and initializes them to local methods that can be self-recursive and mutually recursive.	391
let handler	Establishes a condition handler for the duration of the execution of smallest enclosing implicit body.	392

---

let   **[Local Declaration]**

Creates and initializes new local bindings within the smallest enclosing implicit body.

Macro Call: let *variables* = *init* ;

Arguments: *variables*   variable$_{bnf}$ | (variable-list$_{bnf}$)

                       init   expression$_{bnf}$

Description: let creates local bindings for the *variables*, and initializes them to the values returned by *init*. The bindings are visible for the remainder of the smallest enclosing implicit body.

The first value returned by the *init* is bound to the first *variable*, the second value to the second *variable*, etc. The last *variable* may be preceded by #rest, in which case it is bound to a sequence containing all the remaining values.

Each *variable* is a variable-name or a variable-name followed by a specializer.

If more than one binding is defined, the *variables* are enclosed in parentheses and separated by commas.

```
let start = 0;

let (whole-part, remainder) = truncate(amount);

let (first-value, #rest rest-values) = get-initial-values();
```

Local variables may be specialized. This ensures that their value will always be of a given type. An attempt to initialize or assign the variable to a value not of that type will signal an error of type <type-error>.

```
let elapsed-time :: <integer> = 0;

let the-front-window :: <window> = front-window();

let(whole-part :: <integer>, remainder :: <real>) = truncate(amount);
```

---

local   **[Local Declaration]**

Creates new local bindings within the smallest enclosing implicit body and initializes them to local methods that can be self-recursive and mutually recursive.

Macro Call: local { [method] *name parameter-list* [*body*] end [method] [*name*] } , [+]

Arguments: *name*   variable-name$_{bnf}$

                     parameter-list   parameter-list$_{bnf}$

                     body   body$_{bnf}$

Description: local creates local methods that may be mutually recursive and self-recursive.

Each *name* creates a new local binding. The binding is initialized to a new method specified by the *parameter-list* and *body*. In addition to being visible for the remainder of the smallest enclosing implicit body, the bindings created for the *names* are visible to the *parameter-lists* and *bodies* of all the methods created by the local declaration.

The *parameter-list* is a standard method parameter list. A complete description of parameter lists is given in "Parameter Lists" on page 84.

The *body* is an implicit body.

---

let handler   [Local Declaration]

Establishes a condition handler for the duration of the execution of smallest enclosing implicit body.

Macro Call: `let handler` *condition* `=` *handler*

Arguments:

condition	*type* | `(` *type* `{ ,` *option* `}*` `)`
type	expression*bnf*
option	*test-option* | *init-option*
test-option	`test:` expression*bnf*
init-option	`init-arguments:` expression*bnf*
handler	expression*bnf*

Description: `let handler` establishes a new condition handler that is in effect for the duration of the execution of the remainder of the smallest enclosing implicit body. Unlike the local declarations `let` and `local`, `let handler` does not create any bindings.

- The *condition* describes the conditions for which the handler is applicable.
  - ☐ The *type* is the type of the applicable conditions. The handler will be applicable to conditions that are general instances of *type*.
  - ☐ The *test-option* is a function that is called to further test the applicability of the handler. When a condition of type *type* is signaled, the test function will be called with that condition as an argument. If the test returns true, the handler is considered applicable to the condition. If the test returns false, the handler is considered to be inapplicable to the condition. The default value of this option is a function that always returns true. There can be at most one *test-option*.

    An example use for this feature is a restart handler for restarting only from a particular condition object, for example restarting from an unbound-slot error by setting the slot and retrying the invocation of the accessor. The `<set-and-continue>` restart condition will have the signaled `<unbound-slot>` condition in a slot, and the handler's test will check for it. (These class names are invented for this example and are not part of the specification.)

◻ The *init-option* is a sequence of alternating keywords and objects that can be used as initialization arguments to construct a condition to which the handler is applicable. For example, if the handler is a restart handler, a program could retrieve the *init-option* by calling `do-handlers`, and could then use them to construct a corresponding restart. There can be at most one *init-option*. *init-option* defaults to an empty sequence.

■ The *handler* is function called to handle a condition that matches *type* and passes *test-option*. The function should accept two arguments. The first argument will be the condition being signaled, and the second argument will be a next-handler function. The handler handles the condition by taking a nonlocal exit, returning values according to the condition's recovery protocol, or tail-recursively calling `signal` of a restart. The function can decline to handle the condition by tail-recursively calling the next-handler function with no arguments.

test-option and *handler* are distinct so that handler applicability can be tested without actually handling (which might take a nonlocal exit). One use for this is constructing a list of available restart handlers.

There is no "condition wall," i.e., when executing *handler* the set of available handlers is not reset to the handlers that were in effect when the `let handler` was entered.

Implementations are encouraged to implement `let handler` in a way that optimizes establishing a handler for both speed and space, even if that increases the cost of signaling. The assumption is that most of the time a handler will never be used, because the exception it is looking for will never occur.

type, *handler*, *test-option*, and *init-option* are executed before execution of the rest of the enclosing body begins.

Statements

Statements are used to implement a variety of program constructs.

Many statements include an optional implicit body, which may contain one or more constituents separated by semicolons. When an implicit body is executed, the expressions in the implicit body are executed in order (left to right). The values of the implicit body are the values of the last expression. If the optional implicit body is not present or contains no expressions, the return value is #f.

Table 14-3   Statements

Macro	Description	Page
if	Executes an implicit body if the value of a test is true or an alternate if the test is false.	395
unless	Executes an implicit body unless the value of a test is true.	396
case	Executes a number of tests until one is true, and then executes an implicit body associated with the true test.	397
select	Compares a target object to a series of potential matches, and executes an implicit body associated with the first match found.	398
while	Repeatedly executes a body until a test expression is false.	399
until	Repeatedly executes a body until a test expression is true.	400
for	Performs general iteration over a body, updating bindings and performing end tests on each iteration.	400
begin	Executes expressions in a body, in order.	404
block	Executes a body with several options for nonstandard flow of control.	404
method	Creates and returns a method.	408

Conditionals

The following statements are used to perform conditional execution.

The Built-In Macros and Special Definitions

---

if   **[Statement]**

Executes an implicit body if the value of a test is true or an alternate if the test is false.

Macro Call:

if (*test*) [*consequent*]
  { elseif (*elseif-test*) [*elseif-consequent*] }*
  [else [*alternate*]]
end [if]

Arguments:

test	expression$_{bnf}$
consequent	body$_{bnf}$
elseif-test	expression$_{bnf}$
elseif-consequent	body$_{bnf}$
alternate	body$_{bnf}$

Values: Zero or more instances of <object>.

Description: if executes one or more expressions, executing and returning the values of a body following the first test that returns true.

test is the first expression to be executed. If its value is true, if executes and returns the values of the *consequent*. If the value of *test* is false, if proceeds with the optional elseif-tests and alternate.

First the elseif clauses are tried in order. The first *elseif-test* is executed. If its value is true, the corresponding *elseif-consequent* is executed and its values are returned as the value of the if statement. If its value is false, the next *elseif-test* is tried. This continues until a true *elseif-test* is found, or until there are no more elseif clauses.

If the *test* and all the *elseif-tests* are false, the *alternate* is executed and its values are returned as the value of the if statement. If there is no alternate, the if statement returns #f.

```
if ( x < 0 )
  - x;
end if;
```

```
if ( heads?(flip(coin)) )
  start(black);
else
  start(white);
end if

if (player1.money <= 0)
  end-game(player1)
elseif (player2.money <= 0)
  end-game(player2)
else
  move(player1);
  move(player2);
end if

if ( camel.humps = 1 )
  "dromedary"
elseif ( camel.humps = 2 )
  "bactrian"
else
  "not a camel"
end if;
```

unless   **[Statement]**

Executes an implicit body unless the value of a test is true.

| Macro Call: | `unless ( test )`
`  [ body ]`
`end [ unless ]` |

Arguments:	*test*	expression$_{bnf}$
	body	body$_{bnf}$

Values: Zero or more instances of `<object>`.

Description: `unless` executes *test*. If the value of *test* is false, then the *body* is executed and its values are returned by `unless`. If the value of *test* is true, the *body* is not executed and `unless` returns #f.

If there are no expressions in the *body*, then #f is returned.

```
unless(detect-gas? (nose))
    light(match)
end unless
```

---

case   **[Statement]**

Executes a number of tests until one is true, and then executes an implicit body associated with the true test.

Macro Call:
```
case
{ test => consequent } *
[ otherwise [ => ] alternate ]
end [ case ]
```

Arguments:

test	expression$_{bnf}$
consequent	[constituents$_{bnf}$] ;
alternate	[constituents$_{bnf}$] ;

Values: Zero or more instances of `<object>`.

Description: `case` executes the *test* in order, until it reaches a test that returns true. When it reaches a test that returns true, it executes the corresponding *consequent* and returns its values. Subsequent tests are not executed. If the corresponding *consequent* is empty, the first value of the successful test is returned.

As a special case, the name `otherwise` may appear as a *test*. This *test* always succeeds if there is no preceding successful *test*.

If no *test* is true, then `case` returns #f.

```
case
    player1.money <= 0
        => end-game(player1);
    player2.money <= 0
```

```
    => end-game(player2);
  otherwise
    => move(player1);
       move(player2);
end case;
```

select   [Statement]

Compares a target object to a series of potential matches, and executes an implicit body associated with the first match found.

Macro Call: select (*target* [by *test*])
                   { *matches* => *consequent* }*
                   [otherwise [=>] *alternate*]
                   end [select]

Arguments: *target*   expression*bnf*

                  test   expression*bnf*

                  matches   { expression*bnf* } , + | ({ expression*bnf* } , +)

                  consequent   [constituents*bnf*] ;

                  alternate   [constituents*bnf*] ;

Values: Zero or more instances of <object>.

Description: select generates a target object and then compares it to a series of potential matches, in order. If it finds a match, it executes the corresponding *consequent* and returns the values of the *consequent*. If no match is found, an error is signaled.

The *target* is executed to produce the match object.

The *test*, if supplied, is a function used to compare the target object to the potential matches. The default *test* is ==.

One at a time, each *match* is executed and its value compared to *target*, in order. If a match is found, the corresponding *consequent* is executed and its values are returned. If the corresponding *consequent* is empty, #f is returned.

Once a match is found, subsequent *matches* and the corresponding bodies are not executed.

The Built-In Macros and Special Definitions

As a special case, the name `otherwise` may appear instead of a *matches*. This will be considered a match if no other match is found.

If there is no matching clause, an error is signaled. Because an `otherwise` clause matches when no other clause matches, a `select` form that includes an `otherwise` clause will never signal an error for failure to match.

Since testing stops when the first match is found, it is irrelevant whether the test function would also have returned true if called on later matches of the same clause or on matches of later clauses.

```
select ( career-choice(student) )
   art:, music:, drama:
     => "Don't quit your day job";
   literature:, history:, linguistics:
     => "That really is fascinating";
   science:, math:, engineering:
     => "Say, can you fix my VCR?";
   otherwise => "I wish you luck";
end select;

select ( my-object by instance? )
  <window>, <view>, <rectangle> => "a graphical object";
  <number>, <string>, <list> => "a computational object";
  otherwise => "I don't know";
end select
```

Iteration Constructs

---

while   [Statement]

Repeatedly executes a body until a test expression is false.

Macro Call:
```
while ( test )
  [ body ]
end [ while ]
⇒ #f
```

Arguments: *test*   expression*bnf*

                 body   body*bnf*

Values: #f

Description: while loops over *body* until *test* returns false.

Each pass through the loop begins by executing *test*. If *test* returns a true value, the expressions in the *body* are executed and the looping continues. If *test* returns false, the loop terminates and while returns #f.

---

until   (*test*)   [Statement]

Repeatedly executes a body until a test expression is true.

Macro Call: until (*test*)
                   [*body*]
                  end [until]
                  ⇒ #f

Arguments: *test*   expression*bnf*

                 body   body*bnf*

Values: #f

Description: until loops over *body* until *test* returns true.

Each pass through the loop begins by executing *test*. If *test* returns false, the expressions in the *body* are executed and the looping continues. If *test* returns true, the loop terminates and until returns #f.

---

for   [Statement]

Performs general iteration over a body, updating bindings and performing end tests on each iteration.

Macro Call:

```
for ( { for-clause } , * |
        { { for-clause , }* end-clause })
  [ loop-body ]
  [ finally [ result-body ] ]
  end [ for ]
```

Arguments:

for-clause	*explicit-step-clause* |
	collection-clause |
	numeric-clause
end-test	expression$_{bnf}$
loop-body	body$_{bnf}$
result-body	body$_{bnf}$
explicit-step-clause	variable$_{bnf}$ = *init-value* then *next-value*
collection-clause	variable$_{bnf}$ in *collection*
numeric-clause	variable$_{bnf}$ from *start* [[{ to | above | below } *bound*] [by *increment*]
end-clause	{ until: | while: } *end-test*
init-value	expression$_{bnf}$
next-value	expression$_{bnf}$
collection	expression$_{bnf}$
start	expression$_{bnf}$
bound	expression$_{bnf}$
increment	expression$_{bnf}$

Values: Zero or more instances of `<object>`.

Description: `for` iterates over *loop-body*, creating and updating iteration bindings on each iteration according to the *for-clauses*. Iteration ends when one of the *for-clauses* is exhausted, or when the optional *end-test* is satisfied.

Each *for-clause* controls one iteration binding. The optional *end-test* does not control any iteration bindings.

There are three kinds of for-clauses: *explicit-step-clauses, collection-clauses,* and *numeric-clauses:* An *explicit-step-clause* creates bindings for the results of executing an expression. A *collection-clause* creates bindings for successive elements of a collection. A *numeric-clause* creates bindings for a series of numbers.

Execution of a `for` statement proceeds through the following steps:

1. Execute the expressions that are executed just once, in left to right order as they appear in the `for` statement. These expressions include the types of all the bindings, and the expressions *init-value, collection, start, bound,* and *increment.* If the value of *collection* is not a collection, an error is signaled. The default value for *increment* is 1.

2. Create the iteration bindings of explicit step and numeric clauses.

   □ For each explicit step clause, create the binding for the value of *init-value.* If the binding is typed and the value is not of the specified type, signal an error.

   □ For each numeric clause, create the binding for the value of *start.* If the binding is typed and the value is not of the specified type, signal an error.

3. Check numeric and collection clauses for exhaustion. If a clause is exhausted, go to step 9.

   □ A collection clause is exhausted if its collection has no next element.

   □ A numeric clause is exhausted if a *bound* is supplied and the value of the clause is no longer in bounds. If `above` is specified, the clause will be in bounds as long as the value is greater than the *bounds.* If `below` is specified, the clause will be in bounds as long as the value is less than the *bounds.* If `to` is specified with a positive or zero *increment,* the clause will be in bounds as long as it is less than or equal to the *bounds.* If `to` is specified with a negative *increment,* the clause will be in bounds as long as it is greater than or equal to the *bounds.*

4. For each collection clause create the iteration binding for the next element of the collection for that clause. Fresh bindings are created each time through the loop (i.e., the binding is not assigned the new value). If the binding is typed and the value is not of the specified type, signal an error.

5. If *end-test* is supplied, execute it. If the value of *end-test* is false and the symbol is `while:`, go to step 9. If the value of *end-test* is true and the symbol is `until:`, go to step 9.

6. Execute the expressions in the *body* in order. The expressions in the *body* are used to produce side-effects.

7. Obtain the next values for explicit step and numeric clauses. Values are obtained in left to right order, in the environment produced by step 6.

   ☐ For each explicit step clause, execute *next-value*.

   ☐ For each numeric clause, add the *increment* to the current value of the binding, using +.

8. Create the iteration bindings of explicit step and numeric clauses for the values obtained in step 7. For each clause, if a binding type is supplied and the next value for that clause is not of the specified type, signal an error. Fresh bindings are created each time through the loop (i.e., the binding is not assigned the new value). After the bindings have been created, go to step 3.

9. Execute the expressions in the *result-body* in order. Bindings created in step 2 and 8 are visible during the execution of *result-body*, but bindings created in step 4 (the iteration bindings of collection clauses) are not visible during the execution of *result-body*. The values of the last expression in the *result-body* are returned as the values of the `for` statement. If there are no expressions in the *result-body*, `for` returns #f.

```
for ( thing = first-thing then next(thing),
      until: done?(thing) )
  do-some(thing)
end;

for (j :: <integer> from 0 to height)
  for (i :: <integer> from 0 to width)
    erase(i,j);
    plot (i,j);
  end for;
end for;

for (city in olympic-cities,
     year from start-year by 4)
  schedule-olympic-game(city, year)
  finally notify(press);
         sell(tickets);
end;
```

```
for (i from 0 below 100,
     zombies from 0 below 100,
     normals from 100 above 0 by -1)
   population[i] := zombies + normals
end;
```

Other Statement Macros

begin   [Statement]

Executes expressions in a body, in order.

Macro Call: begin [*body*] end

Arguments: *body*   body*bnf*

Values: Zero or more instances of <object>.

Description: Begin executes the expressions in a body, in order. The values of the last
                  expression are returned. If there are no expressions in the body, #f is returned.

block   [Statement]

Executes a body with several options for nonstandard flow of control.

Macro Call: block ([*exit-variable*])
                  [*block-body*]
                  [afterwards [*afterwards-clause*]]
                  [cleanup [*cleanup-clause*]]
                  { exception *exception-clause* }*
                  end [block]

Arguments: *exit-variable*   variable-name*bnf*

                  block-body   body*bnf*

                  afterwards-   body*bnf*
                  clause

cleanup-clause body*bnf*

exception-clause ([*name* ::] *type* { , *exception-options* }*)
[body*bnf*]

name   variable-name*bnf*

type   expression*bnf*

exception-options
      { test: expression*bnf* } | { init-arguments: expression*bnf* }

Values: Zero or more instances of <object>.

Description: block executes the expressions in the *block-body* in order, and then executes the optional *afterwards-clause* and *cleanup-clause*. Unless there is a nonlocal exit, block returns the values of the *block-body*, or #f if there is no *block-body*.

If *exit-variable* is provided, it is bound to an exit procedure (an object of type <function>) that is valid during the execution of the block body and the clauses. At any point in time before the last clause returns, the exit procedure can be called. Calling the exit procedure has the effect of immediately terminating the execution of the block, and returning as values the arguments to the exit procedure.

The body of the *afterwards-clause*, if provided, is executed after the *block-body*. The values produced by the *afterwards-clause* are ignored. This is useful when you want to execute an expression for side-effect after the *block-body* has executed, but still want to return the values of the last expression in the *block-body*.

The body of the *cleanup-clause*, if provided, is executed after the *block-body* and *afterwards-clause*. Its values are also ignored. The cleanup clause differs from the afterwards clause in that its body is guaranteed to be executed, even if the execution of the block is interrupted by a nonlocal exit. There is no such guarantee for the *afterwards-clause*.

For example, the following code fragment ensures that files are closed even in the case of an error causing a nonlocal exit from the block body:

```
block (return)
  open-files();
  if (something-wrong)
    return("didn't work");
  end if;
```

```
  compute-with-files()
cleanup
  close-files();
end block
```

The *exception-clauses*, if supplied, install exception handlers during the execution of the *block-body*, *afterwards-clause*, and *cleanup-clause*. If one of these handlers is invoked, it never declines but immediately takes a nonlocal exit to the beginning of the block, executes the expressions in its body and returns the values of the last expression or #f if the body is empty. Note that when the expressions in an exception body are executed, all handlers established by the block are no longer active. Note also that the cleanup clause of the block will be executed before the expressions of the handler body are executed.

The *type* and *exception-options* are as for let handler. If present, *name* is bound to the condition during the execution of the handler's body.

The exception clauses are checked in the order in which they appear. That is, the first handler will take precedence over the second, the second over the third, etc.

The following is a trivial use of an exception clause.

```
block ()
  open-files();
  compute-with-files()
exception (<error>)
  "didn't work";
cleanup
  close-files();
end block
```

Dynamic Extent of Block Features

A block installs features that are active for different portions of the execution of the block.

- During the execution of the block body and the afterwards clause the exit procedure, exception clauses, and cleanup clauses are active.

- During the execution of the cleanup clause, the exit procedure and exception clauses are active.

The Built-In Macros and Special Definitions

- During the execution of a handler installed by an exception clause, the exit procedure is active.

Intervening Cleanup Clauses

When an exit procedure is called, it initiates a nonlocal exit out of its establishing block. Before the nonlocal exit can complete, however, the cleanup clauses of intervening blocks (blocks that have been entered, but not exited, since the establishing block was entered) must be executed, beginning with the most recently entered intervening block. Once the cleanup clauses of an intervening block have been executed, it is an error to invoke the exit procedure established by that block. The cleanup clauses of the establishing block are executed last. At that point, further invocation of the exit procedure becomes invalid, and the establishing block returns with the values that were passed to the exit procedure.

Note that a block statement may also be exited due to the execution of a handler clause. Before the exception clause is executed, intervening cleanup clauses are executed as described above (including any clause for the establishing block.) The exit procedure may be invoked during execution of exception clauses, in which case the argument values are immediately returned from the block (the cleanup clause already having been executed).

During the process of executing the cleanup clauses of the intervening blocks, any valid exit procedure may be invoked and may interrupt the current nonlocal exit.

All exception clauses are executed in the same dynamic environment. None of the handlers established in the block are visible during the execution of one of the handlers. This can be thought of as parallel installation of the handlers.

Restrictions on the use of exit procedures

The exit procedure is a first-class object. Specifically, it can be passed as an argument to functions, stored in data structures, and so on. Its use is not restricted to the lexical body of the block in which it was established. However, invocation of the exit procedure is valid only during the execution of the establishing block. It is an error to invoke an exit procedure after its establishing block has returned, or after execution of the establishing block has been terminated by a nonlocal exit.

In the following example, the `block` establishes an exit procedure in the binding `bar`. The `block` returns a method containing a call to `bar`, and the method is stored in the binding `foo`. Calling `foo` is an error because it is no longer valid to invoke `bar` after its establishing `block` has returned.

```
define constant foo =
  block (bar)
     method (n) bar(n) end;
  end block;
foo(5)
  {error or other undefined consequences}
```

`method`	**[Statement]**

Creates and returns a method.

Macro Call: method *parameter-list* [*body*] end [method]

Arguments: *parameter-list* parameter-list*bnf*

  body body*bnf*

Values: An instance of <method>.

Description: method creates and returns a method specified by the *parameter-list* and *body*. For a complete description of methods, see "Methods" on page 80.

Function Macros

Function macros provide syntax for assignment and for conditional execution.

Table 14-4   Function Macros

Macro	Description	Page
: =	Stores a new value in a location.	409
|	Returns the value of the first of two operands that is true.	412
&	If the value of a first operand is true, executes a second operand and returns its values.	412

These three built-in function macros may be called using function-call syntax or operator syntax.

Assignment

: =	**[Function Macro]**

Stores a new value in a location.

Macro Call: *place* : = *new-value*

Arguments: *place*   expression$_{bnf}$

             new-value   expression$_{bnf}$

Values: *new-value*, an instance of `<object>`.

Description: : = stores *new-value* in *place* and returns *new-value*.

place may be a variable, a getter function or macro call with a corresponding setter, a slot access, or an element reference.

new-value may be any operand. It is executed, and its value is stored in *place*.

In all cases, *new-value* must be an appropriate type for *place* or an error is signaled.

The *new-value* of an assignment statement is executed first, followed by the *place* (assuming the *place* requires any execution, which will only be true if it is not a binding name).

Assignment to a binding

If *place* is a binding name, then *new-value* is stored in the binding. It is an error if there is no binding corresponding to *place*. (: = cannot be used to create bindings, only to change their values.) An error is also signaled if *place* is a binding specialized to a type and the *new-value* is not of that type.

```
define variable *number* = 10;
*number*
  ⇒  10
*number* := *number* + 10;
  ⇒  20
*number*
  ⇒  20
```

Assignment to a function or function macro

If *place* has the syntax of a function call, then : = will invoke the corresponding setter function. Given a binding named *fun*, the corresponding setter is the binding named *fun*-setter in the current environment.

: = maps *place* to *place*-setter without regard for whether *place* is a function or a macro. It does not expand a macro call on the left-hand side before determining the setter.

With the exception of the order of execution and a guaranteed return value, the following three expressions are equivalent:

The Built-In Macros and Special Definitions

```
*top-view*.subviews := generate-subviews()
subviews(*top-view*) := generate-subviews()
subviews-setter(generate-subviews(), *top-view*)
```

(The differences are as follows: the execution time of `subviews-setter` is undefined in the first two expressions but defined in the last; the first two expressions will return the value of the call to `generate-subviews` while the last will return the value of the call to `subviews-setter`.)

```
name(arg1,...argn ) := new-value
```

behaves exactly the same as

```
begin
  let temp = new-value;
  name-setter(temp, arg1,...argn );
  temp
end
```

This is true regardless of whether `name` and `name-setter` are functions or macros. Here *temp* stands for a variable with a unique name. If `name-setter` is a macro, it is responsible for the order of execution of `arg1,...argn`.

The same considerations apply to `arg.name := new-value`.

Assignment to element references

Just as `[]` can be used as syntax for `element` and `aref`, `[]` and `:=` can be used as syntax for `element-setter` and `aref-setter`. For example, the following three expressions are equivalent:

```
foo[2] := "quux"
element (foo, 2) := "quux"
element-setter ("quux", foo, 2).
```

Conditional Execution

| **[Function Macro]**

Returns the value of the first of two operands that is true.

Macro Call: *one* | *another*

Arguments: *one*   expression$_{bnf}$

                 another   expression$_{bnf}$

Values: Zero or more instances of <object>.

Description: | (logical or) executes *one*. If the first value of *one* is true, that value is returned and *another* is not executed. Otherwise *another* is executed and its values are returned.

&   **[Function Macro]**

If the value of a first operand is true, executes a second operand and returns its values.

Macro Call: *one* & *another* ⇒ *values*

Arguments: *one*   expression$_{bnf}$

                 another   expression$_{bnf}$

Values: Zero or more instances of <object>.

Description: & (logical and) executes *one*. If the first value returned by *one* is false, #f is returned and *another* is not executed. Otherwise, *another* is executed and its values are returned.

BNF

General Notes

Dylan syntax can be parsed with an LALR(1) grammar.

This appendix uses some special notation to make the presentation of the grammar more readable.

- The *opt* suffix means that the preceding item is optional.

- A trailing ellipsis (...) is used in two different ways to signal possible repetition.

  - If there is only one item on the line preceding the ellipsis, the item may appear one or more times.

  - If more than one item precedes the ellipsis, the last of these items is designated a separator; the rest may appear one or more times, with the separator appearing after each occurrence but the last. (When only one item appears, the separator does not appear.)

- Identifiers for grammar rules are written with uppercase letters when the identifier is used in the phrase grammar but defined in the lexical grammar.

- The grammar does not use distinct identifiers for grammar rules that differ only in alphabetic case.

In the following grammar, some tokens are used multiple ways. For example the hyphen, "-," is punctuation, a unary operator, and a binary operator; also, "method" is a BEGIN-WORD and a DEFINE-BODY-WORD. In some parsing implementations such multiple meanings of a token may not be possible. However this is just an implementation issue since the meaning of the grammar is clear. method is used as punctuation in *local-methods* and *method-definition*; since method is not a core reserved word, this typically has to be implemented by accepting any MACRO-NAME and checking semantically that the word used is "method." The grammar as presented is not obviously LALR(1), since the required changes would tend to obscure the readability for human beings (especially in macro definitions and case-body). The grammar can be made LALR(1) through well-known standard transformations implemented by most parser generators.

Lexical Notes

In the lexical grammar, the various elements that come together to form a single token on the right-hand sides of rules must *not* be separated by whitespace, so that the end result will be a single token. This is in contrast to the phrase grammar, where each element is already a complete token or a series of complete tokens.

Arbitrary whitespace is permitted between tokens, but it is required only as necessary to separate tokens that might otherwise blend together.

Case is not significant except within character and string literals. The grammars do not reflect this, using one case or the other, but it is still true.

Lexical Grammar

Comments

comment:
    // ...the rest of the line
    /* ...everything even across lines, including nested comments... ***/**

Tokens

TOKEN:
    NAME
    SYMBOL
    NUMBER
    CHARACTER-LITERAL
    STRING
    UNARY-OPERATOR
    BINARY-OPERATOR

punctuation
    #-word

punctuation:
    one of   `( ) , . ; [ ] { } :: - = == =>`
    one of   `#( #[ ## ? ?? ?= ...`

#-word:
    one of   `#t #f #next #rest #key #all-keys #include`

Reserved Words

reserved-word:
    core-word
    BEGIN-WORD
    FUNCTION-WORD
    DEFINE-BODY-WORD
    DEFINE-LIST-WORD

core-word:
    one of   `define end handler let local macro otherwise`

The following reserved words are exported by the Dylan module:

BEGIN-WORD:
    one of `begin block case for if method`
    one of `select unless until while`

FUNCTION-WORD:
    (none)

DEFINE-BODY-WORD:
    one of `class library method module`

DEFINE-LIST-WORD:
    one of `constant variable domain`

Names, Symbols and Keywords

NAME:
    word

BNF

```
         \ word
         operator-name
```

UNRESERVED-NAME:
  any *word* that is not also a *reserved-word*
  **** *word*
  operator-name

ORDINARY-NAME:
  UNRESERVED-NAME
  DEFINE-BODY-WORD
  DEFINE-LIST-WORD

CONSTRAINED-NAME:
  NAME **:** *word*
  NAME **:** BINARY-OPERATOR
  : *word*

operator-name:
  **** UNARY-OPERATOR
  **** BINARY-OPERATOR

MACRO-NAME:
  ORDINARY-NAME
  BEGIN-WORD
  FUNCTION-WORD

NAME-NOT-END:
  MACRO-NAME
  one of **define handler let local macro otherwise**

SYMBOL:
  word **:**
  # STRING

word:
  leading-alphabetic
  leading-numeric alphabetic-character leading-alphabetic
  leading-graphic leading-alphabetic

leading-alphabetic:
  alphabetic-character
  leading-alphabetic any-character

BNF

leading-numeric:
    numeric-character
    leading-numeric word-character-not-double-alphabetic

leading-graphic:
    graphic-character
    leading-graphic word-character-not-alphabetic

word-character-not-alphabetic:
    numeric-character
    graphic-character
    special-character

word-character-not-double-alphabetic:
    alphabetic-character word-character-not-alphabetic
    numeric-character
    graphic-character
    special-character

any-character:
    alphabetic-character
    numeric-character
    graphic-character
    special-character

alphabetic-character:
    one of **a b c d e f g h i j k l m n o p q r s t u v w x y z**

numeric-character:
    one of   **0 1 2 3 4 5 6 7 8 9**

graphic-character:
    one of   **! & * < > | ^ $ % @ _**

special-character:
    one of   **- + ~ ? / =**

Operators

UNARY-OPERATOR:
    one of   **- ~**

BINARY-OPERATOR:
    one of   **+ - * / ^ = == ~= ~== < <= > >= & | :=**

Character and String Literals

CHARACTER-LITERAL:
    ' *character* **'**

character:
    any printing character (including space) except for **'** or ****
    **** *escape-character*

STRING*:*
    " *more-string*

more-string:
    string-character more-string
    "

string-character:
    any printing character (including space) except for **"** or ****
    **** *escape-character*

escape-character:
    one of   **\ ' " a b e f n r t 0**
    < *hex-digits* **>**

Numbers

NUMBER:
    integer
    ratio
    floating-point

integer:
    binary-integer
    octal-integer
    $sign_{opt}$ *decimal-integer*
    hex-integer

binary-integer:
    #b *binary-digit*
    binary-integer binary-digit

octal-integer:
    #o *octal-digit*
    octal-integer octal-digit

decimal-integer:
    decimal-digit
    decimal-integer decimal-digit

hex-integer:
    #x *hex-digit*
    hex-integer hex-digit

hex-digits:
    hex-digit ...

binary-digit:
    one of   **0 1**

octal-digit:
    one of   **0 1 2 3 4 5 6 7**

decimal-digit:
    one of   **0 1 2 3 4 5 6 7 8 9**

hex-digit:
    one of   **0 1 2 3 4 5 6 7 8 9 A B C D E F**

ratio:
    $sign_{opt}$ *decimal-integer* **/** *decimal-integer*

floating-point:
    $sign_{opt}$ *decimal-integer$_{opt}$* **.** *decimal-integer exponent$_{opt}$*
    $sign_{opt}$ *decimal-integer* **.** *decimal-integer$_{opt}$ exponent$_{opt}$*
    $sign_{opt}$ *decimal-integer exponent*

exponent:
    E $sign_{opt}$ *decimal-integer*

sign:
    one of   **+ −**

Phrase Grammar

Program Structure

source-record:
    body$_{opt}$

body:
    constituents **;**$_{opt}$

constituents:
    constituent **;** ...

constituent:
    definition
    local-declaration
    expression

macro:
    definition-macro-call
    statement
    function-macro-call

    parsed-macro-call

Property Lists

comma-property-list:
    , *property-list*

property-list:
    property **,** ...

property:
    SYMBOL *value*

value:
    basic-fragment

Fragments

body-fragment:
    non-statement-body-fragment
    statement   non-statement-body-fragment$_{opt}$

list-fragment:
    non-statement-list-fragment
    statement   non-statement-list-fragment$_{opt}$

basic-fragment:
    non-statement-basic-fragment
    statement   non-statement-basic-fragment$_{opt}$

non-statement-body-fragment:
    definition   semicolon-fragment$_{opt}$
    local-declaration   semicolon-fragment$_{opt}$
    simple-fragment   body-fragment$_{opt}$
    ,   *body-fragment$_{opt}$*
    ;   *body-fragment$_{opt}$*

semicolon-fragment:
    ; *body-fragment$_{opt}$*

non-statement-list-fragment:
    simple-fragment   list-fragment$_{opt}$
    ,   *list-fragment$_{opt}$*

non-statement-basic-fragment:
    simple-fragment   basic-fragment$_{opt}$

simple-fragment:
    variable-name
    constant-fragment
    BINARY-OPERATOR
    UNARY-OPERATOR
    bracketed-fragment
    function-macro-call
    #-word
    one of   `.  ::  =>  ?  ??  ?=  ...  ##  otherwise`
    parsed-function-call
    parsed-macro-call

bracketed-fragment:
    (*body-fragment$_{opt}$* **)**
    [*body-fragment$_{opt}$* **]**
    { *body-fragment$_{opt}$* **}**

constant-fragment:
    NUMBER
    CHARACTER-LITERAL
    STRING
    SYMBOL
    #(*constants* **.** *constant* **)**
    #(*constants$_{opt}$* **)**
    #[*constants$_{opt}$* **]**
    parsed-list-constant
    parsed-vector-constant

Definitions

definition:
    definition-macro-call
    define macro *macro-definition*
    parsed-definition

definition-macro-call:
    define *modifiers$_{opt}$* DEFINE-BODY-WORD *body-fragment$_{opt}$* *definition-tail*
    define *modifiers$_{opt}$* DEFINE-LIST-WORD *list-fragment$_{opt}$*

modifier:
    UNRESERVED-NAME

modifiers:
    modifier …

definition-tail:
    end
    end MACRO-NAME
    end DEFINE-BODY-WORD MACRO-NAME

Local Declarations

local-declaration:
    let *bindings*
    let handler *condition* **=** *handler*
    local *local-methods*
    parsed-local-declaration

condition:
    type
    (*type comma-property-list* **)**

handler:
    expression

local-methods:
    method$_{opt}$ *method-definition* **,** ...

bindings:
    variable **=** *expression*
    (*variable-list* **)** **=** *expression*

variable-list:
    variables
    variables **, #rest** *variable-name*
    #rest *variable-name*

variables:
    variable **,** ...

variable:
    variable-name
    variable-name **::** *type*

variable-name:
    ORDINARY-NAME

type:
    operand

Expressions

expressions:
  expression **,** ...

expression:
  binary-operand BINARY-OPERATOR ...

expression-no-symbol:
  binary-operand-no-symbol
  binary-operand-no-symbol BINARY-OPERATOR *expression*

binary-operand-no-symbol:
  UNARY-OPERATOR$_{opt}$ *operand*

binary-operand:
  SYMBOL
  UNARY-OPERATOR$_{opt}$ *operand*

operand:
  operand **(** *arguments$_{opt}$* **)**
  operand **[** *arguments$_{opt}$* **]**
  operand **.** *variable-name*
  leaf

function-macro-call:
  FUNCTION-WORD **(** *body-fragment$_{opt}$* **)**

leaf:
  literal
  variable-name
  (*expression* **)**
  function-macro-call
  statement
  parsed-function-call
  parsed-macro-call

arguments:
  argument **,** ...

argument:
  SYMBOL *expression*
  expression-no-symbol
  SYMBOL

literal:
    NUMBER
    CHARACTER-LITERAL
    string-literal
    #t
    #f
    #(*constants* **.** *constant* **)**
    #(*constants*$_{opt}$ **)**
    #[*constants*$_{opt}$ **]**
    parsed-list-constant
    parsed-vector-constant

string-literal:
    STRING ...

constants:
    constant **,** ...

constant:
    literal
    SYMBOL

Statements

statement:
    BEGIN-WORD *body-fragment*$_{opt}$ *end-clause*

end-clause:
    end BEGIN-WORD$_{opt}$

case-body:
    cases **;**$_{opt}$

cases:
    case-label constituents$_{opt}$ **;** ...

case-label:
    expressions **=>**
    (*expression* **,** *expressions* **)** **=>**
    otherwise =>$_{opt}$

Methods

method-definition:
    variable-name parameter-list body$_{opt}$ **end method**$_{opt}$ *variable-name*$_{opt}$

parameter-list:
    (*parameters*$_{opt}$ **)** **;**$_{opt}$
    (*parameters*$_{opt}$ **)** **=>** *variable* **;**
    (*parameters*$_{opt}$ **)** **=>** **(** *values-list*$_{opt}$ **)** **;**$_{opt}$

parameters:
    required-parameters
    required-parameters **,** *next-rest-key-parameter-list*
    next-rest-key-parameter-list

next-rest-key-parameter-list:
    #next *variable-name*
    #next *variable-name* **,** *rest-key-parameter-list*
    rest-key-parameter-list

rest-key-parameter-list:
    #rest *variable-name*
    #rest *variable-name* **,** *key-parameter-list*
    key-parameter-list

key-parameter-list:
    #key *keyword-parameters*$_{opt}$
    #key *keyword-parameters*$_{opt}$ **,** **#all-keys**

required-parameters:
    required-parameter **,** ...

required-parameter:
    variable
    variable-name **==** *expression*

keyword-parameters:
    keyword-parameter **,** ...

keyword-parameter:
    SYMBOL$_{opt}$ *variable default*$_{opt}$

default:
    = *expression*

values-list:
    variables
    variables **, #rest** *variable*
    #rest *variable*

Macro Definitions

macro-definition:
    MACRO-NAME *main-rule-set aux-rule-sets*$_{opt}$ **end macro**$_{opt}$ MACRO-NAME$_{opt}$

main-rule-set:
    body-style-definition-rule ...
    list-style-definition-rule ...
    statement-rule ...
    function-rule ...

body-style-definition-rule:
    { define *definition-head*$_{opt}$ MACRO-NAME *pattern*$_{opt}$ **;**$_{opt}$ **end } =>** *rhs*

list-style-definition-rule:
    { define *definition-head*$_{opt}$ MACRO-NAME *pattern*$_{opt}$ **} =>** *rhs*

rhs:
    { *template*$_{opt}$ **} ;**$_{opt}$

definition-head:
    modifier-pattern ...

modifier-pattern:
    modifier
    pattern-variable

statement-rule:
    { MACRO-NAME *pattern*$_{opt}$ **;**$_{opt}$ **end } =>** *rhs*

function-rule:
    { MACRO-NAME **(** *pattern*$_{opt}$ **) } =>** *rhs*

Patterns

pattern:
    pattern-list **;** *...*

BNF

pattern-list:
   pattern-sequence
   property-list-pattern
   pattern-sequence **,** *pattern-list*

pattern-sequence:
   simple-pattern ...

simple-pattern:
   NAME-NOT-END
   =>
   bracketed-pattern
   binding-pattern
   pattern-variable

bracketed-pattern:
   (*pattern*$_{opt}$ **)**
   [*pattern*$_{opt}$ **]**
   { *pattern*$_{opt}$ **}**

binding-pattern:
   pattern-variable **::** *pattern-variable*
   pattern-variable **=** *pattern-variable*
   pattern-variable **::** *pattern-variable* **=** *pattern-variable*

pattern-variable:
   ? NAME
   ? CONSTRAINED-NAME
   ...

property-list-pattern:
   #rest *pattern-variable*
   #key *pattern-keywords*$_{opt}$
   #rest *pattern-variable* **,** **#key** *pattern-keywords*$_{opt}$

pattern-keywords:
   #all-keys
   pattern-keyword
   pattern-keyword **,** *pattern-keywords*

pattern-keyword:
   ? NAME *default*$_{opt}$
   ? CONSTRAINED-NAME *default*$_{opt}$

?? NAME *default_{opt}*
?? CONSTRAINED-NAME *default_{opt}*

Templates

template:
    template-element ...

template-element:
    NAME
    SYMBOL
    NUMBER
    CHARACTER-LITERAL
    STRING
    UNARY-OPERATOR
    separator
    #-word
    one of   **. :: =>**
    (*template_{opt}* **)**
    [*template_{opt}* **]**
    { *template_{opt}* **}**
    #(*template_{opt}* **)**
    #[*template_{opt}* **]**
    parsed-list-constant
    parsed-vector-constant
    substitution

separator:
    one of   **; ,**
    BINARY-OPERATOR

substitution:
    name-prefix_{opt} **?** *name-string-or-symbol name-suffix_{opt}*
    ?? NAME *separator_{opt}* **...**
    ...
    ?= NAME

name-prefix:
    STRING **##**

name-suffix:
    ## STRING

name-string-or-symbol:
    NAME
    STRING
    SYMBOL

Auxiliary Rule Sets

aux-rule-sets:
    aux-rule-set ...

aux-rule-set:
    SYMBOL *aux-rules*

aux-rules:
    aux-rule ...

aux-rule:
    { *pattern$_{opt}$* **}** **=>** *rhs*

Parsed Fragments

parsed-definition:
    (no external representation)

parsed-local-declaration:
    (no external representation)

parsed-function-call:
    (no external representation)

parsed-macro-call:
    (no external representation)

parsed-list-constant:
    (no external representation)

parsed-vector-constant:
    (no external representation)

Exported Names

Overview

This appendix lists the names exported from the Dylan module. In a conforming implementation, the Dylan module should export exactly these names, and the names should be bound exactly as described in this book.

There are, in total, 243 names exported from the Dylan module.

Exported Classes

Fifty-two names exported from the Dylan module are bound to classes.

```
<abort>
<array>
<boolean>
<byte-string>
<character>
<class>
<collection>
<complex>
<condition>
<deque>
<double-float>
<empty-list>
<error>
<explicit-key-collection>
<extended-float>
<float>
<function>
<generic-function>
<integer>
<list>
<method>
<mutable-collection>
<mutable-explicit-key-collection>
<mutable-sequence>
<number>
<object-table>
<object>
<pair>
<range>
<rational>
<real>
<restart>
<sealed-object-error>
```

<sequence>
<serious-condition>
<simple-error>
<simple-object-vector>
<simple-restart>
<simple-vector>
<simple-warning>
<single-float>
<singleton>
<stretchy-collection>
<stretchy-vector>
<string>
<symbol>
<table>
<type-error>
<type>
<unicode-string>
<vector>

Exported Functions

One hundred sixty-nine names exported
from the Dylan module are bound to
functions.

*
\+
\-
\/
\<
\<=
\=
\==

\>
\>=
\^
\~
\~=
\~==
abort
abs
add
add!
add-method
add-new
add-new!
all-superclasses
always
any?
applicable-method?
apply
aref
aref-setter
as
as-lowercase
as-lowercase!
as-uppercase
as-uppercase!
ash
backward-iteration-protocol
break
ceiling
ceiling/
cerror
check-type
choose
choose-by
complement

compose
concatenate
concatenate-as
condition-format-arguments
condition-format-string
conjoin
copy-sequence
curry
default-handler
dimension
dimensions
direct-subclasses
direct-superclasses
disjoin
do
do-handlers
element
element-setter
empty?
error
even?
every?
fill!
find-key
find-method
first
first-setter
floor
floor/
forward-iteration-protocol
function-arguments
function-return-values
function-specializers
gcd

generic-function-mandatory-
    keywords
generic-function-methods
head
head-setter
identity
initialize
instance?
integral?
intersection
key-sequence
key-test
last
last-setter
lcm
limited
list
logand
logbit?
logior
lognot
logxor
make
map
map-as
map-into
max
member?
merge-hash-codes
min
modulo
negative
negative?
object-class
object-hash

Exported Functions

odd?

pair

pop

pop-last

positive?

push

push-last

range

rank

rcurry

reduce

reduce1

remainder

remove

remove!

remove-duplicates

remove-duplicates!

remove-key!

remove-method

replace-elements!

replace-subsequence!

restart-query

return-allowed?

return-description

return-query

reverse

reverse!

round

round/

row-major-index

second

second-setter

shallow-copy

signal

singleton

size

size-setter

slot-initialized?

sort

sort!

sorted-applicable-methods

subsequence-position

subtype?

table-protocol

tail

tail-setter

third

third-setter

truncate

truncate/

type-error-expected-type

type-error-value

type-for-copy

type-union

union

values

vector

zero?

Exported Constants

One name exported from the Dylan module is bound to the distinguished permanent hash state.

    $permanent-hash-state

Exported Defining Macros

Eight names exported from the Dylan
module are bound to defining macros.

```
class-definer
constant-definer
domain-definer
generic-definer
library-definer
method-definer
module-definer
variable-definer
```

Exported Function Macros

Three names exported from the Dylan
module are bound to function macros.

```
:=
|
&
```

Exported Statement Macros

Ten names exported from the Dylan module
are bound to statement macros.

```
begin
block
case
for
if
method
select
unless
until
while
```

Glossary

abstract class
A class that cannot have **direct instances**. The opposite of an abstract class is a **concrete class**.

accepts a variable number of arguments
The shape of the parameter list of a function that accepts a rest argument but does not accept keyword arguments.

accepts all keyword arguments
The shape of the parameter list of a function that specifies #all-keys in addition to #key.

accepts keyword arguments
The shape of the parameter list of a function that accepts keyword arguments (specifies #key). It may or may not specify #rest.

access
1. (a slot) To retrieve (**get**) or replace (**set**) the value of the slot. 2. (a collection element) To retrieve or replace the collection element.

accessor
A **slot accessor** (a **getter** or **setter**).

accessible
(from a module) A binding that is either **owned** by the module or imported into the module from another module.

alignment
See **collection alignment**.

ambiguous methods
(for a particular function call) Two methods that are both **applicable** for the function call, but neither of which is more specific than the other.

anonymous
1. (~ method) Created by a method statement, as opposed to having been created and named by a define method or local definition, or having been **implicitly defined**. Compare with **bare method**. 2. (~ class) Created by calling the make function on the class <class>, as opposed to having been created and named by a define class definition. 3. (~ generic function) Created by calling the make function on the class <generic-function>, as opposed to having been created and named by a define generic definition.

applicable
1. (~ method, during a generic function call) Having a **parameter list** that matches the supplied arguments. 2. (~ handler, when a condition is signaled) Matching the signaled condition by type and by an optional test function associated with the handler.

apply
1. (a function to arguments) To call the function with the arguments. 2. The function apply (see page 350).

argument

An object that is supplied to a function in a function call. In other languages, this is sometimes called an "actual argument" or "actual parameter."

array

An instance of <array>.

assign

1. (a variable) To change the value of the variable. 2. (a slot) To set the value of the slot. 3. (a collection element) To change the value of a collection element.

bare method

1. A method that is not part of a generic function. 2. A method that is invoked directly rather than through a generic function.

base type

(of a type): Every type has a base type. The base type for a class is the class itself. The base type of a singleton is the singleton itself. The base type of a union is the union of the base types of its component types. The base type of a limited type limited(C, …) is C.

bind

(a variable) To establish a **binding**.

binding

An association between a name and a value.

body

A grammatical element of a Dylan program, consisting of zero or more constituents. If any of the constituents are expressions, the body returns the values of the last expression.

bound

(~ name) Having a **binding** that associates the name with a value.

call

(a function) To invoke a function on a set of arguments. If the function is a generic function, it will dispatch to an appropriate method. If the function is a method, its body will be executed within an environment in which its **parameters** are bound to the **arguments** of the function call.

circular list

A list that has no last element, because the tail of every pair in the list is another pair in the list. Compare with **improper list**, **dotted list**.

class

1. A **type** that specifies the structure of **instance** and categorizes objects. Each Dylan object is a **direct instance** of exactly one class. 2. (of an object) The class of which the object is a **direct instance**.

class hierarchy

A directed acyclic graph (DAG) that describes the subclass/superclass relationships among classes. Each node represents a class, the children of a node represent the direct subclasses of a class, and the parents of a node represent the direct superclasses of a class.

class precedence list

(of a class) A total ordering on the class and its superclasses that is consistent with the local precedence orders for the class and each of its superclasses. The class precedence list is used in determining method specificity. See "Computing the Class Precedence List" on page 54.

cleanup clause
A clause in a `block` statement that is guaranteed to be executed, even if the execution of the `block` statement is terminated by a **nonlocal exit**.

closed over
(~ binding) A local binding which is referenced by a **closure**.

closure
A function which references local variables created by a local declaration surrounding the function definition.

code body
That portion of a source code file in **Dylan interchange format** which follows the **file header** and consists of program **constituents**.

coerce
(an object to a type) To produce a new object of the specified type, without modifying the original object. The intent is to produce an object that preserves the meaning of the original object, but is an instance of the specified type.

collection
An aggregate data structure such as a list, a table, or an array. A collection is an instance of `<collection>`.

collection alignment
A technique of preparing two or more collections for an iteration over those collections, ensuring that elements are paired in a consistent way.

collection key
(of a collection) An object that can be passed to random-access operations (such as `element` or `element-setter`) to access an element of the collection.

concrete class
A class that can have direct instances. The opposite of a concrete class is an **abstract class**.

condition
An object that is signaled in an exceptional situation, and used to determine which **handlers** are applicable in the situation. Conditions are instances of `<condition>`.

congruent
(two or more ~ parameter lists) Having compatible parameters. The parameter lists of a generic function and its methods must be congruent. See "Parameter List Congruency" on page 93.

constant
1. A **constant binding**. 2. A **literal constant**. 3. (~ binding) Read-only. 4. (~ slot) Not assignable. Constant slots do not have setter functions.

constant binding
A binding that cannot be assigned a new value.

constituent
A portion of a Dylan program; either a definition, a local declaration, or an expression.

contents
1. (of a collection) The elements of the collection. 2. (of an object) The values stored in the object's slots.

copy
1. (of an object) A new object that has similar structure and **contents** as the original object. A copy may be an instance of the same class as the original object, or it may be an instance of the **type-for-copy** of the object. A copy may or may not share structure with the original object. Compare **fresh copy**, **shallow copy**. 2. (an object) To create a copy of the object.

default method
(of a generic function) The method with the most general parameter specializers for the generic function, intended for use when no more specific method is defined.

defaulted initialization arguments
The sequence of keyword/value pairs used to initialize the slots of an object. This sequence consists of the **supplied initialization arguments** augmented by any additional initialization arguments for which default values are defined by the class or any of its superclasses. See also "Instance Creation and Initialization" on page 64.

definition
A syntax form that denotes a declarative part of a program. Definitions are restricted to be top level expressions, and do not return values.

destructive
(~ function) Capable of modifying its arguments.

destructive modification
1. A change to the contents of a collection, as described on page 119. 2. Any visible change made to an object.

direct instance
(of a class C) An object whose class is C itself, rather than some subclass of C.

direct subclass
(of a class C_1) A class C_2 such that C_1 is a direct superclass of C_2.

direct superclass
(of a class C_1) A class C_2 that is listed as a superclass of C_1 in the definition of C_1, or that was passed as one of the superclass: arguments to make when C_1 was created.

disjoint
(of types): Informally, two types are disjoint if there can be no object that is an instance of both types. A formal definition is given in "Type Disjointness" on page 51.

dotted list
A list that has something other than the **empty list** as the tail of its last pair. Compare **proper list**, **improper list**.

Dylan interchange format
A standard file format for Dylan source code, as described on page 21.

element
(of a collection) An object that is stored in the collection. It can be identified by a **collection key**.

element reference syntax
The shorthand syntax for accessing an element of an array or of any other collection. x[y], x[y, z].

element type
(of a collection) A specification of the **types** of objects which may be stored in the collection, as described in "Element Types" on page 124.

empty list
The list that contains no elements. It is the unique instance of the class `<empty-list>`.

environment
1. A set of **bindings**. 2. The set of **bindings** that are available to a particular part of a program.

equivalence class
(for an **equivalence predicate**) A set of objects, or potential objects, that are all the same under the specified **equivalence predicate** and different under that predicate from all objects not in the equivalence class. See also "Tables" on page 122.

equivalence predicate
A boolean function of two arguments that returns true if and only if the arguments are "the same" according to some specified criteria. For a function to be used as an equivalence predicate, it must be reflexive, commutative, and transitive. See also "Tables" on page 122 and **hash function**.

equivalent types
Two types, each of which is a subtype of the other.

error
1. A **condition** that represents an **error situation**. 2. An **error situation**.

error situation
A situation in which there is something invalid about the program.

exceptional situation
A situation that is not conceptually part of the normal execution of the program, but must be handled some other way. Exceptional situations are represented by **conditions**.

execute
The action of running an **expression** to produce its values.

exit
A transfer of control to an **exit point**, bypassing normal flow of control.

exit procedure
A function that can be called explicitly, during the execution of a `block` statement, to terminate the execution of the `block` statement, transfer control to its associated exit point, and return zero or more values.

exit point
A point through which control may be transferred. An exit point established by a `block` statement may have an associated **exit procedure**.

explicit definition
A definition created by `define constant`, `define variable`, `define generic`, `define macro` and the class name in `define class`. See also **implicit definition**.

explicit key collection
A collection that is not constrained to using integers as keys. The objects that may be used as keys are defined by the collection class. Contrast **sequence**.

explicitly defined
(of a class or generic function) defined by an **explicit definition**.

explicitly known
1. (of a class in a library) A class defined by `define class` in the library or in one of the libraries it uses. 2. (of a generic function in a library) A generic function explicitly defined by `define generic` in the library or in one of the libraries it uses, or a generic function implicitly defined by the definition of a method explicitly known in the library or by a slot specification for a class explicitly known in the library. 3. (of a method in a library) A method defined by `define method` in the library or in one of the libraries it uses, or defined by a slot specification for a class explicitly known in the library.

export
1. (~ a binding from a module) To make a binding available for import into other modules. 2. (~ a module from a library) To make a module available for import into other libraries.

expression
A construct that is executed for the values it returns and/or the side-effects that it performs.

false
The unique false object, #f.

file header
The portion of a source code file in **Dylan interchange format** that specifies the library, module, and possibly other characteristics of the remaining source code in the file.

first-class object
An **object**. The adjective "first-class" is used to emphasize that the object may be stored in a variable or data structure, may be passed as an argument to a function, and may be returned as the value of a function.

format arguments
A series of objects that are used to construct a message from a **format string**, as described in "Condition Messages" on page 112.

format directives
Two-character sequences in a **format string** which are replaced with representations of the **format arguments** to construct the format message, as described in "Condition Messages" on page 112.

format string
A string template into which values can be inserted to construct a message. Format strings are used by the condition system, as described in "Condition Messages" on page 112.

free class
A class that may be used freely in multiple inheritance. The opposite of a free class is a **primary class**.

fresh
A collection C is fresh if modification of any pre-existing collection's contents can never modify the contents of C and if modifications to C can never modify the contents of any pre-existing collection. Immutable collections cannot be modified, so a fresh immutable collection can share structure with other immutable collections.

fresh copy
A **copy** that does not share structure.
Compare with **shallow copy**.

freshly allocated
See **fresh**.

function
An object used for performing actions and
returning values. Functions have a
parameter list and an optional **return value
declaration**, which together define the
function's **signature**. There are two kinds of
functions: **methods** and **generic functions**.
A method has a body of code that is
executed to compute the method's values
when the method is called. A generic
function consists of a set of methods, and
computes its values by selecting and calling
an appropriate method based on the types
of the arguments.

general instance
(of a type) An object that is either a **direct
instance** or **indirect instance** of the type.

general subclass
(of a class) A class that is either a **direct
subclass** or **indirect subclass** of the class.

general superclass
(of a class) A class that is either a **direct
superclass** or **indirect superclass** of the
class.

generic function
A function consisting of a set of methods
with a common calling protocol. A generic
function computes its value by selecting
and calling an appropriate method based
on the types of the arguments. See also
method dispatch.

generic function dispatch
See **method dispatch**.

get
(the value of a slot) To retrieve the value of
the slot.

getter
A function that is applied to an object and
returns the value of one of the object's slots.

getter method
A method that returns the value of a slot.

handler
A function that is used to respond to a
signaled **condition**.

hash code
A conceptual object consisting of a **hash id**
and its associated **hash state**.

hash function
A function, associated with a table, that
computes **hash code**. All hash functions
have one argument, a key, and return two
values, a **hash id** and a **hash state**, which
together represent the **hash code**. See also
equivalence predicate.

hash id
An integer encoding of an object.

hash state
An object of implementation-dependent
type that is associated with a particular
hash id and can be used by the
implementation to determine whether the
hash id has been invalidated.

hash table
A **table**.

hygiene
The property that each named value reference in a macro expansion means the same thing as it meant at the place in the original source code from which it was copied into the macro expansion. See "Hygiene" on page 161.

identical
(of two objects) Computationally equivalent. That is, there is no way for any portable Dylan program to distinguish them; they are the same under the **equivalence predicate** ==.

immutable
Not capable of being modified after it is created. It is an error to attempt to modify an immutable object, though Dylan implementations are not required to detect this error. The opposite of **immutable** is **mutable**.

implicit body
A series of one or more constituents separated by semicolons. When an implicit body is executed, the expressions in the implicit body are executed in order (left to right). The values of the implicit body are the values of the last expression, or #f if the implicit body contains no expressions.

implicit definition
A definition created by define method or by the slot specifications of define class.

implicitly defined
1. (of a generic function) Created by an **implicit definition** rather than by define generic. 2. (of a method) Created by a slot specification in a define class definition, rather than by define method.

import
1. (~ a binding into a module *M*) To make a binding exported by another module accessible in the module *M*. 2. (~ a module into a library *L*) To make a module exported by another library accessible in the library *L*.

improper list
A list that does not have the **empty list** as the tail of its last pair. An improper list is either a **dotted list** or a **circular list**.

indirect instance
(of a type) A **direct instance** of one of the **proper subclasses** of the type.

indirect subclass
(of a class) A class that is a **general subclass** of one of the class's **direct subclasses**.

indirect superclass
(of a class) A class that is a **general superclass** of one of the class's **direct superclasses**.

infix operator
A function or function macro that is normally called using infix notation.

init expression
An **init specification** that specifies an expression to be executed to generate a value used to initialize a slot. Each time the slot needs to be initialized, the expression is executed and its value is used. This allows slots to be initialized to fresh values, or to values computed from the current program state. See also **init function** and **init value**.

init function
An **init specification** that specifies a function to be called to generate a value used to initialize a slot. Each time the slot needs to be initialized, the function is called

and its value is used. This allows slots to be initialized to fresh values, or to values computed from the current program state. See also **init value** and **init expression**.

init keyword

A keyword specified in a class definition, used to initialize a slot. An init keyword may be required or optional.

init specification

An init specification provides an initial value for the slot or a default value for an init-keyword. There are three kinds of init specifications. See page 59 for a complete description.

init value

An **init specification** that specifies a particular value used to initialize a slot. Each time the slot needs to be initialized, the identical value is used. See also **init function** and **init expression**.

initialization argument

A keyword argument supplied to `make`, used to initialize a **keyword initializable** slot.

initialization protocol

The protocol by which newly allocated instances are made ready for use, as described in "Instance Creation and Initialization" on page 64.

initialize

1. (an object) To prepare an object for use, by initializing its slots and calling the initialize function on the object. All Dylan objects are automatically initialized immediately after they are allocated. 2. (a slot) To give the slot its initial value. A program can test to see whether a slot has

been initialized by calling the function `slot-initialized?` There is no mechanism for resetting a slot to the uninitialized state. 3. (a variable) To bind the variable to its initial value.

instance

(of a type) A **general instance** of the type.

instantiable class

A class that can be used as the first argument to `make`. The opposite of an instantiable class is an uninstantiable class. Note that an abstract class may be instantiable.

iteration protocol

A protocol that is common to collections, consisting of the functions `forward-iteration-protocol` and `backward-iteration-protocol`. All collections must implement `forward-iteration-protocol`. Collections that are stable under iteration may also implement `backward-iteration-protocol`.

iteration stability

The property of being **stable under iteration**.

iteration binding

A binding associated with a clause in a `for` statement. Each iteration binding is associated with only one clause.

key

An object used to indicate a particular element of a collection.

key test

The test used to determine whether a given object matches a key in a collection. See "Collection Keys" on page 118.

keyword

A symbol literal, represented in source code as a name followed by a colon. Keywords are used as program constants, and for naming keyword arguments in function calls.

keyword argument list

A **sequence** containing an even number of **elements** that are alternating keywords and values (i.e., a sequence of **keyword/value pairs**). When there is more than one keyword/value pair with the same keyword, the first such pair determines the value associated with that keyword in the keyword argument list.

keyword initializable

(of a slot) A slot that may be given an initial value by a keyword argument in a call to make. See also **initialization arguments**.

keyword parameter

(of a function) A parameter that corresponds to an optional **keyword/value pair**. Keyword parameters are specified by name rather than position.

keyword/value pair

Two successive arguments (a keyword and a value, respectively) supplied in a function call.

library

A set of modules and code, which is available for use by Dylan programs. Libraries are the unit of compilation, sealing, and optimization.

limited

(~ type) A type used to indicate objects that are instances of another type and have additional constraints. There are several kinds of limited types. (~ collection) A limited collection type. (~ integer) A limited integer type. See "Limited Types" on page 73 for a complete description of limited types.

literal constant

An object that is specified explicitly in program text. Literal constants are immutable.

local scope

A scope that includes a limited section of program text.

local binding

A binding created by a local declaration. Local bindings are visible within the remainder of the smallest enclosing body containing the declaration that creates the bindings.

local precedence order

The ordering of a class and its direct superclasses specified by the class definition. See also "Computing the Class Precedence List" on page 54 and **class precedence list**.

macro

An extension to the core language that can be defined by the user, by the implementation, or as part of the Dylan language specification. Much of the grammatical structure of Dylan is built with macros.

mandatory keyword

(of a generic function) A keyword that must be recognized by all of the methods of that generic function. Mandatory keywords are specified in the generic function's parameter list, after `#key` or as the `key:` initialization argument to `make` of `<generic-function>`.

method
A basic callable unit of code. It includes a **parameter list**, a **return value declaration** and a **body**.

method dispatch
The process of determining which method to call when a generic function is applied to arguments.

module
A namespace of bindings.

module binding
A binding that can be referenced from all code associated a particular module.

most specific method
The method whose specializers most closely match the arguments of a function call. A method specialized on a subclass is more specific than a method specialized on superclasses.

multimethod
A method that has more than one **specialized** parameter.

multiple inheritance
Inheritance from more than one direct superclass. See also **single inheritance**.

multiple values
Zero or more values returned by an expression. This term makes explicit the fact that Dylan expressions are not required to return exactly one value. They may also return zero or more than one value.

mutable
Capable of being modified after it is created. The opposite of mutable is **immutable**.

named value reference
An **expression** that is a reference to a **binding**.

natural order
The order in which elements of a collection are traversed by the iteration protocol for a particular iteration. If a collection is stable under iteration, every iteration over the collection has the same natural order.

next method
(during a generic function call) The method that is next most specific, after the method that is currently executing, in the sequence of applicable methods for that generic function call.

next-method parameter
A parameter, usually called `next-method`. The value of the next-method parameter is automatically supplied by the generic function dispatch mechanism. It is either `#f` (if there is no **next method**) or a function that calls the next method after defaulting any unsupplied arguments. There is no way for a program to specify the value of the next method parameter explicitly.

nonlocal exit
A transfer of control, through an **exit point**, out of a local region of code. The nonlocal exit terminates the normal execution of the code.

normal exit
Completing execution and returning without taking a **nonlocal exit**.

object
A unit of data in a Dylan program. Objects are instances of classes, may be stored in variables, slots, and collections, may be passed as arguments to functions, and may be returned as values of functions.

open class
A class that may have subclasses that are not explicitly defined in the same library. The opposite of an open class is a **sealed class**.

open generic function
A generic function that may have methods that are not explicitly defined in the same library. The opposite of an open generic function is a **sealed generic function**.

owned
(of a binding, by a module) Created by a `create` clause in the module's `define module` definition, or by a definition associated with the module.

pair
An instance of `<pair>`.

parameter
(of a function) A variable that is declared in the parameter list of a function and specifies part of the function's calling protocol. Parameters are lexically bound within the function body, and are bound to their initial values when the function is called. Dylan supports required parameters, rest parameters, keyword parameters, and next-method parameters.

parameter list
The part of a function definition that specifies the function's arguments and return values. See also **signature**.

predicate function
A function that returns a true or false value. By convention, the names of predicate functions end in a question mark.

primary class
A class that may be used only as the primary superclass in multiple inheritance. A class may not have two primary superclasses unless one is a subclass of the other. The opposite of a primary class is a **free class**.

proper list
A list that has the **empty list** as the tail of its last pair.

proper subclass
(of a class) A class that is a subclass of the class, but is not identical to the class.

proper subtype
(of a type) A type that is a subtype of the type, but is not equivalent to the type. See also **equivalent types**.

protocol
1. (of a class) The methods that all subclasses of the class either implement or inherit. 2. (of a function, esp. a generic function) The **signature** of the function.

pseudosubtype
A relation between types. The type T_1 is a pseudosubtype of the type T_2 if T_1 is a subtype of the base type of T_2 and T_1 and T_2 are not disjoint.

required parameter
(of a function) A parameter that corresponds to an argument that must be supplied when the function is called. Required parameters are specified in a fixed order before other parameters, and their corresponding arguments must be supplied in the same order. Required parameters may be specialized or unspecialized. Compare **rest parameter**, **keyword parameter**, and **next-method parameter**.

requires a fixed number of arguments
The shape of the parameter list of a function that accepts neither keyword arguments nor a rest argument.

rest parameter
(of a function) A parameter that allows a function to accept a variable number of arguments following those that correspond to the required parameters. The additional arguments are stored in a sequence.

return value declaration
An optional part of a function definition that specifies the number and types of the values returned by the function. See also **signature**.

sealed class
A class that cannot have direct subclasses other than those explicitly defined in the same library. The opposite of a sealed class is an **open class**.

sealed domain
A portion of a generic function and a portion of the class hierarchy which are declared to be invariant. See "Define Sealed Domain" on page 135 for a complete description of sealed domains.

sealed generic function
A generic function that cannot have methods that are not explicitly defined in the same library. The opposite of a sealed generic function is an **open generic function**.

sealing directive
A definition or adjective within a definition that specifies a sealing-related characteristic of the object being defined. See "Sealing" on page 133.

sequence
An instance of `<sequence>`, a type of collection which uses successive nonnegative integers as keys.

set
(the value of a slot) To replace the value of the slot with a new value.

setter
A function used to set the value of a slot. By convention, the name of a setter is the name of the getter concatenated with the suffix `-setter`.

setter method
A method that sets the value of a slot.

shadow
(a binding) To hide the binding within a portion of program text, by creating a new local binding with the same name.

shallow copy
(of an object) A new object that has the same **contents** as the object. The contents are not copied, but are the same objects contained in the original object.

signature
(of a function) The **parameter list** of the function, including its **return value declaration**.

single inheritance
Inheritance from only one direct superclass. See also **multiple inheritance**.

singleton
A type used to indicate an individual object. A singleton has only one instance.

slot
A unit of local storage available within an instance or a class, which is used to store state in the instance or class.

slot accessor
A **getter** or **setter**.

slot reference syntax
The shorthand syntax for invoking a function of one argument.
`window.position` is equivalent to `position(window)`.

source record
An implementation-defined unit of source program text.

specialize
1. (a variable) To restrict the variable to values that are general instances of a particular type. 2. (a generic function) To define a method for the generic function that is applicable only to instances of a particular type or types. 3. (a method) To specify the types of the parameters of the method.

specializer
A type, especially when it is used to specialize a parameter, variable, or slot.

stable under iteration
(of a collection) The property of a collection that any two iterations over the collection are guaranteed to produce the same values in the same order (unless, of course, the collection has been modified). See also **natural order** and **sequence**.

statement
A call to a statement macro. See page 15 for a description of statement macros.

stretchy collection
A collection that may grow or shrink to accommodate adding or removing elements.

supplied initialization arguments
The keyword arguments values supplied in a call to `make`. See also "Instance Creation and Initialization" on page 64 and **defaulted initialization arguments**.

table
An object, also known as a hash table, that maps arbitrary keys to objects. Each table has an associated **equivalence predicate** that is used to compare keys. The table maps keys that are equivalent under the predicate to the same table element.

true
1. The canonical true value, `#t`. 2. Any object other than the unique false value, `#f`.

type
A Dylan object that categorizes objects. See page 49.

type equivalent
See **equivalent types**.

type-for-copy
(of an object) An instantiable type suitable for making copies of an object. Instances of the **type-for-copy** must be mutable.

unbounded sequence
A sequence that is infinite or circular.

uninstantiable class
A class that cannot be used as the first argument to `make`. The opposite of an uninstantiable class is an instantiable class.

union type
A type used to indicate objects that are instances of one of a set of specified types. See page 72 for a complete description of union types.

unique string
A symbol literal represented in source code as a sharp sign "#" followed immediately by a string literal. These are semantically identical to **keywords**; the distinct syntax is provided for program readability.

value declaration
See **return value declaration**.

value type
The type of a return value of a function, as defined in the function's **parameter list**.

variable
A **variable binding**.

variable binding
A **binding** that can be assigned a new value.

visible modification
(with respect to an **equivalence predicate**) A modification that changes the equivalence class of the object. The modifications that are visible to an **equivalence predicate** are determined by the definition of the predicate. See also "Tables" on page 122.

whitespace
Any number of contiguous space, tab, newline, and newpage characters. Except within string literals, the amount of contiguous whitespace is not significant in program code.

Index

Symbols

* 277
- 278
/ 278
!, function name convention 24
#(), the empty list 369
#(...), list literal syntax 13
#[...], vector literal syntax 13
#"...", unique string literal syntax 19
#all-keys 86–87
#f 13, 40, 369
  as the default for missing return values 92
  as the default value for keyword
      parameters 89
#key 86, 86–87
  in macro definitions 154
#next 86
#rest 86, 86–87
  in macro definitions 154
#t 13, 40, 369
#-words 17
$, constant name convention 24
$permanent-hash-state 369
%, used in format directives 113
&, logical 'and' 412
  sample definition of 177
+ 277
//, single-line comment syntax 16
., slot reference syntax 15, 34
*, variable name convention 23
:, in keyword syntax 19
:= 38, 409
  sample definition of 177
< 271
<= 273
<...>, type name convention 23
<abort> 253
<array> 218
<boolean> 40, 197
<byte-string> 233
<character> 195
  subclasses of 125
<class> 191
<collection> 117, 208
  and limited collection types 75
<complex> 199
<condition> 105, 245
<deque> 225
<double-float> 203
<empty-list> 229
<error> 247
<explicit-key-collection> 117, 210
<extended-float> 203
<float> 202
<function> 79, 238
<generic-function> 79, 241
<integer> 204
  and limited integer types 74
<list> 227
<method> 79, 243
<mutable-collection> 119, 121, 214
<mutable-explicit-key-collection> 215
<mutable-sequence> 216
<number> 198
<object> 187
  as the root of the type hierarchy 50
<object-table> 237
<pair> 229
<range> 230
<rational> 203
<real> 200
<restart> 111, 251
<sealed-object-error> 249
<sequence> 117, 211
<serious-condition> 247

`<simple-error>` 248
`<simple-object-vector>` 224
`<simple-restart>` 252
`<simple-vector>` 222
`<simple-warning>` 250
`<single-float>` 202
`<singleton>` 71, 194
`<stretchy-collection>` 119, 217
  and collection alignment 121
`<stretchy-vector>` 224
`<string>` 232
`<symbol>` 196
`<table>` 122, 235
`<type>` 190
`<type-error>` 248
`<unicode-string>` 234
`<vector>` 221
`<warning>` 249
= 269
== 268
> 272
>= 273
?
  in macros 154
  predicate name convention 24
??
  in macros 155
[...], element reference syntax 15, 35
  in macro calls 146, 163
  order of execution of 44
\, escape character 18, 20, 36, 149
^ 283
|, logical 'or' 412
  sample definition of 177
~, logical negation 40, 268
~= 271
~== 269
'...', character literal syntax 18
/*...*/, delimited comment syntax 16
"...", string literal syntax 18

A

`<abort>` 253
abort 360
aborting code 41
abs 284
abstract classes 52, 134
  supporting instantiation of 64
accept all keyword arguments 86
accept a variable number of arguments 87
accept keyword arguments 86
accessible bindings in a module 27
accessing slots 57
accessor name convention 24
add 309
  default method of 211
add! 310
adding keys to a collection 119
add-method 352
  disallowed on sealed generic functions 135
add-new 311
  default method of 211
add-new! 312
adjectives
  in class definitions 134
  used to express sealing directives 133
alignment, of collections during
    iteration 120–121
allocation
  of collections 119–120
  of slots 59, 60–61
all-superclasses 344
alphabetic characters 17
always 350
ambiguous methods 96
and, logical operator 412
angle bracket, <...>, type name convention 23
any? 330
applicable handler, locating 106
applicable-method? 355
applicable methods 95
apply 350
  used with next-method 99
aref 302

`aref-setter` 302
  shortand syntax for 38
argument lists
  See parameter lists
argument order
  and method dispatch 98
arguments
  accepted by functions 79
  to a macro call 144
arithmetic operations 274–287
`<array>` 218
array reference syntax 20
  in macros 163
`as` 288
`ash` 286
`as-lowercase` 291
`as-lowercase!` 291
assignment 38–39, 409–411
assignment operator
  in macros 163
  order of execution of 44
asterisk, variable name convention 23
`as-uppercase` 290
`as-uppercase!` 290
`author:`, interchange format keyword 23
auxiliary rule sets 161
  BNF of 430

constant 148
  created by `define class` 380
  created by `define constant` 375
  created by `define generic` 376
  created by `define variable` 374
  created by definitions 28
  defining in modules 27
  names of 23
  of local methods 81–82
bitwise operations 284–286
blank lines, in interchange format 22
blending of tokens 16, 20, 35
`block` 41, 105, 109, 404
  sample definition of 166
body 11
`<boolean>` 197
boolean values
  as literal constants 13
  See also true and false
bracketed fragments 145
bracketed-patterns, matching of 153
`break` 359
built-in definition macros 11
built-in macros
  sample definitions of 165–177
built-in modules 29
built-in statement macros 15
`<byte-string>` 233

B

backslash escape sequence 18, 149
`backward-iteration-protocol` 121, 339
bare methods 82–83
  See also local methods
base types 50–51
`begin` 404
  sample definition of 166
`begin` … `end` bracketing in macros 145
binary operator call 14
binding-patterns, matching of 153
bindings 10
  and multiple values 42

C

calling exception systems 104
`case` 397
  sample definition of 167
catch 103
`ceiling` 280
`ceiling/` 281
`cerror` 359
changing
  collections during iteration 117
  the value of a module binding 38
`<character>` 195

`<character>` (*continued*)
  subclasses of 125
characters
  as literal constants 13, 18
  in the lexical syntax 17
  literal constant BNF 418
  operations on 290–292
`check-type` 360
`choose` 333
  default method of 211
`choose-by` 333
  default method of 211
circularity
  in class inheritance 53
  in library use relationships 28
  in module use relationships 27
circular references
  See infinite recursion
`<class>` 191
class allocated slots, initialization of 66–67
classes 52–56
  abstract or concrete 134
  as a kind of type 49
  built-in 187–253
    collection classes 206–237
    condition classes 244–253
    function classes 238–244
    number classes 197–205
    object classes 187–188
    simple object classes 195–197
    type classes 189–195
  characteristics of 134–135
  created by `define class` 380
  disjointness rule for 51
  explicitly known 133
  features of 52
  inheritance of 53
  overview of 52
  primary or free 134
  restrictions on built-in 187
  sealed or open 134
  sealing 134–135
class precedence lists
  computation of 54–56

definition of 54
`class` slot allocation 60
cleanup clauses 41, 405
closed over bindings 83
closures 83–84
code body, in interchange format 21
coercing objects 287–294
`<collection>` 117, 208
  and limited collection types 75
collections 117–129
  adding and removing elements 119, 309–316
  alignment of 120–121
  allocation of 119–120
  alteration of 119–120
  copying 323
  defining new classes of 121–122
  destructive operations on 120
  element types of 124–126
  freshness of 120
  instability under iteration 118
  iteration protocol of 117–118, 337–343
  keys of 117, 118
  key tests of 118
  limited 126–129
  mapping and reducing 327–337
  modifying during iteration 117
  mutability of 119, 120
  natural order of iteration 118
  operations on 294–343
  properties of 294–299
  removing elements from 119, 312–316
  reordering 316–319
  searching 330, 331, 333, 334, 335
  selecting elements of 300–309
  sorting 333
  stability under iteration 118
  testing 330, 331, 334, 335
  that may grow and shrink 218
  user-defined 126
comments 16
  BNF of 414
comparison operations 267–274
compilation, and macros 143–146
`complement` 346

`<complex>` 199
compose 346
computational equivalence 269
concatenate 323
   default method of 211
concatenate-as 324
concrete classes 52, 134
`<condition>` 105, 245
conditional execution 39
   statements implementing 394–399
condition-format-arguments 364
condition-format-string 364
condition messages 112–114
conditions 103–114
   establishing local handlers for 12, 13, 392
   operations on 357–365
   See also handlers
condition system 105
congruency
   of parameter lists 93–94
   of value declarations 92, 94
conjoin 347
consistency among class precedence lists 54
constant bindings 10, 148
   created by define class 380
   created by define constant 375
   created by define generic 376
constants
   name convention of 24
   See also literal constants
constant slots 59, 61
constituents 11
   at top-level 21
   order of execution of 43
control characters 19
controlling access to bindings and objects 27
conventions for binding names 23
copying objects 287–294
copyright:, interchange format keyword 23
copy-sequence 323
   default method of 211
create clause of a module definition 28
creating
   classes 52–53

instances 64–71, 258–267
limited collections 128
limited types 74
See also initialization protocol
curry 348

D

data structures, collections as 117
deallocating objects 4
debuggers 112
declaring
   characteristics of classes 134–135
   characteristics of generic functions 135
   ownership of module variables 28
   sealing information 133
   types of slots 61
declining to handle a condition 106
defaulted initialization arguments 64
default-handler 106, 361
default values
   of initialization arguments 69
   of keyword parameters 89
   of missing return values 92
   of slot names 58
define as a reserved word 14
define class 52, 378
   sample definition of 173
   used to create explicit definitions 28
   used to create implicit definitions 28
define constant 375
   sample definition of 174
   used to create explicit definitions 28
   used to receive multiple values 42
define domain
   sample definition of 175
define generic 376
   sample definition of 175
   used to create explicit definitions 28
define inert domain 388
define library 386
   sample definition of 175

`define macro` 389
  used to create explicit definitions 28
`define method` 377
  sample definition of 176
  used to add methods to a generic function 80
  used to create implicit definitions 28
  used to create implicit generic functions 79
`define module` 380
  sample definition of 176
`-definer` suffix 148
`define sealed domain` 135
  sample definition of 175
`define sealed method` 138
`define variable` 374
  sample definition of 176
  used to create explicit definitions 28
  used to receive multiple values 42
defining
  classes 52–53
  generic functions 79
  libraries 28
  modules 27
definition macros 147
  built-in 11
  user-defined 11
definitions 11
  BNF of 422
  built-in 373–389
  processing of 143
  said not to execute 43
  special rules for pattern matching of 155–156
  top-level 21
  used to create module bindings 28
delimited comments 16
`<deque>` 225
destructive operations
  naming convention for 24
  on collections 120
`dimension` 298
`dimensions` 297
  and the array protocol 219
direct instance relationship 52
`direct-subclasses` 345
direct subclass relationship 53

`direct-superclasses` 345
direct superclass relationship 53
`disjoin` 347
disjointness of types 51
  implied by slot duplication 58
division by zero 279
division of integers 204, 279
`do` 327
`do-handlers` 114, 362
dollar-sign, constant name convention 24
`<double-float>` 203
duplicate keywords
  in arguments to next-method 99
  in function calls 88
  in initialization arguments 65
Dylan interchange format 21
`dylan` library 29
`dylan` module 29
`dylan` module and operator names 35
Dylan programming language ix–451
`dylan-user` module 29
dynamic condition handlers 103

E

`each-subclass` slot allocation 60
efficiency
  of simple-vectors 223
  See also sealing
`element` 118, 121, 300
  and arrays 219
  and simple-vectors 223
  and the element type of a collection 124
element reference syntax 15, 35
  in macro calls 146, 163
  order of execution of 44
`element-setter` 119, 121, 301
  and `<mutable-collection>` 214
  and `<stretchy-collection>` 218
  and arrays 219
  and simple-vectors 223
  and the element type of a collection 124

`element-setter` (*continued*)
  shortand syntax for 38
elements of collections 117
element types of collections 124–126
  and subclassing 128
  and user-defined collections 126
`empty?` 294
`<empty-list>` 229
`end` as a reserved word 14
equality 269
equality testing operations 267–274
equivalence classes 122
equivalence predicates 122
equivalent types 50
`<error>` 247
`error` 358
errors, as a kind of condition 105
escape characters 20
escape sequence 18
escaping names 20
`even?` 275
`every?` 331
`exception` clause of the `block` statement 105
exceptions 103–114
  background 103–104
  which are not errors 104
exception system 105
exclamation point, name convention 24
execution of expressions 42
exiting exception system 104
exits 105, 108–111
  nonlocal 41, 107, 108, 111, 405
explicit definitions 28
`<explicit-key-collection>` 117, 210
explicit key collections 117
explicitly known objects 133–134
exponentiation 283
export information of a library 29
exporting
  bindings 27
  modules 29
  reserved words 20
expressions 13
  BNF of 424

execution of 42
order of execution within 44
`<extended-float>` 203
extensible grammar 147–148

F

false and true 40
false object, `#f` 40
'field,' as a synonym for 'slot' 57
file header, in interchange format 21
`fill!` 337
filtering slot values 62
`find-key` 335
`find-method` 356
`first` 303
first class
  methods 82–83
  objects 4
  types 49
`first-setter` 304
`<float>` 202
floating point numbers, combined with
    nonfloats 274
`floor` 279
`floor/` 281
flow of control, nonstandard 405
  See also exits, nonlocal exits
`for` 400
  sample definition of 167
formal recovery 104
format arguments 112
format directives 112
format strings 112
`forward-iteration-protocol` 121, 337
forward references 43
fragments
  and macro expansion 144
  BNF of 421
free classes 52, 134
freshly allocated collections 120
`<function>` 79, 238

`function-arguments` 354
function calls 14, 33–35
   and method dispatch 95–99
   order of execution of 44
   shorthand for 20
function macros 147, 148
   built-in 409–412
   calls to 146
   special rules for pattern matching 156–157
`function-return-values` 354
functions 79–100
   built-in 257–365
   introspection of 351–357
   operations on 100, 346–357
`function-specializers` 353

G

garbage collection 4
`gcd` 287
general subclass relationship 53
general superclass relationship 52
`<generic-function>` 79, 241
`generic-function-mandatory-keywords` 353
`generic-function-methods` 351
generic functions 79, 79–80
   calling 95
   characteristics of 135
   created by `define generic` 376
   created implicitly with `define method` 378
   defining 79
   explicitly known 134
   parameter lists of 85, 94–95
   sealed or open 135
   sealing 135
   specializing 88
   with no required parameters 81
getter methods 57
   effect of slot specialization on 61
getter name convention 24
getters 24
goals of the language 3

grammar
   and macros 143
   extensibility of 147–148
   LALR(1) 413
graphic characters 17
greater than comparitor 272
greater than or equal to comparitor 273

H

`handler` as a reserved word 14
handlers 105, 105–106
   established by `let handler` 392
   for restarts 111
handling 103
   by returning 111
   declining to 106
hash codes 123
hash functions 123
hash ids 123
hash states 123, 369
hash tables
   See tables
`head` 307
header files 29
`head-setter` 308
heads of lists 226
hygiene in macros 161–165
   intentional violation of 163
   versus module encapsulation 163–165

I

identity
   and computational equivalence 269
   property of comparitors 267
`identity` 287
IEEE floating point numbers 202–203
   comparisons of 268
`if` 395
   sample definition of 171

immutability
    as a property of literal constants 14
    as a property of types 50
    of some collections 120
    of the values of rest parameters 85
implicit
    definitions 28
    generic function parameter lists 94–95
    generic functions 79
importing
    bindings 27
    macros 149
    modules 29
    reserved words 20
improper lists 227
incremental compilation 9
indefinite element types 124
indirect subclass relationship 53
inequality 271
infinite recursion
    See circular references
inheritance 53
    of initialization arguments 70–71
    of slots 58, 71
inherited slot specifications 67–68
init expressions of slots 59
init functions of slots 59
initialization arguments 60
    inheritance of 70–71
    specification of 68–70
    validity of 65
initialization of instances 53, 64–71
initialization protocol 52, 64–71, 258–261
initialize 260
    used in the initialization protocol 64
    used to initialize virtual slots 61
    additional behavior of 66
initializing instances
    See initialization protocol
initial value of a slot 58
init-keywords
    declaring required 68
    of slots 58, 60
    providing default values for 68–70

    restricting the types of 68–70
    used to initialize constant slots 61
init specifications
    of class allocated slots 67
    of slots 58, 59–60
    overriding in subclasses 67–68
    used to initialize constant slots 61
init values of slots 59
inside stack 107
instability under iteration 118
instance? 343
    in the type protocol 49
    of limited collection types 127
    of union types 72
instance creation
    See initialization protocol
instance slot allocation 60
'instance variable,' as a synonym for 'slot' 57
instantiable classes 52
instantiation, as part of the type protocol 49
<integer> 204
    and limited integer types 74
integers
    division of 204, 279
    precision of 204
integral? 276
interchange format 21
intermediate words in macros 158–159
intersection 319
    default method of 211
introspection 27
    of conditions 104, 114, 362–365
    of functions 351–357
    on types 343–345
iteration 40–41
    collection alignment during 120–121
    natural order of 118
    stability of 118
    statements supporting 399–404
    using mapping functions 327
    using recursion 41
iteration protocol 117–118, 121, 337–343
    and the element type of a collection 124
    of tables 122

J

java 89

K

key-sequence 299
keys of collections 117, 118
key-test 118, 121, 298
key tests of collections 118
   and collection alignment 121
   and tables 122
keyword 70
keyword arguments
   required format of 87
   See also duplicated keywords, keyword
      parameters
keyword initializable
   class allocated slots 67
   slots 60
keyword parameters 85, 89–91
   default values of 89
   names of, shadowing module variables 90
   types of 90–91
keywords 19
   as literal constants 14
   BNF of 415
   in interchange format 21
   mandatory 87
   permitted 87
   recognized 87

L

LALR(1) grammar 413
language:, interchange format keyword 22
last 306
last-setter 306
lcm 286
left-associativity of most operators 35
less than comparitor 271

less than or equal to comparitor 273
let 390
   as a reserved word 14
   used to receive multiple values 42
let handler 105, 392
lexical notes 414
lexical syntax 16–20
   bnf of 414–419
liberality 187, 257, 258
libraries 28–29
   and cross-library definitions 139
   as components of a program 9
   created by define library 386
   definitions of 28
library export information 149
limited 74, 263
limited collections 75, 126–129
   creating 128
   disjointness rule for 51
   instantiable 129
   subclassing 128
   uninstantiable 129
limited integer types 74–75
limited types 73–75
   as kinds of types 49
   constructor for 263
   creating 74
<list> 227
list 261
list literal constants 13, 145, 146
lists 226–230
   constructors for 261, 262
   empty list 369
literal constants 13–14
   parsing of 145
local 81–82, 391
   as a reserved word 14
   used to define local methods 80
local bindings 12
   and macros 149
   created by let 390
local declarations 12
   as macro calls 147
   BNF of 423

local declarations (*continued*)
  built-in 389–393
  parsing of 145
local methods 13, 81–82
  created by `local` 391
local precedence order of superclasses 54
`logand` 285
`logbit?` 285
logical 'and' 412
logical negation 40, 268
logical 'or' 412
`logior` 284
`lognot` 285
`logxor` 284
looping
  See iteration

M

macro system 143–183
`macro` as a reserved word 14
macro definitions
  BNF of 427
macros 143
  and local bindings 149
  and module encapsulation 163–165
  and the creation of reserved words 149
  arguments to 144
  as extensions to the core language 10
  assignment operator in 163
  auxiliary rule sets in 161
  `begin` ... `end` bracketing in 145
  binding-pattern matching in 153
  bracketed-pattern matching in 153
  calls to 143
  captured bindings in 162
  created by `define macro` 389
  definition macros 147
  definitions of 144
  element reference syntax in 163
  examples of 165–183
  expansion of 10, 143
  delaying 145
  exporting 148
  function macros 148
  hygiene in 161–165
  importing 149
  intentional hygiene violation in 163
  intermediate words in 158–159
  kinds of 147
  named value references in 161
  named value references to 149
  names of 148–149
  parsed expression fragments in 146
  parsing and 145
  pattern-list matching in 152
  pattern-sequence matching in 152
  patterns in 151–157
  pattern variable constraints in 157–159
  pattern variable matching in 153
  processing of 143–146
  property-list-pattern matching in 154
  reparsing of 145
  simple-pattern matching in 152
  special rules for definitions 155–156
  special rules for function macros 156–157
  special rules for statements 156
  statement macros 148
  templates in 159–161
  temporary variables in 162
  that contain macros 159
`make` 258
  in the initialization protocol 64
  in the type protocol 49
  used to create classes 52, 134
  used to create generic functions 79, 135
  additional behavior of 66
mandatory keywords 87
`map` 328
`map-as` 328
`map-into` 329
`max` 274
`member?` 334
`merge-hash-codes` 341
`<method>` 79, 243
`method` 408

method (*continued*)
    sample definition of 171
    used to create bare methods 80, 82
method dispatch 79, 95–99
    controlled through specialization 88
    order of arguments and 98
methods 79, 80–84
    ambiguous 96
    applicable to a function call 95
    bare 82–83
    BNF of 426
    built-in, manual notation of 257
    created by `define method` 378
    created by `local` 391
    explicitly known 134
    in generic functions 81
    parameter lists of 85
    restrictions on defining 139
    sealed, manual notation of 257
    selecting 96–98
    specializing 88
    specificity of 96–98
middle stack 107
`min` 274
`module:`, interchange format keyword 22
module bindings
    changing the value of 38
    constant 148
modules 27–28
    and hygiene 163–165
    as units of modularity 9
    built-in 29
    created with `define module` 381
    definitions of 27
    reserved words in 149
`modulo` 282
multiple inheritance
    and primary classes 134
    and slot inheritance 58, 71
multiple values 42–43, 288, 405
    received by `let` 390
mutability
    of collections 119
        during iteration 117

`<mutable-collection>` 119, 121, 214
`<mutable-explicit-key-collection>` 215
`<mutable-sequence>` 216

N

name-based exception systems 104
name character 17
named value references 14
    as macro calls 147
    in macros 161
    to macros 149
    within a module 27
names 17
    BNF of 415
    conventions for 23
    escaping 20
    of macros 148–149
    special treatment of 20
namespace of bindings, modules as 27
natural order, of collection iteration 118
negation, logical 40, 268
`negative` 279
`negative?` 276
new value argument, returned by a setter 58
next-method 98–99
next-method parameter 85
nonlocal exits 41, 107, 108, 111, 405
notation
    of built-in class reference 187
    of built-in function reference 257
    of the BNF 413
    of the manual 6
`<number>` 198
numbers, BNF of 418
numeric
    characters 17
    classes, sealed 199
    literal constants 13, 18
    operations, default implementations of 199

O

`<object>` 187
object-based exception system 104
`object-class` 344
`object-hash` 342
`<object-table>` 237
`odd?` 275
on-unit 103
open classes 52, 134
open generic functions, manual notation of 257
operand 13
operations
  arithmetic 274–287
  equality testing 267–274
  on collections 294–343
  on conditions 357–365
  on functions 346–357
  on sets 319–323
  on strings and characters 290–292
  on types 343–345
operator calls 14, 146
  order of execution of 36, 44
operators 18, 35–37
  and token blending 35
  binding names of 35–37
  BNF of 417
  order of execution of 36, 44
  precedence of 36
  stripping special syntactic properties from
    names of 20
optimization
  as an inappropriate use of macros 143
  See also sealing
optional arguments 85
optional initialization argument
    specifications 68–69
or, logical operator 412
order of arguments and method dispatch 98
order of collection iteration 118
order of execution 43–45
  of operators 36, 44
`otherwise` as a reserved word 14

outside stack 107
owned module bindings 27

P

`<pair>` 229
`pair` 262
pairs
  as literal constants 13
  constructors for 262
  See also lists
parallel binding 42
parameter lists 16, 79, 84–95
  congruency of 93–94
  kinds of 86–88
  of generic functions 79, 85
  of methods 85
parameters
  closed over 83
  kinds of 85–86
  of methods 80
  specializing 88–89
parenthesized expressions 15
parsed expression fragments 146
parsing 143
pattern-lists, matching of 152
pattern matching
  special rules for definitions 155–156
  special rules for function macros 156–157
  special rules for statements 156
patterns
  BNF of 427
  in macros 144, 151–157
pattern-sequences, matching of 152
pattern variables
  constraints of 157–159
  in macros 144
  matching of 153
`$permanent-hash-state` 369
permited keywords 87
`pop` 315
`pop-last` 315

positive? 276
precedence
    of operators 36
    of slot reference syntax 36
precision of integers 204
predicate name convention 24
primary classes 52, 134
printf 113
privacy and encapsulation 27
program control 33–45
program structure 9–24, 27–29
    BNF of 420
proper lists 227
proper subtypes 50
properties
    of collections 294–299
    of numbers 275–277
property-list-patterns, matching of 154
property lists
    BNF of 420
protected regions 41, 405
pseudosubtypes 50–51
    examples of 138
punctuation 19
push 314
push-last 315

Q

question mark
    in macros 154, 155
    predicate name convention 24

R

raise 103
<range> 230
range 263
ranges, constructor for 263
rank 296
<rational> 203

rcurry 349
readability 23
read-only bindings 10
<real> 200
recognized keywords 87
recovery 104, 105, 108–111
    formal 104
    protocols for 111–112
recursion 41
recursive functions
    created by local 391
recursive methods 81–82
reduce 331
reduce1 332
referential transparency 162
remainder 283
remove 312
    default method of 211
remove! 313
remove-duplicates 321
    default method of 211
remove-duplicates! 322
remove-key! 119, 335
remove-method 357
    disallowed on sealed generic functions 135
removing keys from a collection 119
reparsing of macros 145
replace-elements! 336
replace-subsequence! 325
require a fixed number of arguments 86
required initialization argument
        specifications 68–69
required-init-keyword: 70
required keyword 70
required parameters 85
required value declarations 91
reserved words 14
    BNF of 415
    created by macros 149
    exporting and importing 20
    stripping of special syntactic properties 20
<restart> 111, 251
restart handlers 111
restart-query 361

restarts 111
  as an example of conditions 105
rest-binding, used to receive multiple values 43
rest parameters 85
restrictions on method definitions 139
rest value declarations 91
return-allowed 363
return-description 363
returning from exceptions 104, 111
returning multiple values 42
return-query 362
return value declarations 85, 91
  of getters and setters 61
return values of methods 80
reverse 316
  default method of 211
reverse! 317
rewrite rules 150–151
right-associativity of := and ^ 35
root of the type hierarchy, <object> as 50, 188
round 280
round/ 282
row-major-index 297

S

sealed domains 135–140
  abbreviations for 138–139
  constraints implied by 136
  created by define sealed domain 388
  rationale for 136–138
sealed methods, manual notation of 257
<sealed-object-error> 249
sealed slot option to define class 139
sealing 133–140
  classes 52, 53, 134–135
  generic functions 135
  restrictions, violations of 139
  slots 59
sealing directives 133
second 304
second-setter 305

select 398
  sample definition of 172
send super
  See next-method
<sequence> 117, 211
sequences 117
<serious-condition> 247
set operations 319–323
setter function shorthand syntax 38
setter methods 57
  effect of slot specialization on 61
setter name convention 24
setters 24
-setter suffix 38
shadowing macros 12
shadowing names accidently 90
shallow-copy 292
signal 103
signal 106, 357
signaler 105
signaling unit 107
signal system 105
<simple-error> 248
<simple-object-vector> 224
simple-patterns, matching of 152
<simple-restart> 252
<simple-vector> 222
<simple-warning> 250
<single-float> 202
single inheritance and primary classes 134
single-line comments 16
<singleton> 71, 194
singleton 263
singletons 71–72
  as a kind of type 49
  constructor for 263
  disjointness rule 51
  subtype? defined on 50
singleton syntax 20
size 295
  and vectors 221
size-setter 296
slot access 57
slot-initialized? 67, 261

slot reference syntax 15, 34–35
  in macro calls 146
  order of execution of 44
  precedence of 36
slots 52, 57–64
  accessed through functions 62
  allocation of 60–61
  constant 61
  default names of 58
  duplication of 58
  efficiency of 134
  implicitly creating generic functions 79
  inheritance of 58, 70–71
  init expressions of 59
  init functions of 59
  initialization argument specifications of 68–70
  initialization of class allocated 66–67
  init values of 59
  overriding 62
  sealed 139
  specialization of 61–62
  specification of 53
  specifying with define class 380
  testing the initialization of 67, 261
  using 62–64
sort 318
  default method of 211
sort! 318
sorted-applicable-methods 356
sorting applicable methods 96
source code associated with a library 28
source code format 21
source records 9
  in interchange format 21
special definitions 12
  parsing of 145
specializers
  of methods 80
  types used as 49
specializing
  bindings 10
  constant bindings 376
  keyword arguments 85
  local bindings 391

parameters 85
parameters of generic functions 88
parameters of methods 88
required parameters 88–89
slots 59, 61–62
to control method dispatch 88
variable bindings 375
stability under iteration 118
  as a property of seqences 211
stack model 107–108
statement macros 15, 147, 148
statements 15, 146
  BNF of 425
  built-in 393–408
  special rules for pattern matching 156
state of an iteration 117
static nature of definitions 21
<stretchy-collection> 119, 217
  and collection alignment 121
<stretchy-vector> 224
<string> 232
string literal constants 13, 18, 146
  BNF of 418
strings
  classes of 232–235
  operations on 290–292
structure of Dylan programs 9–24
subroutines in macros
  See auxiliary rule sets
subsequence-position 326
subtype? 343
  defined for union types 72
  defining a partial ordering on types 50
  in the type protocol 49
  of limited collection types 127–128
subtypes, proper 50
superclasses, specification of 53
supplied initialization arguments 64
<symbol> 196
symbol literal constants 13, 19
symbols
  BNF of 415
  used to specify keyword arguments 85

syntax
 BNF of 413–430
 of function calls 33
 of the language 9–24

T

`<table>` 122, 235
`table-protocol` 122, 340
tables 122–123, 235–237
`tail` 307
tail recursion 41
 used when calling next-handler 106
`tail-setter` 308
tails of lists 226
templates 159–161
 BNF of 429
 in macros 144
`third` 304
`third-setter` 305
throw 103
token blending
 See blending of tokens
tokens 17
 BNF of 414
top-level constituents 21
top-level definitions 21
total ordering, of classes in a class precedence
 list 54
transfer of control 41, 108
 See also exits, nonlocal exits
transitivity, property of comparitors 267
trichotomy, property of comparitors 267
true and false 40
`truncate` 280
`truncate/` 282
`<type>` 190
`type:` argument in initialization argument
 specifications 70
`<type-error>` 248
`type-error-expected-type` 365
`type-error-value` 365

`type-for-copy` 121, 292
 used to generate the return value of sequence
 operations 211
type protocol 49–51, 343–345
 of limited collection types 127–128
 of limited integer types 74–75
type restrictions
 on init-keywords 68
 on slots 59
types 49–75
 disjointness of 51
 equality of 50
 equivalence of 50
 equivalence of, in method dispatch 96
 introspection on 343–345
 limited collection types 126–129
 limited types 73–75
 naming convention for 23
 of keyword parameters 90–91
 of return values 91
 overview of 49
 relationships among 50
 union types 72–73
 unordered, in method dispatch 96
`type-union` 72, 266

U

unary operator calls 14
Unicode character literal constants 19
`<unicode-string>` 234
uninstantiable classes 52
`union` 320
 default method of 211
union types 72–73
 as a kind of type 49
 constructor for 266
 disjointness rule 51
unique strings 19
 as literal constants 14
 See also keywords

`unless` 396
   sample definition of 172
`until` 400
   sample definition of 173
used modules 27
user-defined definition macros 11
user-defined statement macros 15

V

value declarations 91
values
   returned by functions 79
   returned by handlers 111
`values` 42, 288
value types 91
variable bindings 10
   created by `define variable` 374
   naming convention for 23
   See also bindings
`<vector>` 221
`vector` 267
vector literal constants 13, 145, 146, 223
vectors 221–225
   as single-dimensional arrays 219
   constructor for 267
`version:`, interchange format keyword 23
`virtual` slot allocation 60
virtual slot initialization 65
visible bindings in a module 27
visible modification 122

W

`<warning>` 249
warnings, as kinds of conditions 105
whales 89
`while` 399
   sample definition of 173
whitespace 16
   used around operators 35
wildcard constraints 151–158

Z

`zero?` 275

This Apple manual was written, edited, and composed on a desktop publishing system using Apple Macintosh computers and FrameMaker software. Line art was created using Adobe Illustrator™ and Adobe Photoshop™.

Text type is Palatino® and display type is Helvetica®. Bullets are ITC Zapf Dingbats®. Some elements, such as program listings, are set in Apple Courier.

WRITER
Andrew Shalit, with contributions by Orca Starbuck and David Moon.

ILLUSTRATOR
Steve Strassmann

PRODUCTION EDITOR
Lorraine Findlay

The Dylan project received many years of generous funding from Apple Computer. Without Apple's vision and investment, Dylan would never have been created.

Special thanks are due to Kim Barrett for his timely commentary on many language design questions, to Paul Haahr, David Moon, and Keith Playford for last-minute heroic contributions, to Sonya Keene for the HTML version of this book, to James Joaquin for a great language name, and to Russ Daniels and Ricardo Gonzalez for seeing things through to the end.

Heartfelt acknowledgments are due to the many people who contributed to the design and validation of Dylan over the years. The final Apple Dylan team consisted of Kim Barrett, Rick Bryan, Glenn Burke, Bob Cassels, John Hotchkiss, Jeremy Jones, Phil Kania, Ross Knights, Mike Lockwood, Robin Mair, Dave Moon, Paige Parsons, Kálmán Réti, Carl Schwarcz, Andrew Shalit, David Sotkowitz, Bill St. Clair, Steve Strassmann, Derek White and Gail Zacharias. Past members include Stoney Ballard, Rick Fleischman, Alice Hartley, Mike Kahl, Robyn Kozierok, Larisa Matejic, Neil Mayle, Richard Mlynarik, Robert Muller, Ike Nassi, Tom Parmenter, Jeff Piazza, Mark Preece, David Rosenfeld, Orca Starbuck and Oliver Steele. Contributing members of the Gwydion group include Bill Chiles, Scott E. Fahlman, Paul Gleichauf, Nick Kramer, William Lott, Rob MacLachlan and Robert Stockton. Contributing members of the Harlequin Dylan team include Jonathan Bachrach, Roman Budzianowski, Chris Fry, Paul Haahr, Sonya Keene, Tony Mann, Jo Marks, Robert Mathews, Scott McKay, Tim McNerney, Eliot Miranda, Peter Norvig, Keith Playford, Andy Sizer, Toby Weinberg, and P. Tucker Withington. Among the independent Dylan Partners who contributed are Jim Allard, Patrick C. Beard, Mark C. Chu-Carroll, Mutsumi Komuro, Jonathan Sobel, Joseph N. Wilson and Paul R. Wilson. Important feedback on the language design was provided by our ever-patient early users, including Fritz Anderson, Gary Beaver, Edward Cessna, Geoffrey Clements, Enrico Colombini, Donn Denman, Ken Dickey, Mikel Evins, Mark Gavin, James C. Grandy, Wayne Johnson, Scott Joy, Bo Klintberg, Gabriel Lawrence, Ted Lowery, Matthew MacLaurin, Claes-Fredrik Mannby, Stephen McConnell, Nick Nallick, Carl Nelson, Steve Palmen, Paul R. Potts, Mike Rossetti, Larry Tesler and Andrew Wason.